Puppet 5 Cookbook
Fourth Edition

Jump start your Puppet 5.x deployment using engaging and
practical recipes

Thomas Uphill

BIRMINGHAM - MUMBAI

Puppet 5 Cookbook
Fourth Edition

Copyright © 2018 Packt Publishing

Commissioning Editor: Vijin Boricha
Acquisition Editor: Namrata Patil
Content Development Editor: Deepti Thore
Technical Editors: Cymon Pereira, Varsha Shivhare
Copy Editor: Safis Editing
Project Coordinator: Kinjal Bari
Proofreader: Safis Editing
Indexer: Tejal Daruwale Soni
Graphics: Jisha Chirayil
Production Coordinator: Shantanu Zagade

First published: October 2011

Second edition: August 2013

Third edition: February 2015

Fourth edition: June 2018

Production reference: 1250618

Published by Packt Publishing Ltd.
Livery Place
35 Livery Street
Birmingham
B3 2PB, UK.

ISBN 978-1-78862-244-8

www.packtpub.com

mapt.io

Mapt is an online digital library that gives you full access to over 5,000 books and videos, as well as industry leading tools to help you plan your personal development and advance your career. For more information, please visit our website.

Why subscribe?

- Spend less time learning and more time coding with practical eBooks and Videos from over 4,000 industry professionals

- Improve your learning with Skill Plans built especially for you

- Get a free eBook or video every month

- Mapt is fully searchable

- Copy and paste, print, and bookmark content

PacktPub.com

Did you know that Packt offers eBook versions of every book published, with PDF and ePub files available? You can upgrade to the eBook version at www.PacktPub.com and as a print book customer, you are entitled to a discount on the eBook copy. Get in touch with us at service@packtpub.com for more details.

At www.PacktPub.com, you can also read a collection of free technical articles, sign up for a range of free newsletters, and receive exclusive discounts and offers on Packt books and eBooks.

Contributors

About the author

Thomas Uphill is a Puppet engineer in a large corporate environment. He's been using Puppet for several years now, starting as a system administrator. He's written several books on Puppet as well as given talks at LISA and Puppetconf. He lives and works in Seattle. When not at a computer, he enjoys mountain biking, hiking, and camping.

I'd like to thank my wife, Priya, for her support and helping me find the time to finish this book, my co-workers and meetup companions for some great feedback, and thanks to you, for purchasing this book.

About the reviewer

Subhash Vasarapu is a DevOps and CloudOps engineer, as well as an ethical hacker, who works for mindtree. He loves automating things, pushing production code, testing network penetration tools, working with containerized microservice solutions. He is familiar with the design, build, and deployment of scalable solutions that use sophisticated and complex implementation. He is also a gym rat, coach, swimmer, boxer, anime watcher, pet lover, nutritionist, traveler, and the kitchen is his laboratory.
You can contact him on linkedin— Subhash Vasarapu

Packt is searching for authors like you

If you're interested in becoming an author for Packt, please visit authors.packtpub.com and apply today. We have worked with thousands of developers and tech professionals, just like you, to help them share their insight with the global tech community. You can make a general application, apply for a specific hot topic that we are recruiting an author for, or submit your own idea.

Table of Contents

Preface

Configuration management has gone from something that few organizations practiced to a necessity. Today, every organization I visit is using configuration management in some form or another. The range of tools available has expanded as well. A few years ago, there were only two or three viable options for cross-platform configuration management. Now, there are many more options, including Salt, Chef, Ansible, and Puppet.

In the move to the cloud, it is important to be able to automate building nodes; manual tasks are no longer acceptable. Using Configuration management to automate the building of your nodes is now a requirement of the DevOps engineer.

This book takes you beyond the basics of Puppet and starts to explore the power of customizing Puppet to suit your needs. The book consists of mostly atomic recipes, which can be read independently to tackle a variety of real-world problems. The examples are structured so that you can dip in at any point and try out a recipe without having to work your way through the book from cover to cover. Code samples are included in each example. The book will take you from a rudimentary knowledge of Puppet to a more complete and expert understanding of Puppet's latest features and community best practices.

The open source version of Puppet was used throughout the book; you will not require Puppet Enterprise to complete the examples.

Puppet 5 is still changing rapidly, and I've included what I believe to be the most important parts of this release in this book. For up-to-the-minute information on the latest releases, I suggest you subscribe to the Puppet Developers mailing list at `https://groups.google.com/forum/#!forum/puppet-dev`, the Puppet Slack Channel at `https://slack.puppet.com/`, and the puppetlabs blog at `https://puppet.com/blog`.

Who this book is for

This book assumes a familiarity with Linux administration. The examples require some experience with command-line usage and basic text file editing. Although beneficial, previous coding experience is not required. This book is for the Puppet engineer that is looking for a book that covers a wide range of Puppet topics. This book is also for the system administrator looking for a guide to Puppet with real-world examples.

What this book covers

Chapter 1, *Puppet Language and Style*, introduces the Puppet language and shows how to write manifests. The Puppet linting tool, puppet-lint, is introduced, and we review best practices to write Puppet code. Metaparameters are shown with examples. We also cover changes in the Puppet language available in versions 4 and 5 of Puppet.

Chapter 2, *Puppet Infrastructure*, explains how to deploy Puppet in your environment. It covers the two main methods of installation, centralized and decentralized (masterless). It shows you how to use Git to centrally manage your code. It will help you configure PuppetDB and Hiera.

Chapter 3, *Writing Better Manifests*, deals with organizing your Puppet manifests. Manifests are used to build modules. This chapter introduces the concept of roles and profiles to abstract how modules are applied to machines. Parameterized classes are introduced. It also shows you how to efficiently define resources with arrays of resources and resource defaults.

Chapter 4, *Working with Files and Packages*, shows you how to manage files using snippets (fragments). It introduces the power of creating files with both Ruby (ERB) and Puppet (EPP) templates. It also helps you explore ways to secure information stored in your Puppet manifests.

Chapter 5, *Users and Virtual Resources*, deals with the advanced topic of virtual and exported resources. Virtual resources are a way of defining resources but not applying them by default. Exported resources are similar but are used to have resources from one machine applied to one or more other machines.

Chapter 6, *Managing Resources and Files*, speaks about dealing with directories and purging resources not controlled by Puppet. It shows you how to have file resources applied differently on different machines. Furthermore, methods for managing host entries in /etc/hosts are shown with exported resources examples.

Chapter 7, *Managing Applications*, shows you how to use Puppet to manage your deployed applications. Using public Forge modules, it helps you configure Apache, NGINX, and MariaDB.

Chapter 8, *Servers and Cloud Infrastructure*, introduces virtual resources and shows how to use them to configure highly available services. It also shows you how to use Puppet to manage Docker and AWS instances. Furthermore, Vagrant is used as a tool to create test environments for your Puppet code.

Chapter 9, *External Tools and the Puppet Ecosystem*, shows you how to extend Puppet with your own types and providers, how to make your own facts, as well as the **Puppet Development Kit (PDK)**.

Chapter 10, *Monitoring, Reporting, and Troubleshooting*, shows you how to leverage Puppet to monitor your infrastructure for problems. We configure Puppet reporting and then discuss some of the common problems with Puppet code.

To get the most out of this book

You will need a computer capable of running Linux virtual machines. The examples in the book use Debian and Enterprise Linux-based distributions (RHEL and CentOS). Some of the examples will require multiple virtual machines to be run concurrently. You will need a host machine capable of running three or four virtual machines simultaneously. A minimum of 8 GB of RAM is suggested for performance reasons. To configure a test environment similar to that used in the production of the book, Vagrant should be used. Vagrant is a tool developed by Hashicorp to enable quick deployment of virtual machines via a definition file, Vagrantfile. More information on Vagrantfile syntax is available at https://www.vagrantup.com/docs/vagrantfile/. Vagrantfile used to build the example systems in this book is provided in the *files* section. To effectively use the Vagrantfile provided, you will need to install the vagrant-hosts plugin. To do so, issue the following command:

```
[t@mylaptop ~] $ vagrant plugin install vagrant-hosts
Installing the 'vagrant-hosts' plugin. This can take a few minutes...
Fetching: vagrant-hosts-2.8.2.gem (100%)
Installed the plugin 'vagrant-hosts (2.8.2)'!
```

This will allow Vagrant to update the /etc/hosts file on your nodes with host entries for the other nodes in your test environment (for example, puppet.example.com and git.example.com). It is also convenient to configure ssh to connect to your test machines. After copying down Vagrantfile into a directory on your machine, cd into that directory. Check whether Vagrant is configured properly using the following command:

```
[t@mylaptop ~/cookbook] $ vagrant status
Current machine states:

cookbook poweroff (virtualbox)
puppet   running (virtualbox)
```

```
This environment represents multiple VMs. The VMs are all listed
above with their current state. For more information about a specific
VM, run `vagrant status NAME`.
```

Now, copy the output of the following command into the `.ssh/config` file in your `home` directory as shown here:

```
[t@mylaptop ~/cookbook] $ vagrant ssh-config puppet >>~/.ssh/config
```

This will enable you to do the following:

```
[t@mylaptop ~/cookbook] $ ssh puppet
Last login: Mon Jun 18 20:13:21 2018 from 10.0.2.2
puppet.example.com
Managed by puppet 5.3.3
[vagrant@puppet ~]$ hostname
puppet.example.com
```

Download the example code files

You can download the example code files for this book from your account at `www.packtpub.com`. If you purchased this book elsewhere, you can visit `www.packtpub.com/support` and register to have the files emailed directly to you.

You can download the code files by following these steps:

1. Log in or register at `www.packtpub.com`.
2. Select the **SUPPORT** tab.
3. Click on **Code Downloads & Errata**.
4. Enter the name of the book in the **Search** box and follow the onscreen instructions.

Once the file is downloaded, please make sure that you unzip or extract the folder using the latest version of:

- WinRAR/7-Zip for Windows
- Zipeg/iZip/UnRarX for Mac
- 7-Zip/PeaZip for Linux

The code bundle for the book is also hosted on GitHub at `https://github.com/PacktPublishing/Puppet-5-Cookbook-Fourth-Edition`. In case there's an update to the code, it will be updated on the existing GitHub repository.

We also have other code bundles from our rich catalog of books and videos available at https://github.com/PacktPublishing/. Check them out!

Download the color images

We also provide a PDF file that has color images of the screenshots/diagrams used in this book. You can download it here: https://www.packtpub.com/sites/default/files/downloads/Puppet5CookbookFourthEdition_ColorImages.pdf.

Conventions used

There are a number of text conventions used throughout this book.

CodeInText: Indicates code words in text, database table names, folder names, filenames, file extensions, pathnames, dummy URLs, user input, and Twitter handles. Here is an example: "Apply this manifest using puppet apply git.pp; this will install Git."

A block of code is set as follows:

```
package {'git':
  ensure => installed
}
```

Any command-line input or output is written as follows:

```
t@mylaptop ~/.ssh $ ssh-copy-id -i git_rsa git@git.example.com
git@git.example.com's password:
Number of key(s) added: 1
```

Bold: Indicates a new term, an important word, or words that you see onscreen. For example, words in menus or dialog boxes appear in the text like this. Here is an example: "Select **System info** from the **Administration** panel."

Warnings or important notes appear like this.

Tips and tricks appear like this.

Sections

In this book, you will find several headings that appear frequently (*Getting ready, How to do it..., How it works..., There's more...,* and *See also*).

To give clear instructions on how to complete a recipe, use these sections as follows:

Getting ready

This section tells you what to expect in the recipe and describes how to set up any software or any preliminary settings required for the recipe.

How to do it...

This section contains the steps required to follow the recipe.

How it works...

This section usually consists of a detailed explanation of what happened in the previous section.

There's more...

This section consists of additional information about the recipe in order to make you more knowledgeable about the recipe.

See also

This section provides helpful links to other useful information for the recipe.

Get in touch

Feedback from our readers is always welcome.

General feedback: Email `feedback@packtpub.com` and mention the book title in the subject of your message. If you have questions about any aspect of this book, please email us at `questions@packtpub.com`.

Errata: Although we have taken every care to ensure the accuracy of our content, mistakes do happen. If you have found a mistake in this book, we would be grateful if you would report this to us. Please visit www.packtpub.com/submit-errata, selecting your book, clicking on the Errata Submission Form link, and entering the details.

Piracy: If you come across any illegal copies of our works in any form on the internet, we would be grateful if you would provide us with the location address or website name. Please contact us at copyright@packtpub.com with a link to the material.

If you are interested in becoming an author: If there is a topic that you have expertise in and you are interested in either writing or contributing to a book, please visit authors.packtpub.com.

Reviews

Please leave a review. Once you have read and used this book, why not leave a review on the site that you purchased it from? Potential readers can then see and use your unbiased opinion to make purchase decisions, we at Packt can understand what you think about our products, and our authors can see your feedback on their book. Thank you!

For more information about Packt, please visit packtpub.com.

Puppet Language and Style

1

We will cover the following recipes in this chapter:

- Adding a resource to a node
- Using facter to describe a node
- Using Puppet facts
- Installing a package before starting a service
- Installing, configuring, and starting a service
- Using community Puppet style
- Installing Puppet
- Creating a manifest
- Checking your manifests with Puppet-lint
- Making modules
- Using standard naming conventions
- Using in-line templates
- Iterating over multiple terms
- Writing powerful conditional statements
- Using regular expressions in `if` statements
- Using selectors and case statements
- Using the `in` operator
- Using regular expression substitutions
- Puppet 5 changes
- Puppet 4/5 Changes

Introduction

In this chapter, we'll start with the basics of the Puppet syntax and show you how some of the syntactic sugar in Puppet is used. We'll then move on to how Puppet deals with dependencies and how to make Puppet do the work for you.

We'll look at how to organize and structure your code into modules following community conventions so that other people will find it easy to read and maintain your code. We will also see some powerful features of the Puppet language, which will let you write concise yet expressive manifests.

Adding a resource to a node

This recipe will introduce the language and show you the basics of writing Puppet code. Puppet code files are called **manifests**; manifests declare resources. A resource in Puppet may be a type, class, or node. A **type** is something like a file or package or anything that has a type declared in the language. The current list of standard types is available on the puppetlabs website at `https://puppet.com/docs/puppet/latest/type.html`. I find myself referencing this site very often. You may define your own types, either using a mechanism, similar to a subroutine, named defined types, extending the language using a custom type. Types are the heart of the language; they describe the things that make up a **node** (node is the word Puppet uses for client computers/devices). Puppet uses **resources** to describe the state of a node; for example, we will declare the following package resource for a node using a site manifest: `site.pp`.

How to do it...

Create a `site.pp` file and place the following code in it:

```
node default {
  package { 'httpd':
    ensure => 'installed'
  }
}
```

How it works...

This manifest will ensure that any node on which this manifest is applied will install a package called `httpd`. The default keyword is a wildcard to Puppet; it applies anything within the node `default` definition to any node. When Puppet applies the manifest to a node, it uses a **Resource Abstraction Layer** (**RAL**) to translate the package type into the package management system of the target node. What this means is that we can use the same manifest to install the `httpd` package on any system where Puppet has a Provider for the package type. Providers are the pieces of code that do the real work of applying a manifest. When the previous code is applied to a node running on a YUM-based distribution, the YUM provider will be used to install the `httpd` RPM packages. When the same code is applied to a node running on an APT-based distribution, the APT provider will be used to install the `httpd` DEB package (which may not exist, as most Debian-based systems call this package `apache2`; we'll deal with this sort of naming problem later).

See also...

- *Puppet 3: Beginner's Guide*, John Arundel, Packt Publishing, in addition to this section

Using facter to describe a node

Facter is a separate utility upon which Puppet depends. It is the system used by Puppet to gather information about the target system (node); `facter` calls the nuggets of information facts. You may run `facter` from the command line to obtain real-time information from the system.

How to do it...

We'll compare the output of facter with that of system utilities:

1. Use `facter` to find the current `uptime` of the system, the `uptime` fact:

```
t@cookbook ~$ facter uptime 0:12 hours
```

2. Compare this with the output of the Linux `uptime` command:

```
t@cookbook ~$ uptime
01:18:52 up 12 min, 1 user, load average: 0.00, 0.00, 0.00
```

How it works...

When `facter` is installed (as a dependency for Puppet), several fact definitions are installed by default. You can reference each of these facts by name from the command line.

There's more...

Running `facter` without any arguments causes `facter` to print all the facts known about the system. We will see in later chapters that `facter` can be extended with your own custom facts. All facts are available for you to use as variables; variables are discussed in the next section.

Variables

Variables in Puppet are marked with a `$` character. Variables are immutable; once assigned a value, they cannot be changed. When using variables within a manifest, it is advisable to enclose the variable within braces, such as `${myvariable}`, instead of `$myvariable`. All of the facts from `facter` can be referenced as top-scope variables (we will discuss scope in the next section). For example, the **Fully Qualified Domain Name (FQDN)** of the node may be referenced by `${::fqdn}`. Variables can only contain alphabetic characters, numerals, and the underscore character, _. As a matter of style, variables should start with an alphabetic character. Never use dashes in variable names.

Scope

In the variable example explained in the previous paragraph, the FQDN was referred to as `${::fqdn}` rather than `${fqdn}`; the double colons are how Puppet differentiates scope. The highest level scope, top-scope, or global is referred to by two colons, as in `::`, at the beginning of a variable identifier. To reduce namespace collisions, always use fully scoped variable identifiers in your manifests. A Unix user can think of top-scope variables such as the / (root) level. You can refer to variables using the double colon syntax, similar to how you would refer to a directory by its full path. A developer can think of top-scope variables as global variables; however, unlike global variables, you must always refer to them with the double colon notation to guarantee that a local variable isn't obscuring the top-scope variable. In Puppet5, it is advisable to use the `$facts` fact, so the previous would be `${facts['fqdn']}`. When referring to a variable, the braces (`{}`) are optional outside of a string, as shown in the following example:

```
$fqdn_ = $facts['fqdn']
notify {"::fqdn is ${::fqdn}": }
notify {"fqdn_ is ${fqdn_}": }
notify {"facts['fqdn'] is ${facts['fqdn']}": }
```

This produces the following output:

```
t@mylaptop ~ $ puppet apply fqdn.pp
Notice: Compiled catalog for mylaptop.example.com in environment production
in 0.01 seconds
Notice: ::fqdn is mylaptop.example.com
Notice: /Stage[main]/Main/Notify[::fqdn is mylaptop.example.com]/message:
defined 'message' as '::fqdn is mylaptop.example.com'
Notice: fqdn_ is mylaptop.example.com
Notice: /Stage[main]/Main/Notify[fqdn_ is mylaptop.example.com]/message:
defined 'message' as 'fqdn_ is mylaptop.example.com'
Notice: facts['fqdn'] is mylaptop.example.com
Notice: /Stage[main]/Main/Notify[facts['fqdn'] is
mylaptop.example.com]/message: defined 'message' as 'facts[\'fqdn\'] is
mylaptop.example.com'
Notice: Applied catalog in 0.02 seconds
```

 `$fqdn_` is used to avoid a namespace collision with the top-scope `::fqdn`.

Using puppet facts

As we'll see in subsequent chapters, `facter` may be extended with custom facts written in Ruby. By default, custom facts are not loaded when you run `facter`.

How to do it...

To pull in the custom facts, you need to specify the `-p` option to `facter`, as shown here:

```
t@cookbook:~$ facter puppetversion

t@cookbook:~$ facter -p puppetversion
5.3.3
```

Although still valid, the `facter -p` syntax is now deprecated in favor of using the Puppet face, facts. Puppet faces are the various sub-applications supported by the `Puppet` command. To see the available faces, run `Puppet help`, as shown here:

```
t@cookbook:~$ puppet help

Usage: puppet <subcommand> [options] <action> [options]

Available subcommands:
  agent               The puppet agent daemon
  apply               Apply Puppet manifests locally
  ca                  Local Puppet Certificate Authority management.
(Deprecated)
  catalog             Compile, save, view, and convert catalogs.
  cert                Manage certificates and requests
  certificate         Provide access to the CA for certificate management.
  certificate_request  Manage certificate requests. (Deprecated)
  certificate_revocation_list  Manage the list of revoked certificates.
(Deprecated)
  config              Interact with Puppet's settings.
  describe            Display help about resource types
  device              Manage remote network devices
  doc                 Generate Puppet references
  epp                 Interact directly with the EPP template parser/renderer.
  facts               Retrieve and store facts.
  filebucket          Store and retrieve files in a filebucket
  generate            Generates Puppet code from Ruby definitions.
  help                Display Puppet help.
  key                 Create, save, and remove certificate keys. (Deprecated)
  lookup              Interactive Hiera lookup
  man                 Display Puppet manual pages.
```

```
master              The puppet master daemon
module              Creates, installs and searches for modules on the Puppet
Forge.
node                View and manage node definitions.
parser              Interact directly with the parser.
plugin              Interact with the Puppet plugin system.
report              Create, display, and submit reports.
resource            The resource abstraction layer shell
status              View puppet server status. (Deprecated)
```

One difference between `facter` and `Puppet facts` is that you may request a single fact from facter, whereas Puppet facts will return all the facts for a node at once as a JSON object (you may request other formats with the `--render-as` option).

Installing a package before starting a service

To show how ordering works, we'll create a manifest that installs `httpd` and then ensures the `httpd` package service is running.

How to do it...

We'll create a manifest to install and start our service:

1. Start by creating a manifest that defines `service`:

```
service {'httpd':
  ensure  => running,
  require => Package['httpd'],
}
```

2. The `service` definition references a `package` resource named `httpd`; we now need to define that resource:

```
package {'httpd':
  ensure => 'installed',
}
```

How it works...

In this example, the package will be installed before the service is started. Using `require` within the definition of the `httpd` service ensures that the package is installed first, regardless of the order within the manifest file.

Capitalization is important in Puppet. In our previous example, we created a package named `httpd`. If we wanted to refer to this package later, we would capitalize its type (package) as follows:

```
Package['httpd']
```

To refer to a class- for example, the `something::somewhere` class, which has already been included/defined in your manifest-you can reference it with the full path as follows:

```
Class['something::somewhere']
```

Let's say you have defined the following type:

```
example::thing {'one':}
```

The preceding line may be referenced later, as follows:

```
Example::Thing['one']
```

Knowing how to reference previously defined resources is necessary for the next section on metaparameters and ordering.

Learning metaparameters and ordering

All the manifests that will be used to define a node are compiled into a catalog. A catalog is the code that will be applied to configure a node. It is important to remember that manifests are not applied to nodes sequentially. There is no inherent order to the application of manifests. With this in mind, in the previous `httpd` example, what if we wanted to ensure that the `httpd` process started after the `httpd` package was installed?

We couldn't rely on the `httpd` service coming after the `httpd` package in the manifests. What we would have to do is use metaparameters to tell Puppet the order in which we want resources applied to the node. Metaparameters are parameters that can be applied to any resource and are not specific to any one resource type. They are used for catalog compilation and as hints to Puppet, but not to define anything about the resource to which they are attached.

When dealing with ordering, there are four metaparameters used:

- `before`
- `require`
- `notify`
- `subscribe`

The `before` and `require` metaparameters specify a direct ordering; `notify` implies `before` and `subscribe` implies require. The `notify` metaparameter is only applicable to services; what `notify` does is tell a service to restart after the notifying resource has been applied to the node (this is most often a package or file resource). In the case of files, once the file is created on the node, a `notify` parameter will restart any services mentioned. The `subscribe` metaparameter has the same effect but is defined on the service; the service will `subscribe` to the file.

Trifecta

The relationship between package and service previously mentioned is an important and powerful paradigm of Puppet. Adding one more resource-type file into the fold creates what puppeteers refer to as the trifecta. Almost all system administration tasks revolve around these three resource types. As a system administrator, you install a package, configure the package with files, and then start the service:

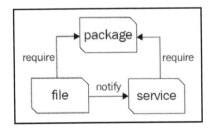

Diagram of the trifecta (files require package for directory: service requires files and package)

Idempotency

A key concept of Puppet is that the state of the system when a manifest is applied to a node cannot affect the outcome of the Puppet run. In other words, at the end of the Puppet run (if the run was successful), the system will be in a known state and any further application of the manifest will result in a system that is in the same state. This property of Puppet is known as idempotency. Idempotency is the property that, no matter how many times you do something, remains in the same state as the first time you did it. For instance, if you had a light switch and you gave the instruction to turn it on, the light would turn on. If you gave the instruction again, the light would remain on.

Installing, configuring, and starting a service

There are many examples of this pattern online. In our simple example, we will create an Apache configuration file under `/etc/httpd/conf.d/cookbook.conf`. The `/etc/httpd/conf.d` directory will not exist until the `httpd` package is installed. After this file is created, we would want `httpd` to restart to notice the change; we can achieve this with a notify parameter.

How to do it...

We will need the same definitions as our last example; we need the package and service installed. We now need two more things. We need the configuration file and index page (`index.html`) created. For this, we follow these steps:

1. As in the previous example, we ensure the service is running and specify that the service requires the `httpd` package:

```
service {'httpd':
  ensure  => running,
  require => Package['httpd'],
}
```

2. We then define `package` as follows:

```
package {'httpd':
  ensure => installed,
}
```

3. Now, we create the `/etc/httpd/conf.d/cookbook.conf` configuration file; the `/etc/httpd/conf.d` directory will not exist until the `httpd` package is installed. We'll use `@heredoc` syntax here to make the code a little more readable, assigning the `cookbook.conf` contents to the `$cookbook` variable. The require metaparameter tells Puppet that this file requires the `httpd` package to be installed before it is created:

```
$cookbook = @(COOKBOOK)
  <VirtualHost *:80>
    Servername cookbook
    DocumentRoot /var/www/cookbook
  </VirtualHost>
  | COOKBOOK
file {'/etc/httpd/conf.d/cookbook.conf':
  content => $cookbook,
  require => Package['httpd'],
  notify  => Service['httpd'],
}
```

4. We then go on to create an `index.html` file for our virtual host in `/var/www/cookbook`. Again, we'll use `@heredoc` syntax to make this more readable. This directory won't exist yet, so we need to create this as well, using the following code:

```
$index = @(INDEX)
  <html>
    <body>
      <h1>Hello World!</h1>
    </body>
  </html>
  | INDEX
file {'/var/www/cookbook':
  ensure  => directory,
  require => Package['httpd'],
}
file {'/var/www/cookbook/index.html':
  content => $index,
  require => File['/var/www/cookbook'],
}
```

How it works...

The require attribute to the file resources tells Puppet that we need the `/var/www/cookbook` directory created before we can create the `index.html` file. The important concept to remember is that we cannot assume anything about the target system (node). We need to define everything on which the target depends. Anytime you create a file in a manifest, you have to ensure that the directory containing that file exists. Anytime you specify that a service should be running, you have to ensure that the package providing that service is installed.

In this example, using metaparameters, we can be confident that no matter what state the node is in before running Puppet, after Puppet runs, the following will be true:

- `httpd` will be running
- The `VirtualHost` configuration file will exist
- `httpd` will restart and be aware of the `VirtualHost` file
- The `DocumentRoot` directory will exist
- An `index.html` file will exist in the `DocumentRoot` directory

Using community Puppet style

If other people need to read or maintain your manifests, or if you want to share code with the community, it's a good idea to follow the existing style conventions as closely as possible. These govern such aspects of your code as layout, spacing, quoting, alignment, and variable references, and the official puppetlabs recommendations on style are available at `https://puppet.com/docs/puppet/latest/style_guide.html`.

How to do it...

In this section, I'll show you a few of the more important examples and how to make sure that your code is style compliant.

Indentation

Indent your manifests using two spaces (not tabs), as follows:

```
service {'httpd':
  ensure => 'running',
}
```

Quoting

Always quote your resource names, as follows:

```
package { 'exim4': }
```

We cannot do this though:

```
package { exim4: }
```

Use single quotes for all strings, except when:

- The string contains variable references, such as ${::fqdn}
- The string contains character escape sequences, such as \n

Consider the following code:

```
file { '/etc/motd':
  content => "Welcome to ${::fqdn}\n"
}
```

Puppet doesn't process variable references or escape sequences unless they're inside double quotes.

Always quote parameter values that are not reserved words in Puppet. For example, the following values are not reserved words:

```
name  => 'Nucky Thompson',
mode  => '0700',
owner => 'deploy',
```

However, these values are reserved words and therefore not quoted:

```
ensure => installed,
enable => true,
ensure => running,
```

false

There is only one thing in Puppet that is `false`, that is, the word `false` without any quotes. The string `false` evaluates to true and the string `true` also evaluates to true. Actually, everything besides the literal false evaluates to true (when treated as a Boolean):

```
if "false" {
  notify { 'True': }
}
if 'false' {
  notify { 'Also true': }
}
if false {
  notify { 'Not true': }
}
```

When this code is run through `puppet apply`, the first two notifies are triggered. The final notify is not triggered; it is the only one that evaluates to false.

Variables

Always include curly braces `{}` around variable names when referring to them in strings, for example, as follows:

```
source => "puppet:///modules/webserver/${brand}.conf",
```

Otherwise, the `Puppet` parser has to guess which characters should be a part of the variable name and which belong to the surrounding string. Curly braces make it explicit.

Parameters

Always end lines that declare parameters with a comma, even if it is the last parameter:

```
service { 'memcached':
  ensure => running,
  enable => true,
}
```

This is allowed by Puppet, and makes it easier if you want to add parameters later, or reorder the existing parameters.

When declaring a resource with a single parameter, make the declaration all on one line and with no trailing comma, as shown in the following snippet:

```
package { 'puppet':
  ensure => installed
}
```

Where there is more than one parameter, give each parameter its own line:

```
package { 'rake':
  ensure   => installed,
  provider => gem,
  require  => Package['rubygems'],
}
```

To make the code easier to read, line up the parameter arrows in line with the longest parameter, as follows:

```
file { "/var/www/${app}/shared/config/rvmrc":
  owner   => 'deploy',
  group   => 'deploy',
  content => template('rails/rvmrc.erb'),
  require => File["/var/www/${app}/shared/config"],
}
```

The arrows should be aligned per resource, but not across the whole file, otherwise it may be difficult for you to cut and paste code from one file to another.

Symlinks

When declaring file resources that are symlinks, use the ensure => link and set the target attribute, as follows:

```
file { '/etc/php5/cli/php.ini':
  ensure => link,
  target => '/etc/php.ini',
}
```

Installing Puppet

You may install Puppet locally on your machine or create a virtual machine and install Puppet on that machine.

How to do it...

For YUM-based systems, use `https://yum.puppetlabs.com/puppet5`, and for APT-based systems, use `https://apt.puppetlabs.com/`. Use the `puppet5-release-[version].deb` package to install Puppet 5. After installing the YUM release RPM or the APT release source package, install the puppet-agent package. The puppet-agent package installs all the files necessary to support Puppet in agent mode on a node.

You may also use `gem` to install Puppet:

1. To use `gem`, we need the `rubygems` package as follows:

```
t@cookbook:~$ sudo yum install rubygems
 Resolving Dependencies
 --> Running transaction check
 ---> Package rubygems.noarch 0:2.0.14.1-30.el7 will be
installed
 ...
 Installed:
  rubygems.noarch 0:2.0.14.1-30.el7
```

2. Now, use `gem` to install Puppet:

```
t@cookbook:~$ gem install puppet

Fetching: facter-2.5.1.gem (100%)
Successfully installed facter-2.5.1
Fetching: hiera-3.4.2.gem (100%)
Successfully installed hiera-3.4.2
Fetching: fast_gettext-1.1.0.gem (100%)
Successfully installed fast_gettext-1.1.0
Fetching: locale-2.1.2.gem (100%)
Successfully installed locale-2.1.2
Fetching: text-1.3.1.gem (100%)
Successfully installed text-1.3.1
Fetching: gettext-3.2.6.gem (100%)
Successfully installed gettext-3.2.6
Fetching: gettext-setup-0.29.gem (100%)
Successfully installed gettext-setup-0.29
Fetching: puppet-5.3.3.gem (100%)
Successfully installed puppet-5.3.3
Parsing documentation for facter-2.5.1
Installing ri documentation for facter-2.5.1
Parsing documentation for hiera-3.4.2
Installing ri documentation for hiera-3.4.2
Parsing documentation for fast_gettext-1.1.0
```

```
Installing ri documentation for fast_gettext-1.1.0
Parsing documentation for locale-2.1.2
Installing ri documentation for locale-2.1.2
Parsing documentation for text-1.3.1
Installing ri documentation for text-1.3.1
Parsing documentation for gettext-3.2.6
Installing ri documentation for gettext-3.2.6
Parsing documentation for gettext-setup-0.29
Installing ri documentation for gettext-setup-0.29
Parsing documentation for puppet-5.3.3
Installing ri documentation for puppet-5.3.3
8 gems installed
```

For the examples in this book, I suggest using the puppet-agent package installation. The package installation method of Puppet uses the **AIO** (**All-In-One**) mentality. The puppet-agent package installs all the necessary support files for Puppet and does not rely on system libraries and applications. The most important dependency is Ruby: the AIO `puppet-agent` package installs a Puppet-specific Ruby that has been tested against the version of Puppet to which it belongs.

Creating a manifest

If you already have some Puppet code (known as a Puppet manifest), you can skip this section and go on to the next. If not, we'll see how to create and apply a simple manifest.

How to do it...

To create and apply a simple manifest, follow these steps:

1. With Puppet installed in the previous section, we can create a directory to contain our Puppet code:

```
t@cookbook:~$ mkdir -p .puppet/manifests
t@cookbook:~$ cd .puppet/manifests
t@cookbook:manifests$
```

2. Within your manifests directory, create the `site.pp` file with the following content:

```
node default {
  file { '/tmp/hello':
    content => "Hello, world!\n",
  }
}
```

3. Test your manifest with the `puppet apply` command. This will tell Puppet to read the manifest, compare it to the state of the machine, and make any necessary changes to that state:

```
t@cookbook:manifests$ puppet apply site.pp
Notice: Compiled catalog for cookbook.example.com in
environment production in 0.05 seconds
Notice:
/Stage[main]/Main/Node[default]/File[/tmp/hello]/ensure:
defined content as '{md5}746308829575e17c3331bbcb00c0898b'
Notice: Applied catalog in 0.07 seconds
```

4. To see if Puppet did what we expected (created the `/tmp/hello` file with the Hello, world! content), run the following command:

```
t@cookbook:manifests$ cat /tmp/hello
Hello, world!
```

Note that creating the file in `/tmp` did not require special permissions. We did not run Puppet via `sudo`. Puppet need not be run through `sudo`; there are cases where running via an unprivileged user can be useful.

There's more...

When several people are working on a code base, it's easy for style inconsistencies to creep in. Fortunately, there's a tool available that can automatically check your code for compliance with the style guide: `puppet-lint`. We'll see how to use this in the next section.

Checking your manifests with puppet-lint

The Puppet official style guide outlines a number of style conventions for Puppet code, some of which we've touched on in the preceding section. For example, according to the style guide, manifests:

- Must use two-space soft tabs
- Must not use literal tab characters
- Must not contain trailing white space
- Should not exceed an 80-character line width
- Should align parameter arrows (=>) within blocks

Following the style guide will make sure that your Puppet code is easy to read and maintain, and if you're planning to release your code to the public, style compliance is essential.

The `puppet-lint` tool will automatically check your code against the style guide. The next section explains how to use it.

Getting ready

Here's what you need to do to install `puppet-lint`:

1. We'll install Puppet-lint using the gem provider because the gem version is much more up to date than the APT or RPM packages available. Create a `puppet-lint.pp` manifest as shown in the following code snippet:

   ```
   package {'puppet-lint':
     ensure   => 'installed',
     provider => 'gem'
   }
   ```

2. Run `puppet apply` on the `puppet-lint.pp` manifest, as shown in the following command:

   ```
   t@cookbook:manifests$ puppet apply puppet-lint.pp
   Notice: Compiled catalog for cookbook.example.com in
   environment production in 1.04 seconds
   Notice: /Stage[main]/Main/Package[puppet-lint]/ensure: created
   Notice: Applied catalog in 0.93 seconds
   ```

How to do it...

Follow these steps to use Puppet-lint:

1. Choose a Puppet manifest file that you want to check with Puppet-lint, and run the following command:

   ```
   t@cookbook:manifests$ puppet-lint puppet-lint.pp
   WARNING: indentation of => is not properly aligned (expected in
   column 12, but found it in column 10) on line 2
   ERROR: trailing whitespace found on line 4
   ```

2. As you can see, Puppet-lint found a number of problems with the manifest file. Correct the errors, save the file, and rerun Puppet-lint to check that all is well. If successful, you'll see no output:

   ```
   t@cookbook:manifests$ puppet-lint puppet-lint.pp
   t@cookbook:manifests$
   ```

There's more...

Should you follow Puppet style guide and, by extension, keep your code lint-clean? It's up to you, but here are a couple of things to think about:

- It makes sense to use some style conventions, especially when you're working collaboratively on code. Unless you and your colleagues can agree on standards for whitespace, tabs, quoting, alignment, and so on, your code will be messy and difficult to read or maintain.
- If you're choosing a set of style conventions to follow, the logical choice would be those issued by Puppet and adopted by the community for use in public modules.

Having said that, it's possible to tell Puppet-lint to ignore certain checks if you've chosen not to adopt them in your code base. For example, if you don't want puppet-lint to warn you about code lines exceeding 80 characters, you can run puppet-lint with the following option:

```
puppet-lint --no-80chars-check
```

Most developers have terminals with more than 80 characters now; the check for 80 characters is generally disabled in favor of a new 140-character limit. You may disable the 140 character check with the following:

```
puppet-lint --no-140chars-check
```

Run `puppet-lint --help` to see the complete list of check configuration commands.

See also

- *You can find out more about* `Puppet-lint` *at* `https://github.com/rodjek/puppet-lint`.

- The *Automatic syntax checking with Git hooks* recipe in `Chapter 2`, *Puppet Infrastructure*

- The *Testing your manifests with rspec-puppet* recipe in `Chapter 9`, *External Tools and the Puppet Ecosystem*

Making modules

One of the most important things you can do to make your Puppet manifests clearer and more maintainable is to organize them into modules.

Modules are self-contained bundles of Puppet code that include all the files necessary to implement a thing. Modules may contain flat files, templates, Puppet manifests, custom fact declarations, augeas lenses, and custom Puppet types and providers.

Separating things into modules makes it easier to reuse and share code; it's also the most logical way to organize your manifests. In this example, we'll create a module to manage `memcached`, a memory caching system commonly used with web applications.

How to do it...

Following are the steps to create an example module:

1. We will use Puppet's module subcommand to create the directory structure for our new module, in our home directory (`/home/vagrant`):

   ```
   [t@cookbook ~]$ puppet module generate thomas-memcached
   ```

2. We need to create a `metadata.json` file for this module. Please answer the following questions; if the question is not applicable to this module, feel free to leave it blank:

   ```
   Puppet uses Semantic Versioning (semver.org) to version
   modules.
   What version is this module? [0.1.0]
   -->
   Who wrote this module? [thomas]
   -->
   What license does this module code fall under? [Apache-2.0]
   -->
   How would you describe this module in a single sentence?
   --> A module to install memcached
   Where is this module's source code repository?
   --> github.com/uphillian/thomas-memcached
   Where can others go to learn more about this module? [https://
   github.com/uphillian/thomas-memcached]
   -->
   Where can others go to file issues about this module? [https://
   github.com/uphillian/thomas-memcached/issues]
   -->
   {
   "name": "thomas-memcached",
   "version": "0.1.0",
   "author": "thomas",
   "summary": "A module to install memcached",
   "license": "Apache-2.0",
   "source": "github.com/uphillian/thomas-memcached",
   "project_page": "https://github.com/uphillian/thomas-
   memcached",
   "issues_url":
   "https://github.com/uphillian/thomas-memcached/issues",
   "dependencies": [
   {
   "name": "puppetlabs-stdlib",
   "version_requirement": ">= 1.0.0"
   }
   ```

```
]
"data_provider": null
}
------------------------------------------
About to generate this metadata; continue? [n/Y]
--> y
Notice: Generating module at /home/vagrant/memcached...
Notice: Populating templates...
Finished; module generated in memcached.
memcached/spec
memcached/spec/spec_helper.rb
memcached/spec/classes
memcached/spec/classes/init_spec.rb
memcached/metadata.json
memcached/manifests
memcached/manifests/init.pp
memcached/Gemfile
memcached/examples
memcached/examples/init.pp
memcached/README.md
memcached/Rakefile
```

This command creates the module directory and creates some empty files as starting points.

3. Now, edit `memcached/manifests/init.pp` and change the class definition at the end of the file to the following. Note that the `puppet module` created many lines of comments; in a `production` module, you would want to edit those default comments:

```
class memcached {
  package { 'memcached': ensure => installed, }
  file { '/etc/memcached.conf':
    source  => 'puppet:///modules/memcached/memcached.conf',
    owner   => 'root',
    group   => 'root',
    mode    => '0644',
    require => Package['memcached'],
  }
  service { 'memcached':
    ensure  => running,
    enable  => true,
    require => [Package['memcached'],
                File['/etc/memcached.conf']],
  }
}
```

4. Create the `modules/thomas-memcached/files` directory and then create a file named `memcached.conf` with the following contents:

```
[t@cookbook memcached]$ mkdir files
[t@cookbook memcached]$ echo "-m 64 -p 11211 -u nobody -l
127.0.0.1" > files/memcached.conf
```

5. We would like this module to install `memcached`. We'll need to run `Puppet` with root privileges, and we'll use `sudo` for that. We'll need `Puppet` to be able to find the module in our home directory; we can specify this on the command line when we run `Puppet`, as shown in the following code snippet:

```
t@cookbook:memcached$ sudo /opt/puppetlabs/bin/puppet apply --
modulepath=/home/vagrant -e 'include memcached'
Warning: ModuleLoader: module 'memcached' has unresolved
dependencies - it will only see those that are resolved. Use
'puppet module list --tree' to see information about modules
   (file &amp; line not available)
Notice: Compiled catalog for cookbook.strangled.net in
environment production in 0.46 seconds
Notice: /Stage[main]/Memcached/Package[memcached]/ensure:
created
Notice:
/Stage[main]/Memcached/File[/etc/memcached.conf]/ensure:
defined content as '{md5}febccf4a987759cf4f1558cc625fbea9'
Notice: /Stage[main]/Memcached/Service[memcached]/ensure:
ensure changed 'stopped' to 'running'
Notice: Applied catalog in 6.99 seconds
```

6. We can verify that `memcached` is running using `systemctl` or `puppet resource`:

```
t@cookbook:memcached$ sudo /opt/puppetlabs/bin/puppet resource
service memcached
service { 'memcached':
 ensure => 'running',
 enable => 'true',
}
t@cookbook:memcached$ sudo systemctl status memcached
memcached.service - Memcached
  Loaded: loaded (/usr/lib/systemd/system/memcached.service;
enabled; vendor preset: disabled)
  Active: active (running) since Thu 2017-12-28 05:17:41 UTC;
3min 28s ago
Main PID: 4057 (memcached)
  CGroup: /system.slice/memcached.service
```

```
        └──4057 /usr/bin/memcached -u memcached -p 11211 -m
    64 -c 1024

    Dec 28 05:17:41 cookbook systemd[1]: Started Memcached.
    Dec 28 05:17:41 cookbook systemd[1]: Starting Memcached...
    Note that /opt/puppetlabs/bin/puppet may not be in root's path,
    use the full path or add the path to a file in /etc/profile.d.
```

How it works...

When we created the module using Puppet's module generate command, we used the name `thomas-memcached`. The name before the hyphen is your username or your username on Puppet forge (an online repository of modules). Modules have a specific directory structure. Not all of these directories need to be present, but if they are, this is how they should be organized:

```
modules/
└─MODULE_NAME/ never use a dash (-) in a module name
└─examples/ example usage of the module
└─files/ flat files used by the module
└─lib/
   └─facter/ define new facts for facter
   └─puppet/
      └─parser/
         └─functions/ define a new puppet function, like sort()
      └─provider/ define a provider for a new or existing type
      └─util/ define helper functions (in ruby)
      └─type/ define a new type in puppet
└─manifests/
└─init.pp class MODULE_NAME { }
└─spec/ rSpec tests
└─templates/ EPP or ERB template files used by the module
```

All manifest files (those containing Puppet code) live in the manifests directory. In our example, the memcached class is defined in the `manifests/init.pp` file, which will be imported automatically.

Inside the memcached class, we refer to the `memcached.conf` file:

```
file { '/etc/memcached.conf':
  source => 'puppet:///modules/memcached/memcached.conf',
}
```

The preceding `source` parameter tells Puppet to look for the file in:

```
MODULEPATH/ (/home/vagrant/)
 └memcached/
    └files/
      └memcached.conf
```

There's more...

Learn to love modules because they'll make your Puppet life a lot easier. They're not complicated, however; practice and experience will help you judge when things should be grouped into modules, and how best to arrange your module structure. Modules can hold more than manifests and files, as we'll see in the next two sections.

Templates

If you need to use a template as a part of the module, place it in the module's templates directory and refer to it as follows:

```
file { '/etc/memcached.conf':
  content => epp('memcached/memcached.conf.epp),
}
```

Puppet will look for the file in:

```
MODULEPATH/memcached/templates/memcached.conf.epp
```

Facts, functions, types, and providers

Modules can also contain custom facts, custom functions, custom types, and providers. For more information about these, refer to Chapter 9, *External Tools and the Puppet Ecosystem*.

Third-party modules

You can download modules provided by other people and use them in your own manifests just like the modules you create. For more on this, see Chapter 7, *Using Public Modules*.

Module organization

For more details on how to organize your modules, see the puppetlabs website: `https://puppet.com/docs/puppet/latest/modules_fundamentals.html`.

See also

- *The Creating custom facts* recipe in `Chapter 9`, *External Tools and the Puppet Ecosystem*
- *The Using public modules* recipe in `Chapter 9`, *External Tools and the Puppet Ecosystem*
- *The Creating your own resource types* recipe in `Chapter 9`, *External Tools and the Puppet Ecosystem*
- *The Creating your own providers* recipe in `Chapter 9`, *External Tools and the Puppet Ecosystem*

Using standard naming conventions

Choosing appropriate and informative names for your modules and classes will be a big help when it comes to maintaining your code. This is even truer if other people need to read and work on your manifests.

How to do it...

Here are some tips on how to name things in your manifests:

1. Name modules after the software or service they manage, for example, `apache` or `haproxy`.
2. Name classes within modules (subclasses) after the function or service they provide to the module, for example, `apache::vhosts` or `rails::dependencies`.
3. If a class within a module disables the service provided by that module, name it `disabled`. For example, a class that disables Apache should be named `apache::disabled`.

4. Create a roles and profiles hierarchy of modules. Each node should have a single role consisting of one or more profiles. Each profile module should configure a single service.

5. The module that manages users should be named user.

6. Within the user module, declare your virtual users within the `user::virtual` class (for more on virtual users and other resources, see the *Using virtual resources* recipe in `Chapter 5`, *Users and Virtual Resources*).

7. Within the user module, subclasses for particular groups of users should be named after the group, for example, `user::sysadmins` or `user::contractors`.

8. When using Puppet to deploy the config files for different services, name the file after the service, but with a suffix indicating what kind of file it is, for example:
   - Apache `init` script: `apache.init`
   - Logrotate config snippet for Rails: `rails.logrotate`
   - Nginx `vhost` file for mywizzoapp: `mywizzoapp.vhost.nginx`
   - MySQL config for standalone server: `standalone.mysql`
   - If you need to deploy a different version of a file depending on the operating system release, for example, you can use a naming convention like the following:

     ```
     memcached.lucid.conf
     memcached.precise.conf
     ```

     - You can have Puppet automatically select the appropriate version as follows:

     ```
     source = > "puppet:///modules/memcached
     /memcached.${::lsbdistrelease}.conf",
     ```

9. If you need to manage, for example, different Ruby versions, name the class after the version it is responsible for; for example, `ruby192` or `ruby186`.

There's more...

Some people prefer to include multiple classes on a node by using a comma-separated list, rather than separate include statements; for example:

```
node 'server014' inherits 'server' {
  include mail::server, repo::gem, repo::apt, zabbix
}
```

This is a matter of style, but I prefer to use separate include statements, one on a line, because it makes it easier to copy and move around class inclusions between nodes without having to tidy up the commas and indentation every time.

I mentioned inheritance in a couple of the preceding examples; if you're not sure what this is, don't worry, I'll explain this in detail in the next chapter.

Using inline templates

Templates are a powerful way of using **Embedded Puppet** (**EPP**) or Embedded Ruby (ERB) to help build config files dynamically. You can also use EPP or ERB syntax directly without having to use a separate file by calling the inline_epp or inline_template function. EPP and ERB allow you to use conditional logic, iterate over arrays, and include variables. EPP is the replacement of ERB; EPP uses native Puppet language. ERB uses Ruby language. ERB allows for using native Ruby functions which may not be available in EPP, so unless you need something Ruby specific, it is better to go with the native EPP templates. In the following example, we'll use a Ruby construct, so we'll use an ERB inline template.

How to do it...

Here's an example of how to use inline_template.

Pass your Ruby code to inline_template within the Puppet manifest, as follows:

```
cron { 'chkrootkit':
  command => '/usr/sbin/chkrootkit > /var/log/chkrootkit.log 2>&amp;1',
  hour    => inline_template('<%= @hostname.sum % 24 %>'),
  minute  => '00',
}
```

How it works...

Anything inside the string passed to inline_template is executed as if it were an ERB template. That is, anything inside the <%= and %> delimiters will be executed as Ruby code, and the rest will be treated as a string.

In this example, we use `inline_template` to compute a different hour for this `cron` resource (a scheduled job) for each machine, so that the same job does not run at the same time on all machines. For more on this technique, see the *Efficiently distributing cron jobs* recipe in `Chapter 5`, *Users and Virtual Resources*.

There's more...

In ERB code, whether inside a template file or an `inline_template` string, you can access your Puppet variables directly by name using an @ prefix, if they are in the current scope or the top scope (facts):

```
<%= @fqdn %>
```

To reference variables in another scope, use `scope.lookupvar`, as follows:

```
<%= "The value of something from otherclass is " +
scope.lookupvar('otherclass::something') %>
```

You should use inline templates sparingly. If you really need to use some complicated logic in your manifest, consider using a custom function instead (see the *Creating custom functions* recipe in `Chapter 8`, *External Tools and the Puppet Ecosystem*). As we'll see later, EPP templates use global scope for their variables; you always refer to variables with their full scope.

See also

- The *Using ERB templates* recipe in `Chapter 4`, *Working with Files and Packages*
- The *Using array iteration in templates* recipe in `Chapter 4`, *Working with Files and Packages*

Iterating over multiple items

Arrays are a powerful feature in Puppet; wherever you want to perform the same operation on a list of things, an array may be able to help. You can create an array just by putting its content in square brackets:

```
$lunch = [ 'franks', 'beans', 'mustard' ]
```

How to do it...

Here's a common example of how arrays are used:

1. Add the following code to your manifest:

```
$packages = [
  'ruby1.8-dev', 'ruby1.8',
  'ri1.8', 'rdoc1.8',
  'irb1.8', 'libreadline-ruby1.8',
  'libruby1.8', 'libopenssl-ruby'
]
package { $packages: ensure => installed }
```

2. Run `Puppet` and note that each package should now be installed.

How it works...

Where Puppet encounters an array as the name of a resource, it creates a resource for each element in the array. In the example, a new package resource is created for each of the packages in the `$packages` array, with the same `ensure => installed` parameters. This is a very compact way to instantiate many similar resources.

There's more...

Although arrays will take you a long way with Puppet, it's also useful to know about an even more flexible data structure: the hash.

Using hashes

A hash is like an array, but each of the elements can be stored and looked up by name (referred to as the key); for example, `hash.pp`:

```
$interface = {
 'name' => 'eth0',
 'ip'   => '192.168.0.1',
 'mac'  => '52:54:00:4a:60:07'
}
notify { "(${interface['ip']}) at ${interface['mac']} on
${interface['name']}": }
```

When we run `Puppet` on this, we see the following notice in the output:

```
t@cookbook:~/.puppet/manifests$ puppet apply hash.pp
Notice: Compiled catalog for cookbook.example.com in environment production
in 0.04 seconds
Notice: (192.168.0.1) at 52:54:00:4a:60:07 on eth0
```

Hash values can be anything that you can assign to variables, strings, function calls, expressions, and even other hashes or arrays. Hashes are useful to store a bunch of information about a particular thing because by accessing each element of the hash using a key, we can quickly find the information we are looking for.

Creating arrays with the split function

You can declare literal arrays using square brackets, as follows:

```
define lunchprint() {
 notify { "Lunch included ${name}":}
}
$lunch = ['egg', 'beans', 'chips']
lunchprint { $lunch: }
```

Now, when we run Puppet on the preceding code, we see the following notice messages in the output:

```
t@cookbook:~$ puppet apply lunchprint.pp
Notice: Compiled catalog for cookbook.strangled.net in environment
production in 0.02 seconds
Notice: Lunch included egg
Notice: Lunch included beans
Notice: Lunch included chips
Notice: Applied catalog in 0.04 seconds
```

However, Puppet can also create arrays for you from strings, using the `split` function, as follows:

```
$menu = 'egg beans chips'
$items = split($menu, ' ')
lunchprint { $items: }
```

Running `puppet apply` against this new manifest, we see the same messages in the output:

```
t@cookbook:~$ puppet apply lunchprint2.pp
Notice: Compiled catalog for cookbook.strangled.net in environment
production in 0.02 seconds
Notice: Lunch included egg
Notice: Lunch included beans
Notice: Lunch included chips
Notice: Applied catalog in 0.21 seconds
```

 The split takes two arguments: the first argument is the string to be split. The second argument is the character to split on. In this example, it's a single space. As Puppet works its way through the string, when it encounters a space, it will interpret it as the end of one item and the beginning of the next. So, given the string egg, beans, and chips, this will be split into three items.

The character to split on can be any character or string:

```
$menu = 'egg and beans and chips' $items = split($menu, ' and ')
```

The character can also be a regular expression, for example, a set of alternatives separated by a | (pipe) character:

```
$lunch = 'egg:beans,chips'
$items = split($lunch, ':|,')
```

Writing powerful conditional statements

Puppet's `if` statement allows you to change the manifest behavior based on the value of a variable or an expression. With it, you can apply different resources or parameter values depending on certain facts about the node; for example, the operating system or the memory size.

You can also set variables within the manifest, which can change the behavior of included classes. For example, nodes in data center A might need to use different DNS servers than nodes in data center B, or you might need to include one set of classes for an Ubuntu system, and a different set for other systems.

How to do it...

Here's an example of a useful conditional statement. Add the following code to your manifest:

```
if $::timezone == 'UTC' {
  notify { 'Universal Time Coordinated':}
} else {
  notify { "$::timezone is not UTC": }
}
```

How it works...

Puppet treats whatever follows an if keyword as an expression and evaluates it. If the expression evaluates to true, Puppet will execute the code within the curly braces.

Optionally, you can add an else branch, which will be executed if the expression evaluates to false.

There's more...

Lets take a look at some more tips on using if statements.

elsif branches

You can add further tests using the elsif keyword, as follows:

```
if $::timezone == 'UTC' {
notify { 'Universal Time Coordinated': }
} elsif $::timezone == 'GMT' {
notify { 'Greenwich Mean Time': }
} else {
notify { "$::timezone is not UTC": }
}
```

Comparisons

You can check whether two values are equal using the == syntax, as in our example:

```
if $::timezone == 'UTC' {
  ...
}
```

Alternatively, you can check whether they are not equal using !=:

```
if $::timezone != 'UTC' {
  ...
}
```

You can also compare numeric values using < and >:

```
if $::uptime_days > 365 {
  notify { 'Time to upgrade your kernel!': }
}
```

To test whether a value is greater (or less) than or equal to another value, use <= or >=:

```
if $::mtu_eth0 <= 1500 {
  notify {"Not Jumbo Frames": }
}
```

Combining expressions

You can put together the kind of simple expressions described previously into more complex logical expressions, using and, or, and not:

```
if ($::uptime_days > 365) and ($::kernel == 'Linux') {
  ...
}
if ($role == 'webserver') and ( ($datacenter == 'A') or ($datacenter ==
'B') ) {
  ...
}
```

See also

- *The Using the in operator* recipe in this chapter
- *The Using selectors and case statements* recipe in this chapter

Using regular expressions in if statements

Another kind of expression you can test in `if` statements and other conditionals is the regular expression. A regular expression is a powerful way to compare strings using pattern matching.

How to do it...

This is one example of using a regular expression in a conditional statement. Add the following to your manifest:

```
if $::architecture =~ /64/ {
  notify { '64Bit OS Installed': }
} else {
  notify { 'Upgrade to 64Bit': }
  fail('Not 64 Bit')
}
```

How it works...

Puppet treats the text supplied between the forward slashes as a regular expression, specifying the text to be matched. If the match succeeds, the if expression will be true and so the code between the first set of curly braces will be executed. In this example, we used a regular expression because different distributions have different ideas on what to call 64 bit; some use `amd64`, while others use `x86_64`. The only thing we can count on is the presence of the number 64 within the fact. Some facts that have version numbers in them are treated as strings to Puppet. For instance, `$::facterversion`. On my test system, this is 3.9.3, but when I try to compare that with 3, Puppet fails to make the following comparison:

```
if $::facterversion > 3 {
  notify {"Facter version 3": }
}
```

Which produces the following output when run with `puppet apply`:

```
t@cookbook:~$ puppet apply version.pp
Error: Evaluation Error: Comparison of: String > Integer, is not possible.
Caused by 'A String is not comparable to a non String'. at
/home/vagrant/version.pp:1:21 on node cookbook.example.com
```

We could make the comparison with =~ but that would match a 3 in any position in the version string. Puppet provides a function to compare versions, versioncmp, as shown in this example:

```
if versioncmp($::facterversion,'3') > 0 {
  notify {"Facter version 3": }
}
```

Which now produces the desired result:

```
t@cookbook:~$ puppet apply version2.pp
Notice: Compiled catalog for cookbook.strangled.net in environment
production in 0.01 seconds
Notice: Facter version 3
```

The versioncmp function returns -1 if the first parameter is a lower version than the second, 0 if the two parameters are equal, or 1 if the second parameter is lower than the first.

If you wanted instead to do something if the text does not match, use !~ rather than =~:

```
if $::kernel !~ /Linux/ {
  notify { 'Not Linux, could be Windows, MacOS X, AIX, or ?': }
}
```

There's more...

Regular expressions are very powerful, but can be difficult to understand and debug. If you find yourself using a regular expression so complex that you can't see at a glance what it does, think about simplifying your design to make it easier. However, one particularly useful feature of regular expressions is their ability to capture patterns.

Capturing patterns

You can not only match text using a regular expression, but also capture the matched text and store it in a variable:

```
$input = 'Puppet is better than manual configuration'
if $input =~ /(.*) is better than (.*)/ {
  notify { "You said '${0}'. Looks like you're comparing ${1} to ${2}!": }
}
```

The preceding code produces this output:

```
Notice: You said 'Puppet is better than manual configuration'. Looks like
you're comparing Puppet to manual configuration!
```

The `$0` variable stores the whole matched text (assuming the overall match succeeded). If you put brackets around any part of the regular expression, it creates a group, and any matched groups will also be stored in variables. The first matched group will be `$1`, the second `$2`, and so on, as shown in the preceding example.

Regular expression syntax

Puppet's regular expression syntax is the same as Ruby's, so resources that explain Ruby's regular expression syntax will also help you with Puppet. You can find a good introduction to Ruby's regular expression syntax at this website: `http://www.tutorialspoint.com/ruby/ruby_regular_expressions.htm`.

See also

- Refer to the *Using regular expression substitutions* recipe in this chapter

Using selectors and case statements

Although you could write any conditional statement using `if`, Puppet provides a couple of extra forms to help you express conditionals more easily: the selector and the case statement.

How to do it...

Here are some examples of selector and case statements:

1. Add the following code to your manifest:

```
$systemtype = $::operatingsystem ? {
    'Ubuntu' => 'debianlike',
    'Debian' => 'debianlike',
    'RedHat' => 'redhatlike',
    'Fedora' => 'redhatlike',
    'CentOS' => 'redhatlike',
```

```
    default  => 'unknown',
  }
  notify { "You have a ${systemtype} system": }
```

2. Add the following code to your manifest:

```
class debianlike {
  notify { 'Special manifest for Debian-like systems': }
}
class redhatlike {
  notify { 'Special manifest for RedHat-like systems': }
}
case $::operatingsystem {
  'Ubuntu', 'Debian': { include debianlike },
  'RedHat', 'Fedora', 'CentOS', 'Springdale': { include
redhatlike }
  default: { notify { "I don't know what kind of system you
have!": } }
}
```

How it works...

Our example demonstrates both the selector and the case statement, so let's see in detail how each of them works.

Selector

In the first example, we used a selector (the ? operator) to choose a value for the $systemtype variable depending on the value of $::operatingsystem. This is similar to the ternary operator in C or Ruby, but instead of choosing between two possible values, you can have as many values as you like.

Puppet will compare the value of $::operatingsystem to each of the possible values we have supplied in Ubuntu, Debian, and so on. These values could be regular expressions (for example, for a partial string match or to use wildcards), but in our case, we have just used literal strings.

As soon as it finds a match, the selector expression returns whatever value is associated with the matching string. If the value of $::operatingsystem is fedora, for example, the selector expression will return the redhatlike string and this will be assigned to the $systemtype variable.

Case statement

Unlike selectors, the case statement does not return a value. Case statements come in handy when you want to execute different code depending on the value of an expression. In our second example, we used the case statement to include either the `debianlike` or `redhatlike` class, depending on the value of `$::operatingsystem`.

Again, Puppet compares the value of `$::operatingsystem` to a list of potential matches. These could be regular expressions or strings, or as in our example, comma-separated lists of strings. When it finds a match, the associated code between curly braces is executed. So, if the value of `$::operatingsystem` is Ubuntu, then the code including `debianlike` will be executed.

There's more...

Once you've got a grip on the basic use of selectors and case statements, you may find the following tips useful.

Regular expressions

As with `if` statements, you can use regular expressions with selectors and case statements, and you can also capture the values of the matched groups and refer to them using `$1`, `$2`, and so on:

```
case $::lsbdistdescription {
  /Ubuntu (.+)/: {
    notify { "You have Ubuntu version ${1}": }
  }
  /CentOS (.+)/: {
    notify { "You have CentOS version ${1}": }
  }
  default: {}
}
```

Defaults

Both selectors and case statements let you specify a default value, which is chosen if none of the other options match (the style guide suggests you always have a default clause defined):

```
$lunch = 'Filet mignon.' $lunchtype = $lunch ? {
  /fries/ => 'unhealthy',
  /salad/ => 'healthy',
  default => 'unknown',
}
notify { "Your lunch was ${lunchtype}": }
```

The output is as follows:

```
t@cookbook:~$ puppet apply lunchtype.pp
Notice: Compiled catalog for cookbook.strangled.net in environment
production in 0.01 seconds
Notice: Your lunch was unknown
```

When the default action dosen't occur, use the `fail()` function to halt the Puppet run.

Using the in operator

The `in` operator tests whether one string contains another string. Here's an example:

```
if 'spring' in 'springfield'
```

The preceding expression is true if the spring string is a substring of `springfield`, which it is. The `in` operator can also test for membership of arrays as follows:

```
if $crewmember in ['Frank', 'Dave', 'HAL' ]
```

When `in` is used with a hash, it tests whether the string is a key of the hash:

```
$ifaces = {
  'lo'   => '127.0.0.1',
  'eth0' => '192.168.0.1'
}
if 'eth0' in $ifaces {
  notify { "eth0 has address ${ifaces['eth0']}": }
}
```

How to do it...

The following steps will show you how to use the `in` operator:

1. Add the following code to your manifest:

```
if $::operatingsystem in [ 'Ubuntu', 'Debian' ] {
  notify { 'Debian-type operating system detected': }
} elsif $::operatingsystem in [ 'RedHat', 'Fedora', 'SuSE',
'CentOS' ] {
  notify { 'RedHat-type operating system detected': }
} else {
  notify { 'Some other operating system detected': }
}
```

2. Run Puppet:

```
t@cookbook:~$ puppet apply in.pp
Notice: Compiled catalog for cookbook.example.com in
environment production in 0.01 seconds
Notice: RedHat-type operating system detected
```

There's more...

The value of an in expression is Boolean (true or false) so you can assign it to a variable:

```
$debianlike = $::operatingsystem in [ 'Debian', 'Ubuntu' ]
if $debianlike {
  notify { 'You are in a maze of twisty little packages, all alike': }
}
```

Using regular expression substitutions

Puppet's `regsubst` function provides an easy way to manipulate text, search and replace expressions within strings, or extract patterns from strings. We often need to do this with data obtained from a fact, for example, or from external programs.

In this example, we'll see how to use `regsubst` to extract the first three octets of an IPv4 address (the network part, assuming it's a /24 class C address).

How to do it...

Follow these steps to build the example:

1. Add the following code to your manifest:

```
$class_c = regsubst($::ipaddress, '(.*)\..*', '\1.0')
notify { "The network part of ${::ipaddress} is ${class_c}": }
```

2. Run Puppet:

```
t@cookbook:~$ puppet apply regsubst.pp
Notice: Compiled catalog for cookbook.strangled.net in environment
production in 0.02 seconds
Notice: The network part of 10.0.2.15 is 10.0.2.0
```

How it works...

The `regsubst` function takes at least three parameters: source, pattern, and replacement. In our example, we specified the source string as `$::ipaddress`, which, on this machine, is as follows:

```
10.0.2.15
```

We specify the pattern function as follows:

```
(.*)\..*
```

We specify the replacement function as follows:

```
\1.0
```

The pattern captures all of the string up to the last period (`\.`) in the `\1` variable. We then match on `.*`, which matches everything to the end of the string, so when we replace the string at the end with `\1.0`, we end up with only the network portion of the IP address, which evaluates to the following:

```
10.0.2.0
```

We could have got the same result in other ways, of course, including the following:

```
$class_c = regsubst($::ipaddress, '\.\d+$', '.0')
```

Here, we only match the last octet and replace it with `. 0`, which achieves the same result without capturing.

There's more...

The pattern function can be any regular expression, using the same (Ruby) syntax as regular expressions in `if` statements.

See also

- The *Importing dynamic information* recipe in `Chapter 3`, *Writing Better Manifests*
- The *Getting information about the environment* recipe in `Chapter 3`, *Writing Better Manifests*
- The *Using regular expressions in if statements* recipe in this chapter

Puppet 5 changes

Prior to Puppet 4, Puppet 3 had a preview of the Puppet 4 language named the future parser. The future parser feature allowed you to preview the language changes that would be coming to Puppet 4 before upgrading. Most of these features were related to iterating on objects and have been carried forward to Puppet 5. In this section, we will cover the major changes in Puppet 5. A good place to check for language changes are the release notes. While writing this book, I'm using Puppet 5.3, so I need to check the release notes for Puppet 5.0 (`https://puppet.com/docs/puppet/5.0/release_notes.html`), 5.1 (`https://puppet.com/docs/puppet/5.1/release_notes.html`), 5.2 (`https://puppet.com/docs/puppet/5.2/release_notes.html`), 5.3 (`https://puppet.com/docs/puppet/5.3/release_notes.html`), and 5.5(`https://puppet.com/docs/puppet/5.5/release_notes.html`).

Using the call function

Puppet 5 adds a new function, `call`. This function is useful for calling a function by name using a variable. In the following example, we change the function we use depending on a variable:

```
if versioncmp($::puppetversion,'4.0') {
   $func = 'lookup'
```

```
} else {
 $func = 'hiera'
}
$val = call($func,'important_setting')
notify {"\$val = $val, \$func = $func": }
```

If the version of Puppet is lower than 4.0, the `hiera` function will be called; if not, `lookup` will be used.

Puppet 4/5 changes

The following changes occured in Puppet 4 and carried forward to Puppet 5.

Appending to and concatenating arrays

You can `conca/home/test/puppet-beginners-guide-3/tenate` arrays with the + operator or append them with the << operator. In the following example, we use the ternary operator to assign a specific package name to the `$apache` variable. We then append that value to an array using the << operator:

```
$apache = $::osfamily ? {
   'Debian' => 'apache2',
   'RedHat' => 'httpd'
}
$packages = ['memcached'] << $apache
package {$packages: ensure => installed}
```

If we have two arrays, we can use the + operator to concatenate the two arrays. In this example, we define an array of system administrators (`$sysadmins`) and another array of application owners (`$appowners`). We can then concatenate the array and use it as an argument to our allowed users:

```
$sysadmins = [ 'thomas','john','josko' ]
$appowners = [ 'mike', 'patty', 'erin' ]
$users = $sysadmins + $appowners
notice ($users)
```

When we apply this manifest, we see that the two arrays have been joined, as shown in the following command-line output:

```
t@cookbook:~$ puppet apply concat.pp
Notice: Scope(Class[main]): [thomas, john, josko, mike, patty, erin]
```

Merging hashes

If we have two hashes, we can merge them using the same + operator we used for arrays. Consider our `$interfaces` hash from a previous example; we can add another interface to the hash:

```
$iface = {'name'  => 'eth0',
          'ip'    => '192.168.0.1',
          'mac'   => '52:54:00:4a:60:07' }
       + {'route' => '192.168.0.254'}
notice ($iface)
```

When we apply this manifest, we see that the route attribute has been merged into the hash (your results may differ; the order in which the hash prints is unpredictable), as follows:

```
t@cookbook:~$ puppet apply merge.pp
Notice: Scope(Class[main]): {name => eth0, ip => 192.168.0.1, mac =>
52:54:00:4a:60:07, route => 192.168.0.254}
```

Using the sensitive type

It is often the case that you wish to store passwords or other credentials in Puppet. There are a few ways to do so with some level of security, such as eyaml or GPG. However, the unencrypted data may still be leaked via reports and logs. Starting in Puppet 4.6, a new `sensitive` type was created to address this problem. Data that is stored in a Sensitive type will not be leaked via reports or logs; when the value needs to be recorded it will be replaced with `value redacted`.

In the following example, we can see how we can output a password to a file but take advantage of the protections of the `Sensitive` type:

```
$secret = Sensitive('My Top Secret Password')
file {'/tmp/passwd':
  content => "${secret.unwrap}\n",
}
notice($secret)
```

When we use `puppet apply` on this code, we see that the notice has the value redacted while the unwrapped value is stored in the file:

```
t@cookbook:~$ puppet apply sensitive.pp
Notice: Scope(Class[main]): Sensitive [value redacted]
Notice: Compiled catalog for cookbook.example.com in environment production
in 0.01 seconds
```

```
Notice: /Stage[main]/Main/File[/tmp/passwd]/content: content changed
'{md5}6d814ec03401f7954ed41306e8848a07' to
'{md5}a4ca22adedac7912cbb7e53ccfba0a9d'
Notice: Applied catalog in 0.03 seconds
t@cookbook:~$ cat /tmp/passwd
My Top Secret Password
```

Lambda functions

Lambda functions are iterators applied to arrays or hashes. You iterate through the array or hash and apply an `iterator` function such as `each`, `map`, `filter`, `reduce`, or `slice` to each element of the array or key of the hash. Some of the lambda functions return a calculated array or value; others such as `each` only return the input array or hash.

Lambda functions such as `map` and `reduce` use temporary variables that are thrown away after the lambda has finished. Use of lambda functions is something best shown by example. In the next few sections, we will show an example usage of each of the lambda functions.

reduce

`reduce` is used to reduce the array to a single value. This can be used to calculate the maximum or minimum of the array, or in this case, the sum of the elements of the array:

```
$count = [1,2,3,4,5]
$sum = reduce($count) | $total, $i | { $total + $i }
notice("Sum is $sum")
```

This preceding code will compute the sum of the $count array and store it in the $sum variable, as follows:

```
t@cookbook:~$ puppet apply reduce.pp
Notice: Scope(Class[main]): Sum is 15
```

filter

`filter` is used to filter the array or hash based on a test within the lambda function. For instance, we filter our $count array as follows:

```
$count = [1,2,3,4,5]
$filter = filter ($count) | $i | { $i > 3 }
notice("Filtered array is $filter")
```

When we apply this manifest, we see that only elements 4 and 5 are in the result:

```
t@cookbook:~$ puppet apply filter.pp
Notice: Scope(Class[main]): Filtered array is [4, 5]
```

map

map is used to apply a function to each element of the array. For instance, if we wanted (for some unknown reason) to compute the square of all the elements of the array, we would use map as follows:

```
$count = [1,2,3,4,5]
$map = map ($count) | $i | { $i * $i }
notice("Square of array is ${map}")
```

The result of applying this manifest is a new array with every element of the original array squared (multiplied by itself), as shown in the following command-line output:

```
t@cookbook:~$ puppet apply map.pp
Notice: Scope(Class[main]): Square of array is [1, 4, 9, 16, 25]
```

slice

slice is useful when you have related values stored in the same array in a sequential order. For instance, if we had the destination and port information for a firewall in an array, we could split them up into pairs and perform operations on those pairs:

```
$firewall_rules = ['192.168.0.1','80',
                   '192.168.0.10','443']
slice ($firewall_rules,2) |$ip, $port| {
  notice("Allow $ip on $port")
}
```

When applied, this manifest will produce the following notices:

```
t@cookbook:~$ puppet apply slice.pp
Notice: Scope(Class[main]): Allow 192.168.0.1 on 80
Notice: Scope(Class[main]): Allow 192.168.0.10 on 443
```

To make this a useful example, create a new firewall resource within the block of the `slice` instead of `notice`:

```
$firewall_rules = ['192.168.0.1','80',
                   '192.168.0.10','443']
slice ($firewall_rules,2) |$ip, $port| {
  firewall { "$port from $ip":
    dport  => $port,
    source => "$ip",
    action => 'accept',
  }
}
```

each

`each` is used to iterate over the elements of the array but lacks the ability to capture the results like the other functions. `each` is the simplest case where you simply wish to do something with each element of the array, as shown in the following code snippet:

```
each ($count) |$c| { notice($c) }
```

As expected, this executes the notice for each element of the `$count` array, as follows:

```
t@cookbook:~$ puppet apply each.pp
Notice: Scope(Class[main]): 1
Notice: Scope(Class[main]): 2
```

Functions in Puppet language

Starting from Puppet 4, you can write functions in the Puppet language instead of Ruby. It is believed at some point that Puppet will move away from using Ruby in the backend, so any new functions you write should use the Puppet language if possible. The interesting thing about writing functions in the Puppet language is that there is no `return` statement; Puppet will return the last expression from a function as the return value. It is still possible to do more advanced programming while remaining within Puppet language. In the following example, we will use a rough estimation algorithm to calculate the square root of a number.

The first function is used to determine if we are close to the square root:

```
function close(Integer $number, Float $guess) {
  if abs(($guess * $guess) - $number ) < 0.01 {
    true
  } else {
    guessAgain($number,$guess)
  }
}
```

This will either return true if $guess^2 is within 0.01 of $number or it will use the next guessAgain function to return the next guess to the main function:

```
function guessAgain($number, $guess) {
  ($guess + ($number / $guess )) / 2.0
}
```

This function is used to make a correction to the current guess, to bring the estimation closer to the square root. The last function is where we do our recursion; recursion is where a function uses itself as part of the algorithm:

```
function sqrt_($number, $guess) {
  if close($number,$guess) == true {
    $guess
  } else {
    sqrt_($number, guessAgain($number, $guess))
  }
}
```

> If you are unfamiliar with recursion, I suggest the Wikipedia article on recursion (https://en.wikipedia.org/wiki/Recursion_(computer_science)).

In this function, if the close function returns true, we know we are close enough to the root and can return $guess to the calling function. If not, we call sqrt_ again with a new guess. The final function is just a wrapper of sqrt_ and is used so the caller need not set an initial guess:

```
function sqrt($number) {
  sqrt_($number,1.0)
}
```

To see this in action, we'll need to call our `sqrt` function and use `notify` to print the values returned:

```
function sqrt_($number, $guess) {
  if close($number,$guess) == true {
    $guess
  } else {
    sqrt_($number, guessAgain($number, $guess))
  }
}
```

Now when we run Puppet, we see the following output:

```
Notice: sqrt(4) = 2.000609756097561
Notice: sqrt(2) = 1.4166666666666665
Notice: sqrt(81) = 9.000011298790216
```

Puppet Infrastructure 2

We will cover the following recipes in this chapter:

- Managing your manifests with Git
- Creating a decentralized Puppet architecture
- Writing a papply script
- Running Puppet from cron
- Bootstrapping Puppet with Bash
- Creating a centralized Puppet infrastructure
- Creating certificates with multiple DNS names
- Setting up the environment
- Configuring PuppetDB
- Configuring Hiera
- Environment-specific Hiera
- Setting node-specific data with Hiera
- Writing a Custom Hiera 5 function
- Storing secret data with hiera-eyaml
- Automatic syntax-checking with Git hooks
- Pushing code around with Git
- Managing environments with Git

Introduction

In this chapter, we will cover how to deploy Puppet in a centralized and decentralized manner. With each approach, we'll see a combination of best practices, my personal experience, and community solutions. We'll configure and use both PuppetDB and Hiera. PuppetDB is used with exported resources, which we will cover in Chapter 5, *Users and Virtual Resources*. Hiera is used to separate variable data from Puppet code. Finally, we will learn about Git and see how to use Git to organize our code and our infrastructure. Because Linux distributions, such as Ubuntu, Red Hat, and CentOS, differ in the specific details of package names, configuration file paths, and many other things, for reasons of space and clarity, the best approach for this book is was pick one distribution (CentOS 7) and stick to that. However, Puppet runs on most popular operating systems, so you should have very little trouble adapting the recipes to your favorite OS and distribution. At the time of writing, Puppet 5.3.3 is the latest stable version available; this is the version of Puppet used in the book. The syntax of Puppet commands changes often, so be aware that while older versions of Puppet are still perfectly usable, they may not support all of the features and syntax described in this book.

Managing your manifests with Git

It's a great idea to put your Puppet manifests in a version-control system, such as Git or Subversion (Git is the *de facto* standard for Puppet). This gives you several advantages:

- You can undo changes and revert to any previous version of your manifest
- You can experiment with new features using a branch
- If several people need to make changes to the manifests, they can make them independently, in their own working copies, and then merge their changes later
- You can use the Git log feature to see what was changed and when (and by whom)

Getting ready

In this section, we'll import your existing manifest files into Git. If you have created a Puppet directory in a previous section, use that, otherwise, use your existing manifest directory.

In this example, we'll create a new Git repository on a server accessible from all our nodes. There are several steps we need to take to have our code held in a Git repository:

1. Install Git on a central server.
2. Create a user to run Git and own the repository.
3. Create a repository to hold the code.
4. Create SSH keys to allow key-based access to the repository.
5. Install Git on a node and download the latest version from our Git repository.

How to do it...

Follow these steps:

1. Install Git on your Git server (git.example.com in our example). The easiest way to do this is using Puppet. Create the following manifest and call it git.pp:

```
package {'git':
  ensure => installed
}
```

2. Apply this manifest using puppet apply git.pp; this will install Git.

3. Create a Git user that the nodes will use to log in and retrieve the latest code. Again, we'll do this with Puppet. We'll also create a directory to hold our repository (/home/git/repos), as shown in the following code snippet:

```
group { 'git': gid => 1111, }
user {'git':
  uid     => 1111,
  gid     => 1111,
  comment => 'Git User',
  home    => '/home/git',
  require => Group['git'],
}
file {'/home/git':
  ensure  => 'directory',
  owner   => 1111,
  group   => 1111,
  require => User['git'],
}
file {'/home/git/repos':
  ensure  => 'directory',
  owner   => 1111,
  group   => 1111,
```

```
require => File['/home/git']
}
```

4. After applying that manifest, log in as the `git` user and create an empty Git repository using the following command:

```
# sudo -iu git
git@git $ cd repos
git@git $ git init --bare puppet.gitInitialized empty Git
repository in /home/git/repos/puppet.git/
```

5. Set a password for the Git user; we'll need to log in remotely after the next step:

```
[root@git ~]# passwd git
Changing password for user git.
New password:
Retype new password:
passwd: all authentication tokens updated successfully.
```

6. Back on your local machine, create an `ssh` key for our nodes to use to update the repository:

```
t@mylaptop ~ $ cd .ssh
t@mylaptop ~/.ssh $ ssh-keygen -b 4096 -f git_rsa
Generating public/private rsa key pair.
Enter passphrase (empty for no passphrase):
Enter same passphrase again:
Your identification has been saved in git_rsa.
Your public key has been saved in git_rsa.pub.
The key fingerprint is:
SHA256:fOnErAM6BKecUQ1Lh9wLqFv9LxICFsMaySc3Ey5LM5I
thomas@mylaptop
```

7. Copy the newly created public key to the `authorized_keys` file. This will allow us to connect to the Git server using this new key:

```
t@mylaptop ~/.ssh $ ssh-copy-id -i git_rsa git@git.example.com
git@git.example.com's password:
Number of key(s) added: 1
```

8. Try logging into the machine with `ssh 'git@git.example.com'` and check to make sure that only the `key(s)` you wanted were added.

9. Configure ssh to use your key when accessing the Git server and add the
   following to your `~/.ssh/config file`:

   ```
   Host git git.example.com
   User git
   IdentityFile /home/thomas/.ssh/git_rsa
   ```

 If you are using vagrant to provision your nodes for this exercise,
use `vagrant ssh-config` to print the extra information required to
connect to your vagrant nodes via ssh.

10. `clone` the repository onto your machine into a directory named Puppet
    (substitute your server name if you didn't use `git.example.com`):

    ```
    t@mylaptop ~$ git clone git@git.example.com:repos/puppet.git
    Cloning into 'puppet'...
    warning: You appear to have cloned an empty repository.
    ```

11. We've created a Git repository; before we commit any changes to the repository,
    it's a good idea to set your name and email in Git. Your name and email will be
    appended to each commit you make. When you are working in a large team,
    knowing who made a change is very important; for this, use the following code
    snippet:

    ```
    t@mylaptop puppet$ git config --global user.email
    "thomas@narrabilis.com"
    t@mylaptop puppet$ git config --global user.name "Thomas
    Uphill"
    ```

12. You can verify your Git settings using the following snippet:

    ```
    t@mylaptop ~$ git config --global --list
    user.name=Thomas Uphill
    user.email=thomas@narrabilis.com
    core.editor=vim
    merge.tool=vimdiff
    color.ui=true
    push.default=simple
    ```

13. Now that we have Git configured properly, change the directory to your
    `repository` directory and create a new site manifest, as shown in the following
    snippet:

    ```
    t@mylaptop ~$ cd puppet
    t@mylaptop puppet$ mkdir manifests
    ```

```
t@mylaptop puppet$ vim manifests/site.pp
node default {
  include base
}
```

14. This site manifest will install our base class on every node; we will create the base class using the Puppet module, as we did in Chapter 1, *Puppet Language and Style*:

```
t@mylaptop puppet$ mkdir modules
t@mylaptop puppet$ cd modules
t@mylaptop modules$ puppet module generate thomas-base --skip-
interview
Notice: Generating module at
/home/thomas/puppet/modules/base...
Notice: Populating templates...
Finished; module generated in base.
base/Gemfile
base/metadata.json
base/spec
base/spec/spec_helper.rb
base/spec/classes
base/spec/classes/init_spec.rb
base/Rakefile
base/examples
base/examples/init.pp
base/manifests
base/manifests/init.pp
base/README.md
```

15. To make sure our module does something useful, add the following to the body of the base class defined in base/manifests/init.pp:

```
class base {
  $content = @(MOTD)
    ${::fqdn}
    Managed by puppet ${::puppetversion}
    | MOTD
  file {'/etc/motd':
    content => $content
  }
}
```

16. Add the new base module and site manifest to Git using `git add` and `git commit`, as follows:

```
t@mylaptop modules$ cd ..
t@mylaptop puppet$ git add modules manifests
t@mylaptop puppet$ git status
On branch master

No commits yet

Changes to be committed:
  (use "git rm --cached <file>..." to unstage)

  new file: manifests/site.pp
  new file: modules/base/Gemfile
  new file: modules/base/README.md
  new file: modules/base/Rakefile
  new file: modules/base/examples/init.pp
  new file: modules/base/manifests/init.pp
  new file: modules/base/metadata.json
  new file: modules/base/spec/classes/init_spec.rb
  new file: modules/base/spec/spec_helper.rb
t@mylaptop puppet$ git commit -m "Initial commit with simple
base module"
[master (root-commit) 0863b71] Initial commit with simple base
module
 9 files changed, 232 insertions(+)
 create mode 100644 manifests/site.pp
 create mode 100644 modules/base/Gemfile
 create mode 100644 modules/base/README.md
 create mode 100644 modules/base/Rakefile
 create mode 100644 modules/base/examples/init.pp
 create mode 100644 modules/base/manifests/init.pp
 create mode 100644 modules/base/metadata.json
 create mode 100644 modules/base/spec/classes/init_spec.rb
 create mode 100644 modules/base/spec/spec_helper.rb
```

17. Your changes to the Git repository have been committed locally; you now need to push those changes back to `git.example.com`, so that other nodes can retrieve the updated files:

```
Counting objects: 18, done.
Delta compression using up to 8 threads.
Compressing objects: 100% (12/12), done.
Writing objects: 100% (18/18), 4.41 KiB | 2.20 MiB/s, done.
```

```
Total 18 (delta 0), reused 0 (delta 0)
To git.example.com:repos/puppet.git
 * [new branch] master -> master
```

How it works...

Git tracks changes to files and stores a complete history of all changes. The history of the repo is made up of commits. A commit represents the state of the repo at a particular point in time, which you create with the `git commit` command and annotate with a message.

You've now added your Puppet manifest files to the repo and created your first commit. This updates the history of the repo, but only in your local working copy. To synchronize the changes with the `git.example.com` copy, we use the `git push` command. This pushes all changes made since the last sync.

There's more...

Now that you have a central Git repository for your Puppet manifests, you can check out multiple copies of it in different places and work on them before committing your changes. For example, if you're working in a team, each member can have their own local copy of the repo and synchronize changes with the others via the central server. You may also choose to use GitHub as your central Git repository server. GitHub offers free Git repository hosting for public repositories, and you can pay for GitHub's premium service if you don't want your Puppet code to be publicly available.

 In addition to GitHub, there are several other web frontends for Git. Gogs is a Git frontend written in go; more information is available at `https://gogs.io/`. Gitlab is a Git frontend similar to github; more information is available at `https://about.gitlab.com/`. Additionally, self-hosted systems, such as gitolite (`http://gitolite.com/gitolite/index.html`), are also available.

In the next section, we will use our Git repository for both centralized and decentralized Puppet configurations.

Creating a decentralized Puppet architecture

Puppet is a configuration management tool that can be used to configure and prevent configuration drift in a large number of client computers. If all your client computers are easily reached via a central location, you may choose to have a central Puppet server control all the client computers. In the centralized model, the Puppet server is known as the Puppet master. Originally, the Puppet master ran a service named `master`, it now runs a service named `puppetserver`, but the name has remained. We will cover how to configure a central Puppet master later.

If your client computers are widely distributed or you cannot guarantee communication between client computers and a central location, then a decentralized architecture may be a good fit for your deployment. In the next few sections, we will see how to configure a decentralized Puppet architecture.

As we have seen, we can run the `puppet apply` command directly on a manifest file to have Puppet apply it. The problem with this arrangement is that we need to have the manifests transferred to the client computers.

We can use the Git repository we created in the previous section to transfer our manifests to each new node we create.

Getting ready

Create a new test node and call this new node whatever you like; I'll use `testnode` for mine. Install Puppet on the machine as we did previously.

How to do it...

Create a `bootstrap.pp` manifest that will perform the following configuration steps on our new node:

1. Install Git using the following code:

```
package {'git':
  ensure => 'installed'
}
```

2. Create a user to connect to the Git server:

```
File {
  owner => '1100',
  group => '1100',
  mode  => '0755',
}
file {'githome':
  ensure => 'directory',
  path   => '/usr/local/git',
}
user {'git':
  uid     => '1100',
  gid     => '1100',
  home    => '/usr/local/git',
  comment => 'GIT User',
}
```

3. Install the ssh key to access git.example.com in the root user's home directory
(/root/.ssh/id_rsa):

```
file {'git-ssh':
  ensure => 'directory',
  path   => '/usr/local/git/.ssh',
  mode   => '0700',
}
$git_id_rsa = @(GIT)
  -----BEGIN RSA PRIVATE KEY-----
  ...
  NIjTXmZUlOKefh4MBilqUU3KQG8GBHjzYl2TkFVGLNYGNA0U8VG8SUJq
  -----END RSA PRIVATE KEY-----
  | GIT
file {'git-id_rsa':
 path    => '/usr/local/git/.ssh/id_rsa',
 content => $git_id_rsa,
 mode    => 0600,
 require => File['git-ssh']
}
```

4. Download the ssh host key from git.example.com (/usr/local/g
it/.ssh/known_hosts):

```
exec {'download git.example.com host key':
  command => 'ssh-keyscan git.example.com
>>/usr/local/git/.ssh/known_hosts',
  path    => '/usr/bin:/usr/sbin:/bin:/sbin',
  unless  => 'grep git.example.com
```

```
/usr/local/git/.ssh/known_hosts',
  user    => 'git',
  require => [ User['git'],
               File['git-ssh']
             ],
}
```

5. Create a directory to contain the Git repository (`/usr/local/git/cookbook`):

```
file {'cookbook':
  ensure => 'directory',
  path   => '/usr/local/git/cookbook'
}
```

6. Clone the Puppet repository onto the new machine:

```
exec {'create cookbook':
  command => 'git clone git@git.example.com:repos/puppet.git
cookbook',
  path    => '/usr/bin:/usr/sbin:/bin:/sbin',
  cwd     => '/usr/local/git',
  user    => 'git',
  require => [ User['git'],
               Package['git'],
               File['git-id_rsa'],
               Exec['download git.example.com host key']
             ],
  unless  => 'test -f /usr/local/git/cookbook/.git/config',
}
```

7. Now, when we run Puppet apply on the new machine, the ssh key will be installed for the Puppet user. The Puppet user will then clone the Git repository into /etc/ puppet/cookbook:

```
Notice: Compiled catalog for testnode.example.com in
environment production in 0.37 seconds
Notice: /Stage[main]/Main/Package[git]/ensure: created
Notice: /Stage[main]/Main/File[githome]/ensure: created
Notice: /Stage[main]/Main/Group[git]/ensure: created
Notice: /Stage[main]/Main/User[git]/ensure: created
Notice: /Stage[main]/Main/File[git-ssh]/ensure: created
Notice: /Stage[main]/Main/File[git-id_rsa]/ensure: defined
content as '{md5}d4b1ca514e782f4c01756fa480cf9ded'
Notice: /Stage[main]/Main/Exec[download git.example.com host
key]/returns: executed successfully
```

```
Notice: /Stage[main]/Main/File[cookbook]/ensure: created
Notice: /Stage[main]/Main/Exec[create cookbook]/returns:
executed successfully
Notice: Applied catalog in 2.45 seconds
```

You may have to disable the tty requirement of sudo. Comment out the line Defaults require tty at /etc/sudoers if you have this line. Alternatively, you can set user => Puppet within the create cookbook exec. Be aware that using the user attribute will cause any error messages from the command to be lost.

8. Now that your Puppet code is available on the new node, you can apply it using puppet apply, specifying that /etc/puppet/cookbook/modules will contain the modules:

```
[root@testnode ~]# puppet apply --
modulepath=/usr/local/git/cookbook/modules
/usr/local/git/cookbook/manifests/site.pp
Notice: Compiled catalog for testnode.example.com in
environment production in 0.02 seconds
Notice: /Stage[main]/Base/File[/etc/motd]/content: content
changed '{md5}d41d8cd98f00b204e9800998ecf8427e' to
'{md5}eafe806b41f4336cec16f12421e8d61e'
Notice: Applied catalog in 0.03 seconds
[root@testnode ~]# cat /etc/motd
testnode.example.com
Managed by puppet 5.3.3
```

How it works...

First, bootstrap.pp ensures that Git is installed. The manifest then goes on to create a git user and ensure that the ssh key for the Git user on git.example.com is installed in the git user's home directory (/usr/local/git). The manifest then ensures that the host key for git.example.com is trusted by the git user. With ssh configured, the bootstrap ensures that /usr/local/git/cookbook exists and is a directory.

We then use an exec to have Git clone the repository into /usr/local/git/cookbook. With all the code in place, we then call puppet apply a final time to deploy the code from the repository. In a production setting, you would distribute the bootstrap.pp manifest to all your nodes, possibly via an internal web server, using a method similar to the following:

```
curl http://puppet/bootstrap.pp >bootstrap.pp && puppet apply bootstrap.pp
```

Writing a papply script

We'd like to make it as quick and easy as possible to apply Puppet on a machine; for this, we'll write a short script that wraps the `puppet apply` command with the parameters it needs. We'll deploy the script where it's needed, with Puppet itself.

How to do it...

Follow these steps to create the `papply` script.

1. In your Puppet repo, create the directories needed for a Puppet module:

   ```
   t@mylaptop ~$ cd puppet/modules
   t@mylaptop modules$ mkdir -p puppet/{manifests,files}
   ```

2. Create the `modules/puppet/files/papply.sh` file with the following contents:

   ```
   #!/bin/sh
   cd /usr/local/git/cookbook
   sudo -u git git pull -q origin master
   sudo /opt/puppetlabs/bin/puppet apply
   /usr/local/git/cookbook/manifests/site.pp \
     --modulepath=/usr/local/git/cookbook/modules $*
   ```

3. Create the `modules/puppet/manifests/init.pp` file with the following contents:

   ```
   class puppet {
     $papply = @("PAPPLY")
       #!/bin/sh
       cd /usr/local/git/cookbook
       sudo -u git git pull -q origin master
       sudo /opt/puppetlabs/bin/puppet apply \
         /usr/local/git/cookbook/manifests/site.pp \
         --modulepath=/usr/local/git/cookbook/modules $*
       | PAPPLY
     file { '/usr/local/bin/papply':
       content => $papply,
       mode    => '0755',
     }
   }
   ```

4. Modify your `manifests/site.pp` file, as follows:

```
node default {
  include base
  include puppet
}
```

5. Add the Puppet module to the Git repository and commit the change, as follows:

```
t@mylaptop puppet$ git add manifests/site.pp modules/puppet
t@mylaptop puppet$ git status
On branch master
Your branch is up-to-date with 'origin/master'.
Changes to be committed:
(use "git reset HEAD <file>..." to unstage)
modified: manifests/site.pp
new file: modules/puppet/files/papply.sh
new file: modules/puppet/manifests/init.pp
t@mylaptop puppet$ git commit -m "adding puppet module to
include papply"
[master 2d5de5f] adding puppet module to include papply
 2 files changed, 32 insertions(+)
 create mode 100644 modules/puppet/manifests/init.pp
```

6. Remember to push the changes to the Git repository on `git.example.com`:

```
t@mylaptop puppet$ git push origin master
Counting objects: 14, done.
Delta compression using up to 4 threads.
Compressing objects: 100% (7/7), done.
Writing objects: 100% (10/10), 894 bytes | 0 bytes/s, done.
Total 10 (delta 0), reused 0 (delta 0) To
git@git.example.com:repos/puppet.git
ea4c536..2d5de5f master -> master
```

7. Back on your new node (`testnode`), pull the latest version of the Git repository, as shown in the following command line:

```
[root@testnode ~]# cd /usr/local/git/cookbook/
[root@testnode cookbook]# sudo -u git git pull origin master
remote: Counting objects: 10, done.
remote: Compressing objects: 100% (6/6), done.
remote: Total 10 (delta 0), reused 0 (delta 0)
Unpacking objects: 100% (10/10), done.
From git.example.com:repos/puppet
 * branch master -> FETCH_HEAD
Updating ea4c536..2d5de5f
```

```
Fast-forward
 manifests/site.pp | 1 +
 modules/puppet/manifests/init.pp | 28
 +++++++++++++++++++++++++++
 2 files changed, 32 insertions(+)
 create mode 100644 modules/puppet/manifests/init.pp
```

8. Apply the manifest manually once to install the `papply` script:

```
[root@testnode cookbook]# puppet apply
/usr/local/git/cookbook/manifests/site.pp --modulepath
/usr/local/git/cookbook/modules
Notice: Compiled catalog for testnode.example.com in
environment production in 0.02 seconds
Notice: /Stage[main]/Puppet/File[/usr/local/bin/papply]/ensure:
defined content as '{md5}785de21fb5f00385068ee2f700af80a8'
Notice: Applied catalog in 0.03 seconds
```

9. Test the script:

```
[root@testnode cookbook]# papply
Notice: Compiled catalog for testnode.example.com in
environment production in 0.02 seconds
Notice: Applied catalog in 0.02 seconds
```

Now, whenever you need to run Puppet, you can simply run `papply`. In future, when we apply Puppet changes, I'll ask you to run `papply` instead of the full `puppet apply` command.

How it works...

As you've seen, to run Puppet on a machine and apply a specified manifest file, we use the `puppet apply` command:

```
puppet apply manifests/site.pp
```

When you're using modules (such as the Puppet module we just created), you also need to tell Puppet where to search for modules, using the `modulepath` argument:

```
puppet apply manifests/site.pp \
  --modulepath=/usr/local/git/cookbook/modules
```

In order to run Puppet with the root privileges it needs, we have to put `sudo` before everything:

```
sudo puppet apply manifests/site.pp \
--modulepath=/home/ubuntu/puppet/modules
```

Finally, any additional arguments passed to `papply` will be passed through to Puppet itself, by adding the `$*` parameter:

```
sudo puppet apply manifests/nodes.pp \
--modulepath=/home/ubuntu/puppet/modules $*
```

That's a lot of typing, so putting this in a script makes sense. Additionally, we want the latest code from our Git repository to be applied, so we first call `git` to update our local copy. We've added a Puppet file resource that will deploy the script to `/usr/local/bin` and make it executable. Since the script is quite short, we use a HEREDOC string to hold the contents of the script:

```
$papply = @("PAPPLY")
#!/bin/sh
cd /usr/local/git/cookbook
sudo -u git git pull -q origin master
sudo /opt/puppetlabs/bin/puppet apply \
/usr/local/git/cookbook/manifests/site.pp \
--modulepath=/usr/local/git/cookbook/modules $*
| PAPPLY

file { '/usr/local/bin/papply':
 content => $papply,
 mode => '0755',
}
```

Finally, we include the Puppet module in our `default` node declaration:

```
node default {
 include base
 include puppet
}
```

You can do the same for any other nodes managed by Puppet.

> In my personal deployments, I would move the `papply` script into the `bootstrap.pp` manifest. This makes it much simpler to deploy, since I only have to run `puppet apply bootstrap.pp` once, and after that I can use `papply`. (I would also rename `papply` to `pa`; I don't like to type.)

Running Puppet from cron

You can do a lot with the setup you already have: work on your Puppet manifests as a team, communicate changes via a central Git repository, and manually apply them on a machine using the `papply` script.

However, you still have to log in to each machine to update the Git repo and rerun Puppet. It would be helpful to have each machine update itself and apply any changes automatically. Then, all you need to do is push a change to the repo, and it will go out to all your machines within a certain time.

The simplest way to do this is with a `cron` job that pulls updates from the repo at regular intervals and then runs Puppet if anything has changed. Since our `papply` script already pulls the latest changes, we can just schedule `cron` to run the `papply` script.

Getting ready

You'll need the Git repo we set up in the *Managing your manifests with Git* and *Creating a decentralized Puppet architecture* recipes, and the `papply` script from the *Writing a papply script* recipe. You'll need to apply the `bootstrap.pp` manifest we created to install `ssh` keys to download the latest repository.

How to do it...

Follow these steps:

1. Copy the `bootstrap.pp` script to any node you want to enroll. The `bootstrap.pp` manifest includes the private key used to access the Git repository; it should be protected in a production environment.

2. Modify the `modules/puppet/manifests/init.pp` file and add the following snippet after the `papply` file definition:

```
cron { 'run-puppet':
  ensure  => 'present',
  user    => 'root',
  command => '/usr/local/bin/papply',
  minute  => '*/10',
  hour    => '*',
}
```

3. Commit the changes as before and push to the Git server, as shown in the following command line:

```
t@mylaptop puppet$ git add modules/puppet
t@mylaptop puppet$ git commit -m "adding cron"
[master cbf08cd] adding cron
 1 file changed, 3 insertions(+), 7 deletions(-)
Counting objects: 6, done.
Delta compression using up to 8 threads.
Compressing objects: 100% (5/5), done.
Writing objects: 100% (6/6), 565 bytes | 565.00 KiB/s, done.
Total 6 (delta 1), reused 0 (delta 0)
To git.example.com:repos/puppet.git
   2d5de5f..cbf08cd master -> master
```

4. Run `papply` on `testnode` to update the local Git clone and then apply the new code:

```
[root@testnode ~]# papply
Notice: Compiled catalog for testnode.example.com in
environment production in 0.04 seconds
Notice: /Stage[main]/Puppet/Cron[run-puppet]/ensure: created
Notice: Applied catalog in 0.04 seconds
```

5. Verify that the `cron` job was created successfully:

```
[root@testnode ~]# crontab -l
# HEADER: This file was autogenerated at 2018-01-20 01:24:03
+0000 by puppet.
# HEADER: While it can still be managed manually, it is
definitely not recommended.
# HEADER: Note particularly that the comments starting with
'Puppet Name' should
# HEADER: not be deleted, as doing so could cause duplicate
cron jobs.
# Puppet Name: run-puppet
*/10 * * * * /usr/local/bin/papply
```

How it works...

When we created the `bootstrap.pp` manifest, we made sure that the git user can check out the Git repository using an `ssh` key. This enables the git user to run `git pull` in the cookbook directory unattended. We've added this to the `papply` script, which does this and runs Puppet after checking for updates

We've created a `cron` job that runs `papply` at regular intervals (every 10 minutes, but feel free to change this if you need to):

```
cron { 'run-puppet':
  ensure  => 'present',
  user    => 'root',
  command => '/usr/local/bin/papply',
  minute  => '*/10',
  hour    => '*',
  require => File['/usr/local/bin/papply'],
}
```

There's more...

Congratulations, you now have a fully-automated Puppet infrastructure! Once you have applied the `bootstrap.pp` manifest, run Puppet on the repository; the machine will be set up to pull any new changes and apply them automatically.

So, for example, if you wanted to add a new user account to all your machines, all you have to do is add the account in your working copy of the manifest, and commit and push the changes to the central Git repository. Within 10 minutes, it will automatically be applied to every machine that's running Puppet.

Bootstrapping Puppet with bash

Previous versions of this book used Rakefiles to bootstrap Puppet. The problem with using Rake to configure a node is that you are running the commands from your laptop; you assume you already have `ssh` access to the machine. Most bootstrap processes work by issuing an easy-to-remember command from a node once it has been provisioned. In this section, we'll show you how to use `bash` to bootstrap Puppet with a web server and a bootstrap script.

Getting ready

Install `httpd` on a centrally accessible server and create a password-protected area to store the bootstrap script. In my example, I'll use the Git server I set up previously, git.example.com. Start by creating a directory in the root of your web server:

```
root@git:~# puppet resource package apache2 ensure=installed
Notice: /Package[apache2]/ensure: created
```

```
package { 'apache2':
 ensure => '2.4.25-3+deb9u3',
}
root@git:~# cd /var/www/html
root@git:/var/www/html# mkdir bootstrap
```

My git node is a Debian-based machine, so the `apache` package name is `apache2`; if you are using a RHEL-based distribution, use the package name `httpd`.

Now perform the following steps:

1. Add the following location definition to your apache configuration (`/etc/apache2/sites-available/000-default.conf` or `/etc/httpd/conf.d/bootstrap.conf`):

    ```
    <Location /bootstrap>
      AuthType basic
      AuthName "Bootstrap"
      AuthBasicProvider file
      AuthUserFile /var/www/puppet.passwd
      Require valid-user
    </Location>
    ```

2. Reload your web server to ensure the location configuration is operating and verify with `curl` that you cannot download from the bootstrap directory without authentication:

    ```
    root@git:~# systemctl restart apache2
    root@git:~# curl http://git.example.com/bootstrap
    <!DOCTYPE HTML PUBLIC "-//IETF//DTD HTML 2.0//EN">
    <html><head>
    <title>401 Unauthorized</title>
    </head><body>
    <h1>Unauthorized</h1>
    <p>This server could not verify that you
    are authorized to access the document
    requested. Either you supplied the wrong
    credentials (e.g., bad password), or your
    browser doesn't understand how to supply
    the credentials required.</p>
    <hr>
    <address>Apache/2.4.25 (Debian) Server at git.example.com Port
    80</address>
    </body></html>
    ```

3. Create the password file you referenced in the apache configuration (`/var/www/puppet.passwd`):

```
root@git:~# cd /var/www
root@git:/var/www# htpasswd -cb puppet.passwd bootstrap
cookbook
Adding password for user bootstrap
```

4. Verify that the username and password permit access to the `bootstrap` directory, as follows:

```
root@git:/var/www# curl --user bootstrap:cookbook
http://git.example.com/bootstrap/
<!DOCTYPE HTML PUBLIC "-//W3C//DTD HTML 3.2 Final//EN">
<html>
 <head>
 <title>Index of /bootstrap</title>
 </head>
 <body>
<h1>Index of /bootstrap</h1>
 <table>
 <tr><th valign="top"><img src="/icons/blank.gif"
alt="[ICO]"></th><th><a href="?C=N;O=D">Name</a></th><th><a
href="?C=M;O=A">Last modified</a></th><th><a
href="?C=S;O=A">Size</a></th><th><a
href="?C=D;O=A">Description</a></th></tr>
 <tr><th colspan="5"><hr></th></tr>
<tr><td valign="top"><img src="/icons/back.gif"
alt="[PARENTDIR]"></td><td><a href="/">Parent
Directory</a></td><td> </td><td align="right"> -
</td><td> </td></tr>
 <tr><th colspan="5"><hr></th></tr>
</table>
<address>Apache/2.4.25 (Debian) Server at git.example.com Port
80</address>
</body></html>
```

How to do it...

Now that you have a safe location to store the bootstrap script, create a bootstrap script for each OS you support in the bootstrap directory. In this example, I'll show you how to do this for a Red Hat Enterprise Linux 7-based distribution.

Although the bootstrap location requires a password, there is no encryption since we haven't configured SSL on our server. Without encryption, the location is not very safe.

Create a script named el7.sh in the bootstrap directory with the following contents:

```bash
#!/bin/bash
# bootstrap for EL7 distributions
SERVER=git.example.com
LOCATION=/bootstrap
BOOTSTRAP=bootstrap.pp
USER=bootstrap
PASS=cookbook
# install puppet
curl -sS http://yum.puppetlabs.com/RPM-GPG-KEY-puppetlabs >/etc/pki/rpm-gpg/RPM-GPG-KEY-puppetlabs
rpm --import /etc/pki/rpm-gpg/RPM-GPG-KEY-puppetlabs
yum -y install
http://yum.puppet.com/puppet5/puppet5-release-el-7.noarch.rpm
yum -y install puppet-agent
# download bootstrap
curl -sS --user $USER:$PASS http://$SERVER/$LOCATION/$BOOTSTRAP >/tmp/$BOOTSTRAP
# apply bootstrap
cd /tmp
/opt/puppetlabs/bin/puppet apply /tmp/$BOOTSTRAP
# apply puppet
/opt/puppetlabs/bin/puppet apply --modulepath
/usr/local/git/cookbook/modules \
   /usr/local/git/cookbook/manifests/site.pp
```

How it works...

The apache configuration only permits access to the bootstrap directory with a username and password combination. We supply these with the --user argument to curl, thereby getting access to the file. We use a pipe (|) to redirect the output of curl into bash. This causes bash to execute the script. We write our bash script as we would any other bash script. The bash script downloads our bootstrap.pp manifest and applies it. Finally, we apply the Puppet manifest from the Git repository and the machine is configured as a member of our decentralized infrastructure:

```
[root@localhost ~]# curl -sS --user bootstrap:cookbook
http://git.example.com/bootstrap/el7.sh |bash
Loaded plugins: fastestmirror
puppet5-release-el-7.noarch.rpm | 7.0 kB 00:00:00
```

```
Examining /var/tmp/yum-root-mt0iaR/puppet5-release-el-7.noarch.rpm:
puppet5-release-5.0.0-1.el7.noarch
Marking /var/tmp/yum-root-mt0iaR/puppet5-release-el-7.noarch.rpm to be
installed
Resolving Dependencies
--> Running transaction check
---> Package puppet5-release.noarch 0:5.0.0-1.el7 will be installed
--> Finished Dependency Resolution
Dependencies Resolved
======================================================================
===========
 Package Arch Version Repository Size
======================================================================
===========
Installing:
 puppet5-release noarch 5.0.0-1.el7 /puppet5-release-el-7.noarch 2.1 k
Transaction Summary
======================================================================
===========
Install 1 Package
Total size: 2.1 k
Installed size: 2.1 k
...
Notice: Compiled catalog for localhost.localdomain in environment
production in 0.05 seconds
Notice: /Stage[main]/Base/File[/etc/motd]/content: content changed
'{md5}d41d8cd98f00b204e9800998ecf8427e' to
'{md5}726a5ba2476213515ba218024ee9aa7e'
Notice: /Stage[main]/Puppet/File[/usr/local/bin/papply]/ensure: defined
content as '{md5}785de21fb5f00385068ee2f700af80a8'
Notice: /Stage[main]/Puppet/Cron[run-puppet]/ensure: created
Notice: Applied catalog in 0.18 seconds
```

There's more...

To support another operating system, we only need to create a new bash script. All Linux distributions will support bash scripting; macOS X does, as well. Since we placed much of our logic into the bootstrap.pp manifest, the bootstrap script is quite minimal and easy to port to new operating systems.

Creating a centralized Puppet infrastructure

A configuration management tool such as Puppet is best used when you have many machines to manage. If all the machines can reach a central location, using a centralized Puppet infrastructure might be a good solution. Unfortunately, Puppet doesn't scale well with a large number of nodes. If your deployment has less than 4,000 servers, a single Puppet master should be able to handle the load, assuming your catalogs are not complex (take less than 10 seconds to compile each catalog). If you have a larger number of nodes, I suggest a load-balancing configuration, described in *Mastering Puppet*.

A Puppet master is a Puppet server that acts as an X509 certificate authority for Puppet and distributes catalogs (compiled manifests) to client nodes. The puppet master runs the `puppetserver` service. Puppetserver is a JRuby application running on a custom Clojure framework known as TrapperKeeper. Many puppet services now run via Trapperkeeper and JRuby. Although slow to start up, the system is far more capable of handling load than the previous versions of the puppet master service.

Getting ready

The puppetserver service is not installed when you install the `puppet-agent` package. The package name is `puppetserver`. To start, install the `puppetserver` package and then start puppetserver. To get started, we'll create a new CentOS 7 server named `puppet.example.com`.

How to do it...

1. Install Puppet on the new server and then use Puppet to install the `puppetserver` package:

```
[root@puppet ~]# puppet resource package puppetserver
ensure='installed'
Notice: /Package[puppetserver]/ensure: created
package { 'puppetserver':
  ensure => '5.1.4-1.el7',
}
```

2. Start the Puppet master service and ensure it will start at boot:

```
[root@puppet ~]# puppet resource service puppetserver
ensure="true" enable="true"
Notice: /Service[puppetserver]/ensure: ensure changed 'stopped'
to 'running'
service { 'puppetserver':
 ensure => 'running',
 enable => 'true',
}
```

If you are running puppetserver from a VM, you may need to increase the memory of the VM. Puppetserver uses 2 GB of memory by default, you can change this by editing the defaults in /etc/sysconfig/puppetserver and changing the setting for JAVA_ARGS. The -Xms and -Xmx options specify the initial heap size for Java.

How it works...

The puppetserver package includes the start and stop scripts for the puppetserver service. We use Puppet to install the package and start the service. Once the service is started, we can point another node at the Puppet master (you might need to disable the host-based firewall on your machine):

1. From another node, run puppet agent to start a puppet agent, that will contact the server and request a new certificate:

```
[vagrant@testnode ~]$ sudo /opt/puppetlabs/bin/puppet agent -t
Info: Creating a new SSL key for testnode.example.com
Info: Caching certificate for ca
Info: csr_attributes file loading from
/etc/puppetlabs/puppet/csr_attributes.yaml
Info: Creating a new SSL certificate request for
testnode.example.com
Info: Certificate Request fingerprint (SHA256):
18:54:C3:82:FB:B3:E4:9F:BF:89:23:DD:CF:A0:80:67:B0:D2:B0:DD:04:
56:EE:16:19:35:68:4A:98:BE:7B:86
Info: Caching certificate for ca
Exiting; no certificate found and waitforcert is disabled
```

2. On the Puppet server, sign the new key:

```
[root@puppet ~]# puppet cert list
"testnode.example.com" (SHA256)
18:54:C3:82:FB:B3:E4:9F:BF:89:23:DD:CF:A0:80:67:B0:D2:B0:DD:04:
56:EE:16:19:35:68:4A:98:BE:7B:86
[root@puppet ~]# puppet cert sign testnode.example.com
Signing Certificate Request for:
"testnode.example.com" (SHA256)
18:54:C3:82:FB:B3:E4:9F:BF:89:23:DD:CF:A0:80:67:B0:D2:B0:DD:04:
56:EE:16:19:35:68:4A:98:BE:7B:86
Notice: Signed certificate request for testnode.example.com
Notice: Removing file Puppet::SSL::CertificateRequest
testnode.example.com at
'/etc/puppetlabs/puppet/ssl/ca/requests/testnode.example.com.pe
m'
```

3. Return to the cookbook node and run Puppet again:

```
[vagrant@testnode ~]$ sudo /opt/puppetlabs/bin/puppet agent -t
Info: Caching certificate for testnode.example.com
Info: Caching certificate_revocation_list for ca
Info: Caching certificate for testnode.example.com
Info: Using configured environment 'production'
Info: Retrieving pluginfacts
Info: Retrieving plugin
Info: Caching catalog for testnode.example.com
Info: Applying configuration version '1516559867'
Notice: Applied catalog in 0.01 seconds
```

There's more...

When we ran puppet agent, Puppet looked for a host named puppet.example.com (since our test node is in the example.com domain); if it couldn't find that host, it would then look for a host named puppet. We can specify the server to contact with the --server option to puppet agent. When we installed the puppetserver package and started the puppetserver service, Puppet created default SSL certificates based on our hostname. In the next section, we'll see how to create an SSL certificate that has multiple DNS names for our Puppet server.

Creating certificates with multiple DNS names

By default, Puppet will create an SSL certificate for your Puppet master that contains the fully-qualified domain name of the server only. Depending on how your network is configured, it can be useful for the server to be known by other names. In this recipe, we'll make a new certificate for our Puppet master that has multiple DNS names.

Getting ready

Install the `Puppet master` package if you haven't already done so. You will then need to start the `Puppet master` service at least once to create a **certificate authority** (CA).

How to do it...

The steps are as follows:

1. Stop the running `puppetserver` process with the following command:

```
[root@puppet ~]# puppet resource service puppetserver
ensure=false
Notice: /Service[puppetserver]/ensure: ensure changed 'running'
to 'stopped'
service { 'puppetserver':
  ensure => 'stopped',
}
```

2. Delete (`clean`) the current server certificate:

```
[root@puppet ~]# puppet cert clean puppet.example.com
Notice: Revoked certificate with serial 2
Notice: Removing file Puppet::SSL::Certificate
puppet.example.com at
'/etc/puppetlabs/puppet/ssl/ca/signed/puppet.example.com.pem'
Notice: Removing file Puppet::SSL::Certificate
puppet.example.com at
'/etc/puppetlabs/puppet/ssl/certs/puppet.example.com.pem'
Notice: Removing file Puppet::SSL::Key puppet.example.com at
'/etc/puppetlabs/puppet/ssl/private_keys/puppet.example.com.pem
'
```

3. Create a new Puppet certificate using `puppet certificate generate` with the `--dns-alt-names` option:

```
[vagrant@puppet ~]$ sudo /opt/puppetlabs/bin/puppet certificate
generate --dns-alt-names
puppet,puppet.example.com,puppet.example.org,puppet.example.net
--ca-location local puppet.example.com
Notice: puppet.example.com has a waiting certificate request
true
```

4. Sign the new certificate:

```
[vagrant@puppet ~]$ sudo /opt/puppetlabs/bin/puppet cert --
allow-dns-alt-names sign puppet.example.com
Signing Certificate Request for:
  "puppet.example.com" (SHA256)
05:E8:0A:D4:A8:4E:DE:67:CF:ED:49:64:7A:6A:A6:6A:60:0B:E2:E0:1C:
DB:D9:3E:EA:74:04:75:49:5B:14:91 (alt names: "DNS:puppet",
"DNS:puppet.example.com", "DNS:puppet.example.net",
"DNS:puppet.example.org") **
Notice: Signed certificate request for puppet.example.com
Notice: Removing file Puppet::SSL::CertificateRequest
puppet.example.com at
'/etc/puppetlabs/puppet/ssl/ca/requests/puppet.example.com.pem'
```

5. Copy the signed certificate into the correct location (when you created it with `puppet certificate generate`, it remained in the `/etc/puppetlabs/puppet/ssl/ca/signed` directory; we need it moved over to `/etc/puppetlabs/puppet/ssl/certs`):

```
[vagrant@puppet ~]$ sudo /opt/puppetlabs/bin/puppet certificate
find puppet.example.com --ca-location local
-----BEGIN CERTIFICATE-----
MIIFzjCCA7agAwIBAgIBDTANBgkqhkiG9w0BAQsFADAoMSYwJAYDVQQDDB1QdXB
w
...
sk3Ba5EYwX15FAh3IE9q512WxaF7leSWHoM5wh9kwzAoYJsw007EIPUvnW6WhFr
A
D+8=
-----END CERTIFICATE-----
```

6. Restart the `puppetserver` process:

```
[vagrant@puppet ~]$ sudo /opt/puppetlabs/bin/puppet resource
service puppetserver ensure=true
Notice: /Service[puppetserver]/ensure: ensure changed 'stopped'
to 'running'
service { 'puppetserver':
  ensure => 'running',
}
```

How it works...

When your puppet agents connect to the Puppet server, they look for a host called `Puppet`; they then look for a host called `Puppet.[your domain]`. If your clients are in different domains, then you need your Puppet master to reply to all the names correctly. By removing the existing certificate and generating a new one, you can have your Puppet master reply to multiple DNS names. We can now connect to our puppetserver using any of the following hostnames `puppet.example.com`, `puppet.example.org`, and `puppet.example.net`:

```
[vagrant@testnode ~]$ sudo /opt/puppetlabs/bin/puppet agent -t --server
puppet.example.org
Info: Using configured environment 'production'
Info: Retrieving pluginfacts
Info: Retrieving plugin
Info: Caching catalog for testnode.example.com
Info: Applying configuration version '1516583887'
Notice: Applied catalog in 0.01 seconds
```

Setting up the environment

Environments in Puppet are directories holding different versions of your Puppet manifests. Whenever a node connects to a Puppet master, it informs the Puppet master of its environment. By default, all nodes report to the production environment. This causes the Puppet master to look in the production environment for manifests. You may specify an alternate environment with the `--environment` setting when running `puppet agent` or by setting `environment = newenvironment` in `/etc/puppet/puppet.conf` in the `agent` section.

Getting ready

Verify `environmentpath` in your installation with the following `puppet config` command:

```
[vagrant@puppet ~]$ sudo /opt/puppetlabs/bin/puppet config print
environmentpath
/etc/puppetlabs/code/environments
```

How to do it...

The steps are as follows:

1. Create a production directory at `/etc/puppetlabs/code/environments` that contains both a modules and manifests directory. Then, create a `site.pp` that creates a file in `/tmp`, as follows:

```
[vagrant@puppet ~]$ sudo mkdir -p
/etc/puppetlabs/code/environments/production/{manifests,modules
}
[vagrant@puppet ~]$ sudoedit
/etc/puppetlabs/code/environments/production/manifests/site.pp
```

2. Create a `site.pp` in `/etc/puppetlabs/code/environments/production/manifests/site.pp` with the following contents:

```
node default {
  $production = @(PROD)
    Hello world!
    This is production
    | PROD
  file {'/tmp/production':
    content => $production,
  }
}
```

3. Run `puppet agent` on the `testnode` to connect to it and verify that the production code was delivered:

```
[vagrant@testnode ~]$ sudo /opt/puppetlabs/bin/puppet agent -t
Info: Using configured environment 'production'
Info: Retrieving pluginfacts
Info: Retrieving plugin
Info: Caching catalog for testnode.example.com
Info: Applying configuration version '1516585242'
```

```
Notice:
/Stage[main]/Main/Node[default]/File[/tmp/production]/ensure:
defined content as '{md5}1aaacf1bc9455ab9b4f14e0b729ef51d'
Notice: Applied catalog in 0.01 seconds
[vagrant@testnode ~]$ cat /tmp/production
Hello world!
This is production
```

4. Configure another `devel` environment and then create a new manifest in the `devel` environment:

```
[vagrant@puppet ~]$ sudo mkdir -p
/etc/puppetlabs/code/environments/devel/{manifests,modules}
[vagrant@puppet ~]$ sudoedit
/etc/puppetlabs/code/environments/devel/manifests/site.pp
```

5. Create `site.pp` for `devel` with the following contents:

```
node default {
  $devel = @(DEVEL)
    Good-bye world!
    This is development
    | DEVEL
  file {'/tmp/devel':
    content => $devel,
  }
}
```

6. Apply the new environment by running `puppet agent` with the `--environment devel` option:

```
[vagrant@testnode ~]$ sudo /opt/puppetlabs/bin/puppet agent -t
--environment devel
Info: Using configured environment 'devel'
Info: Retrieving pluginfacts
Info: Retrieving plugin
Info: Caching catalog for testnode.example.com
Info: Applying configuration version '1516585608'
Notice:
/Stage[main]/Main/Node[default]/File[/tmp/devel]/ensure:
defined content as '{md5}18fa54bdeff51f2b22795b8664ecfae8'
Notice: Applied catalog in 0.01 seconds
[vagrant@testnode ~]$ cat /tmp/devel
Good-bye world!
This is development
```

There's more...

Each environment can have its own module path if you create an `environment.conf` file within the environment directory. More information on environments can be found on the Puppet labs website at `https://docs.puppetlabs.com/puppet/latest/reference/environments.html`.

Configuring PuppetDB

PuppetDB is a database for Puppet that is used to store information about nodes connected to a Puppet master. PuppetDB is also a storage area for exported resources. Exported resources are resources that are defined on nodes but applied to other nodes. The simplest way to install PuppetDB is to use the PuppetDB module from Puppet labs. From this point on, we'll assume you are using the `puppet.example.com` machine running puppetserver.

Getting ready

Install the `PuppetDB` module in the production environment you created in the previous recipe. If you didn't create directory environments, don't worry; using `puppet module install` will install the module to the correct location for your installation with the following command:

```
[vagrant@puppet ~]$ sudo /opt/puppetlabs/bin/puppet module install
puppetlabs-puppetdb
Notice: Preparing to install into
/etc/puppetlabs/code/environments/production/modules ...
Notice: Downloading from https://forgeapi.puppet.com ...
Notice: Installing -- do not interrupt ...
/etc/puppetlabs/code/environments/production/modules
└─┬ puppetlabs-puppetdb (v6.0.2)
  ├── puppetlabs-firewall (v1.11.0)
  ├── puppetlabs-inifile (v2.1.1)
  └─┬ puppetlabs-postgresql (v5.2.1)
    ├── puppetlabs-apt (v4.4.1)
    ├── puppetlabs-concat (v4.1.1)
    └── puppetlabs-stdlib (v4.24.0)
```

How to do it...

Now that our Puppet master has the `PuppetDB` module installed, we need to apply the `PuppetDB` module to our Puppet master; we can do this in the site manifest. Add the following to your (production) `site.pp`:

```
node puppet {
  class { 'puppetdb': }
  class { 'puppetdb::master::config':  }
}
```

Run `puppet agent` to apply the `puppetdb` class and the `puppetdb::master::config` class:

```
[vagrant@puppet ~]$ sudo /opt/puppetlabs/bin/puppet agent -t
Info: Using configured environment 'production'
Info: Retrieving pluginfacts
Info: Retrieving plugin
Notice: /File[/opt/puppetlabs/puppet/cache/lib/facter]/ensure: created
...
Info: Class[Puppetdb::Server::Puppetdb]: Scheduling refresh of
Service[puppetdb]
Notice: /Stage[main]/Puppetdb::Server/Service[puppetdb]/ensure: ensure
changed 'stopped' to 'running'
Info: /Stage[main]/Puppetdb::Server/Service[puppetdb]: Unscheduling refresh
on Service[puppetdb]
Notice:
/Stage[main]/Puppetdb::Master::Routes/File[/etc/puppetlabs/puppet/routes.ya
ml]/ensure: defined content as '{md5}be99db88f4c07058843ea356eb3469bf'
...
Info: Class[Puppetdb::Master::Puppetdb_conf]: Scheduling refresh of
Service[puppetserver]
Notice: /Stage[main]/Puppetdb::Master::Config/Service[puppetserver]:
Triggered 'refresh' from 2 events
Notice: Applied catalog in 118.71 seconds
```

A lot will happen on your puppet master after running `puppet agent` this time. The `puppetdb` service will be configured, puppetserver will be reconfigured to use that `puppetdb` service, and a PostgreSQL database will be created to hold the PuppetDB data.

How it works...

The PuppetDB module is a great example of how a complex configuration task can be puppetized. Simply by adding the `puppetdb` class to our Puppet master node, Puppet installed and configured PostgreSQL and PuppetDB.

The agent run set up the configuration files for PuppetDB and configured Puppet to use PuppetDB. If you look at `/etc/puppet/puppet.conf`, you'll see the following two new lines:

```
storeconfigs = true
storeconfigs_backend = puppetdb
```

There's more...

Now that `PuppetDB` is configured and we've had a successful agent run, `PuppetDB` will have data we can query:

```
[vagrant@puppet ~]$ sudo /opt/puppetlabs/bin/puppet agent -t
Info: Using configured environment 'production'
Info: Retrieving pluginfacts
Info: Retrieving plugin
Info: Loading facts
Info: Caching catalog for puppet.example.com
Info: Applying configuration version '1516587381'
Notice: Applied catalog in 0.68 seconds
[vagrant@puppet ~]$ sudo /opt/puppetlabs/bin/puppet node status
puppet.example.com
Currently active
Last catalog: 2018-01-22T02:16:25.535Z
Last facts: 2018-01-22T02:16:20.832Z
```

We need one more run of `puppet agent` to occur before querying PuppetDB since we need PuppetDB configured at the beginning of the agent run instead of at the end.

Configuring Hiera

Hiera is an information repository for Puppet. Using Hiera, you can have a hierarchical categorization of data about your nodes that is maintained outside of your manifests. This is very useful for sharing code and dealing with exceptions that will creep into any Puppet deployment.

At the time of writing, the current release of Hiera is version 3.4.2, and to make things extra confusing, this version includes Hiera5. Hiera configuration versions do not match the release of Hiera itself. Originally Hiera was just known as Hiera, then incompatible settings were introduced when Puppet4 was released. The Hiera configuration that supported Puppet4 was named Hiera4; now with Puppet5, we have Hiera5, but the actual version number of Hiera is still only 3.x.

Hiera5 introduces to Hiera the ability to run custom puppet functions to lookup information. Hiera5 in conjunction with Puppet5 supports the ability to have custom hiera look up data within Puppet modules. We'll see more of this in the coming sections.

How to do it...

1. Hiera is configured from a YAML file,
   `/etc/puppetlabs/puppet/hiera.yaml`. The installer should have created a template version of `hiera.yaml` for you; replace it with the following:

   ```
   ---
   # Hiera 5 Global configuration file

   version: 5
   hierarchy:
     - name: "Per-OS defaults"
       path: "os/%{facts.os.family}.yaml"

     - name: "Common data"
       path: "common.yaml"
   ```

2. Create the `data` directory to contain the Hiera `yaml` files.:

   ```
   [root@puppet ~]# cd /etc/puppetlabs/puppet
   [root@puppet puppet]# mkdir data
   [root@puppet puppet]# vim data/common.yaml
   ```

3. Create the `common.yaml` file in
   `/etc/puppetlabs/puppet/data/common.yaml` with the following contents:

   ```
   ---
   message: "This is from /etc/puppetlabs/puppet/data/common.yaml"
   ```

4. Edit the `site.pp` file and add a `notify` resource based on the Hiera value:

```
$message = lookup('message',String,first,'unknown')
notify { "Message is ${message}": }
```

5. Apply the manifest to a `test` node:

```
[vagrant@testnode ~]$ sudo /opt/puppetlabs/bin/puppet agent -t
Info: Using configured environment 'production'
Info: Retrieving pluginfacts
Info: Retrieving plugin
Info: Loading facts
Info: Caching catalog for testnode.example.com
Info: Applying configuration version '1516672880'
Notice: Message is This is from
/etc/puppetlabs/puppet/data/common.yaml
Notice: /Stage[main]/Main/Node[default]/Notify[Message is This
is from /etc/puppetlabs/puppet/data/common.yaml]/message:
defined 'message' as 'Message is This is from
/etc/puppetlabs/puppet/data/common.yaml'
Notice: Applied catalog in 0.02 seconds
```

How it works...

Hiera uses a hierarchy to search through a set of YAML files to find the appropriate values. We defined this hierarchy in `hiera.yaml` with the single entry for `common.yaml`. We used the `lookup` function in `site.pp` to look up the value for the message and store that value in the `$message` variable. The values used for the definition of the hierarchy can be any `facter` facts defined on the system. In most companies, a hierarchy is usually based on the following facts:

- `hostname: hosts/%{::facts.hostname}`
- `os.family: os/%{::facts.os.family}`
- `os.release.major: os/%{facts.os.release.major}`
- `network: network/%{::facts.network}`

Using these facts, it is possible to have custom Hiera values for different operating systems (Windows, Red Hat, and Debian), different major releases of operating systems (Red Hat 6,7), and different networks within your organization. If you need to have data specific to a particular node, you can use the hosts directory to contain custom YAML for each host.

There's more...

Hiera can be used for automatic parameter lookup with parameterized classes. For example, if you have a class named `cookbook::example` with a parameter named `publisher`, you can include the following in a Hiera YAML file to automatically set this parameter:

```
cookbook::example::publisher: 'PacktPub'
```

A good rule of thumb is to limit the hierarchy to eight levels or less. Keep in mind that each time a parameter is searched with Hiera, all the levels are searched until a match is found.

The default Hiera function returns the first match to the search key, you can also use `hiera_ array` and `hiera_hash` to search and return all values stored in Hiera.

Hiera can also be searched from the command line, as shown in the following command line using `puppet lookup`:

```
[root@puppet ~]# puppet lookup message
--- This is from /etc/puppetlabs/puppet/data/common.yaml
...
```

Environment-specific Hiera

Each environment can have its own `hiera.yaml` configuration and associated data directory. When we configured Hiera in the previous section, we placed the configuration file in `/etc/puppetlabs/puppet/hiera.yaml`. This is known as the global configuration file for Hiera. Any values you set at this level will override any values we set at the environment level.

Using environment-specific Hiera, we can have different Hiera data values in the production environment than in the devel environment.

Getting ready

Create a `hiera.yaml` file in `/etc/puppetlabs/code/environments/production` with the following contents:

```
---
version: 5
defaults:
hierarchy:
  - name: "Network specific data (yaml version)"
    path: "network/%{::facts.network}.yaml"
  - name: "Common"
    path: "common.yaml"
```

Next, create the `data` directory to contain the environment-specific data:

```
[root@puppet ~]# mkdir /etc/puppetlabs/code/environments/production/data
```

How to do it...

Create the network directory under the data directory in the production environment:

```
[root@puppet ~]# mkdir
/etc/puppetlabs/code/environments/production/data/network
```

Create the network-specific file in the network directory. Make sure it matches the network on your `testnode`:

```
[vagrant@testnode ~]$ sudo /opt/puppetlabs/puppet/bin/facter network
10.0.2.0
```

In my example, I'll create the file as
`/etc/puppetlabs/code/environments/production/`
`data/network/10.0.2.0.yaml` with the following contents:

```
---
msg: "production network"
```

Now we need to modify our `site.pp` and add the following to show the value for `msg`:

```
$msg = lookup('msg',String,first,'unknown')
notify { "Environment specific msg is ${msg}": }
```

Next, run `puppet agent` on our `testnode` to see the new value:

```
Notice: Environment specific msg is production network
Notice: /Stage[main]/Main/Node[default]/Notify[Environment specific msg is
production network]/message: defined 'message' as 'Environment specific msg
is production network'
```

How it works...

When the catalog is compiled on testnode, puppet uses a lookup call to check for a value in the global configuration. If none is found, puppet then looks in the environment for the value. Since we haven't defined a key `msg` in the global configuration, the environment-specific hiera.yaml is read and then the hierarchy searched.

We can see this in action on the master by using the `lookup --explain` puppet. This option to `puppet lookup` will show us which files puppet is using to look up the value. This is very useful when trying to figure out where a value came from or, more commonly, when the value can't be found:

```
[root@puppet ~]# puppet lookup --explain msg
...
Searching for "msg"
 Global Data Provider (hiera configuration version 5)
 Using configuration "/etc/puppetlabs/puppet/hiera.yaml"
 Hierarchy entry "Per-OS defaults"
 Path "/etc/puppetlabs/puppet/data/os/RedHat.yaml"
 Original path: "os/%{::facts.os.family}.yaml"
 No such key: "msg"
 Hierarchy entry "Common data"
 Path "/etc/puppetlabs/puppet/data/common.yaml"
 Original path: "common.yaml"
 No such key: "msg"
 Environment Data Provider (hiera configuration version 5)
 Using configuration
"/etc/puppetlabs/code/environments/production/hiera.yaml"
 Hierarchy entry "Network specific data (yaml version)"
 Path
"/etc/puppetlabs/code/environments/production/data/network/10.0.2.0.yaml"
 Original path: "network/%{::facts.network}.yaml"
 Found key: "msg" value: "production network"
```

Setting node-specific data with Hiera

In our hierarchy defined in `hiera.yaml`, we created an entry based on the hostname fact; in this section, we'll create `yaml` files in the `hosts` subdirectory of Hiera data with information specific to a particular host.

Getting ready

Install and configure Hiera as in the last section, and modify the hierarchy defined in the previous recipe to include a `hosts/%{hostname}` entry, as follows:

```
---
# Hiera 5 Global configuration file

version: 5
hierarchy:
  - name: "Per-host defaults"
    path: "hosts/%{::facts.hostname}.yaml"
  - name: "Per-OS defaults"
    path: "os/%{::facts.os.family}.yaml"
  - name: "Common data"
    path: "common.yaml"
```

How to do it...

1. Create a file at `/etc/puppetlabs/puppet/data/hosts` that is the hostname of your `test` node. For example, if your host is named `testnode`, the file would be named `testnode.yaml`.

2. Insert a specific message in this file:

   ```
   message: 'This is the test node for the cookbook'
   ```

3. Run Puppet on two different test nodes to note the difference:

   ```
   vagrant@git:~$ sudo /opt/puppetlabs/bin/puppet agent -t
   ...
   Info: Caching catalog for git.example.com
   Info: Applying configuration version '1516685029'
   Notice: Message is This is from
   /etc/puppetlabs/puppet/data/common.yaml
   Notice: /Stage[main]/Main/Node[default]/Notify[Message is This
   ```

```
is from /etc/puppetlabs/puppet/data/common.yaml]/message:
defined 'message' as 'Message is This is from
/etc/puppetlabs/puppet/data/common.yaml'
[vagrant@testnode ~]$ sudo /opt/puppetlabs/bin/puppet agent -t
...
Info: Caching catalog for testnode.example.com
Info: Applying configuration version '1516683708'
Notice: Message is This is the test node for the cookbook
Notice: /Stage[main]/Main/Node[default]/Notify[Message is This
is the test node for the cookbook]/message: defined 'message'
as 'Message is This is the test node for the cookbook'
```

How it works...

Hiera searches the hierarchy for files that match the values returned by facter. In this case, the `testnode.yaml` file is found by substituting the hostname of the node into the `/etc/puppetlabs/puppet/data/hosts/%{facts.hostname}.yaml` search path.

Using Hiera, it is possible to greatly reduce the complexity of your Puppet code. Use YAML files for separate values, where previously you had large case statements or nested if statements.

Writing a custom Hiera5 function

Hiera5 includes the ability to run custom functions at each level of the hierarchy. Unlike earlier versions of Hiera, it is now possible to have different backends for each level of the hierarchy. There are three main types of backends available, depending on how you will access data:

- `data_hash`
- `lookup_key`
- `data_dig`

If you are accessing something locally or where it's possible to read all the data at once, use `data_hash`. For remote services, use `lookup_key` and, for databases, use `data_dig`. More information on custom backends is available at `https://puppet.com/docs/puppet/5.3/hiera_custom_backends.html`

In this example, we'll create a custom function that queries the Google News API and returns the first headline.

Getting ready

To start, we'll need to create an API key for our function to contact Google. Obtain your own at `https://newsapi.org/register`. We'll store the API key in the top-level `hiera.yaml` configuration. After obtaining your API key, create the following section in `/etc/puppetlabs/puppet/hiera.yaml`:

```
---
# Hiera 5 Global configuration file
version: 5
hierarchy:
  - name: "Headlines"
    lookup_key: packtnews_lookup_key
    options:
      apikey: 88196...........c6
```

How to do it...

We'll create a news module to hold our `hiera5` function:

1. Create the function file in
   `modules/news/lib/puppet/functions/packtnews_lookup_key.rb`:

```
Puppet::Functions.create_function(:packtnews_lookup_key) do

  dispatch :lookup_key do
    param 'String[1]', :key
    param 'Hash', :options
    param 'Puppet::LookupContext', :context
  end

  def lookup_key(key, options, context)
    unless options.include?('apikey')
      Puppet.info("packtNews_lookup_key: apikey must be set,
get a key at https://newsapi.org/register")
      raise ArgumentError,
        "packtNews_lookup_key: apikey must be set, get a key at
https://newsapi.org/register"
    end

    return nil unless key == 'headline'
    # where to look
url="https://newsapi.org/v2/top-headlines?sources=google-news&a
piKey=#{options['apikey']}"
    timeout = 5
```

```
      uri = URI(url)
      https = Net::HTTP.new(uri.host, uri.port)
      https.use_ssl = true
      https.verify_mode = OpenSSL::SSL::VERIFY_PEER


      # make the request
      begin
        Puppet.info("https #{https.methods.sort -
Object.methods}")
        response = https.request_get(uri.request_uri)
        j=JSON.parse(response.body)
        return {'headline' => j['articles'][0]['title']} rescue
Exception => e
        Puppet.info("packtNews_lookup_key: unable to request JSON
from #{uri} (#{e})")
        raise Puppet::ResourceError, "packtNews_lookup_key:
unable to request JSON from #{uri} (#{e})"
        return nil
      end
    end
end
```

2. Add a notify to your `site.pp` that displays the headline:

```
node default {
  $headline = lookup('headline')
  notify {"headline is $headline":}
}
```

3. Run puppet on a node and observe the headline:

```
[root@cookbook ~]# puppet agent -t
Info: Using configured environment 'production'
Info: Retrieving pluginfacts
Info: Retrieving plugin
Notice:
/File[/opt/puppetlabs/puppet/cache/lib/puppet/functions/packtne
ws_lookup_key.rb]/ensure: defined content as
'{md5}5ba688fdb2583299cd91309379805385'
Info: Loading facts
Info: Caching catalog for test.example.com
Info: Applying configuration version '1524025895'
Notice: headline is {headline => U.S. Holds Back on New Russia
Sanctions}
```

```
Notice: /Stage[main]/Main/Node[default]/Notify[headline is
{headline => U.S. Holds Back on New Russia Sanctions}]/message:
defined 'message' as 'headline is {headline => U.S. Holds Back
on New Russia Sanctions}'
Notice: Applied catalog in 0.03 seconds
```

How it works...

When `puppet agent` is run on your node, the `packtnews_lookup_key` function is run on the Puppet master for each Hiera key. The function is also downloaded to your node, but it is important to know that the function will run on the master. In our example code, when the lookup key is equal to `headline`, our code will query the news API and return the first headline. If the lookup key is not `headline`, our function will return *nil*. When a Hiera function returns *nil*, the next level of the hierarchy is attempted. Returning a hash or an empty hash (`{}`) will cause the lookup to stop. Our code uses the `Ruby Net::Http` method to contact the news API. We put our API key in the `hiera.yaml` configuration file, it is accessible as `options['apikey']`.

There's more...

When the catalog is compiled for a node, the functions are downloaded for the node's particular environment. You can have multiple versions of functions in different environments. This allows you to develop a function without affecting production environments. You may also have multiple functions defined in your Hiera hierarchy.

Storing secret data with hiera-eyaml

If you're using Hiera to store your configuration data, there's a gem available, called `hiera-eyaml`, that adds an encryption backend to Hiera to allow you to protect values stored in Hiera.

Getting ready

`Hiera-eyaml` will run through the puppetserver process on our master, so we need to install the `hiera-eyaml` gem on the puppetserver. `Hiera-eyaml` also provides some command-line utilities, to take advantage of those, we'll install the `puppet gem` installation as well.

To install the gems, do the following:

```
[vagrant@puppet ~]$ sudo /opt/puppetlabs/puppet/bin/gem install hiera-eyaml
...
Done installing documentation for trollop, highline, hiera-eyaml after 0
seconds
3 gems installed

[vagrant@puppet ~]$ sudo /opt/puppetlabs/bin/puppetserver gem install
hiera-eyaml
...
Successfully installed hiera-eyaml-2.1.0
3 gems installed
```

Restart `puppetserver` to take advantage of the new gem:

```
[vagrant@puppet ~]$ sudo systemctl restart puppetserver
```

Create initial keys for your `hiera-eyaml` installation to use:

```
[vagrant@puppet ~]$ sudo mkdir /etc/puppetlabs/puppet/eyaml
[vagrant@puppet ~]$ sudo /opt/puppetlabs/puppet/bin/eyaml createkeys --
pkcs7-private-key /etc/puppetlabs/puppet/eyaml/private_key.pkcs7.pem --
pkcs7-public-key /etc/puppetlabs/puppet/eyaml/public_key.pkcs7.pem
[hiera-eyaml-core] Keys created OK
[vagrant@puppet ~]$ sudo chown -R puppet:puppet
/etc/puppetlabs/puppet/eyaml
```

Now create a directory to store the secret `hieradata`:

```
[vagrant@puppet ~]$ sudo mkdir /etc/puppetlabs/puppet/data/secrets
```

Finally, modify the Hiera hierarchy to use the `eyaml_lookup_key` function when looking for files in the `secrets` directory:

```
  - name: "Secret data"
    lookup_key: eyaml_lookup_key
    paths:
      - "secrets/hosts/%{::facts.hostname}.yaml"
      - "secrets/common.yaml"
    options:
      pkcs7_private_key: /etc/puppetlabs/puppet/eyaml/private_key.pkcs7.pem
      pkcs7_public_key: /etc/puppetlabs/puppet/eyaml/public_key.pkcs7.pem
```

How to do it...

In this example, we'll create a piece of encrypted data and retrieve it using `hiera-eyaml`:

1. Encrypt the `Val Kilmer` value using `eyaml encrypt`:

```
[vagrant@puppet ~]$ sudo /opt/puppetlabs/puppet/bin/eyaml
encrypt --pkcs7-private-key
/etc/puppetlabs/puppet/eyaml/private_key.pkcs7.pem --pkcs7-
public-key /etc/puppetlabs/puppet/eyaml/public_key.pkcs7.pem -s
'Val Kilmer'
string:
ENC[PKCS7,MIIBeQYJKoZIhvcNAQcDoIIBajCCAWYCAQAxggEhMIIBHQIBADAFM
AACAQEwDQYJKoZIhvcNAQEBBQAEggEA45yQmfTarsCS7b4cG2TZ/ifXkuE7pjcP
RJ3t/GU8kXPEIWZvGs8uu15deVue2+C+dlt6SuPwzTZpw6caaNHS73PRcYyZ3XQ
VLbpFGNKKTTkCY1jsLbbLrCRrY4FxLs2jfEtKN7tcvR6uHq6KeqBhWFJIL5rV2C
m8tnm3XPjon9LqYKVlhBmredEPNNg1ayKcWB/OdVAW9R8kdhkM3OCjpAd6t7H5E
RBNoN07gqnkg91gZ8cNjAVHFbmxHW6qnDuU0VtUDPA8XYMZF4YPh8/KPpl895eY
YjNEXfO9hFhgQaEWcOmUJ3surpECoUcSJS2qeil1wAgDHnjQ6mc0rMru4TA8Bgk
qhkiG9w0BBwEwHQYJYIZIAWUDBAEqBBB+56tLOfoqUZtfry8YxdF2gBAEhuVtui
uVZKj1E45x9c7D]

OR

block: >
ENC[PKCS7,MIIBeQYJKoZIhvcNAQcDoIIBajCCAWYCAQAxggEhMIIBHQIBADAFM
AACAQEw
DQYJKoZIhvcNAQEBBQAEggEA45yQmfTarsCS7b4cG2TZ/ifXkuE7pjcPRJ3t
/GU8kXPEIWZvGs8uu15deVue2+C+dlt6SuPwzTZpw6caaNHS73PRcYyZ3XQV
LbpFGNKKTTkCY1jsLbbLrCRrY4FxLs2jfEtKN7tcvR6uHq6KeqBhWFJIL5rV
2Cm8tnm3XPjon9LqYKVlhBmredEPNNg1ayKcWB/OdVAW9R8kdhkM3OCjpAd6
t7H5ERBNoN07gqnkg91gZ8cNjAVHFbmxHW6qnDuU0VtUDPA8XYMZF4YPh8/K
Ppl895eYYjNEXfO9hFhgQaEWcOmUJ3surpECoUcSJS2qeil1wAgDHnjQ6mc0
rMru4TA8BgkqhkiG9w0BBwEwHQYJYIZIAWUDBAEqBBB+56tLOfoqUZtfry8Y
        xdF2gBAEhuVtuiuVZKj1E45x9c7D]
```

2. Copy either the string or block representation to your `secrets/common.yaml`. I prefer the block format myself as it adds linebreaks to the encrypted value for improved readability:

```
---
top_secret: >
ENC[PKCS7,MIIBeQYJKoZIhvcNAQcDoIIBajCCAWYCAQAxggEhMIIBHQIBADAFM
AACAQEw
DQYJKoZIhvcNAQEBBQAEggEA45yQmfTarsCS7b4cG2TZ/ifXkuE7pjcPRJ3t
/GU8kXPEIWZvGs8uu15deVue2+C+dlt6SuPwzTZpw6caaNHS73PRcYyZ3XQV
LbpFGNKKTTkCY1jsLbbLrCRrY4FxLs2jfEtKN7tcvR6uHq6KeqBhWFJIL5rV
```

```
        2Cm8tnm3XPjon9LqYKVlhBmredEPNNg1ayKcWB/OdVAW9R8kdhkM3OCjpAd6
        t7H5ERBNoN07gqnkg91gZ8cNjAVHFbmxHW6qnDuU0VtUDPA8XYMZF4YPh8/K
        Ppl895eYYjNEXfO9hFhgQaEWcOmUJ3surpECoUcSJS2qeil1wAgDHnjQ6mc0
        rMru4TA8BgkqhkiG9w0BBwEwHQYJYIZIAWUDBAEqBBB+56tLOfoqUZtfry8Y
        xdF2gBAEhuVtuiuVZKj1E45x9c7D]
```

3. Modify site.pp to include our secret value:

    ```
    $top_secret = lookup('top_secret',String,first,'Deja Vu')
    notify { "He's The Saint, He's ${top_secret}": }
    ```

4. Run puppet agent on your node to see the secret message:

    ```
    [vagrant@testnode ~]$ sudo /opt/puppetlabs/bin/puppet agent
    -t
    ...
    Info: Caching catalog for testnode.example.com
    Info: Applying configuration version '1516687031'
    ...
    Notice: He's The Saint, He's Val Kilmer
    Notice: /Stage[main]/Main/Node[default]/Notify[He's The
    Saint, He's Val Kilmer]/message: defined 'message' as
    'He\'s The Saint, He\'s Val Kilmer'
    Notice: Applied catalog in 0.02 seconds
    ```

How it works...

When you install hiera-eyaml, it creates a function that can be used as a custom hiera5 backend. hiera.yaml is modified to inform the eyaml backend function where to find the public and private keys used for encryption. puppetserver is then able to decrypt the values stored in our secrets/common.yaml file and deliver the unencrypted string to the client node. Hiera-eyaml is an encrypted-at-rest system. You can safely give out the contents of the secrets/common.yaml file since they are encrypted with pkcs7. Provided you protect access to the private_key.pkcs7.pem file, you can be assured of a moderate level of protection from prying eyes.

There's more...

You can extend hiera5 with your own custom functions. It's possible to query your own internal systems for the data. You can customize Hiera for your environment and take advantage of pre-existing data sources.

Automatic syntax-checking with Git hooks

It would be nice if we knew there was a syntax error in the manifest before we even committed it. You can have Puppet check the manifest using the `puppet parser validate` command:

```
vagrant@git:~$ puppet parser validate git.pp
Error: Could not parse for environment production: Syntax error at
'require' at /home/vagrant/git.pp:16:3
```

This is especially useful because a mistake anywhere in the manifest will stop Puppet from running on any node, even on nodes that don't use that particular part of the manifest. So, checking in a bad manifest can cause Puppet to stop applying updates to production for some time, until the problem is discovered, and this could potentially have serious consequences. The best way to avoid this is to automate the syntax check, by using a precommit hook in your version control repo.

How to do it...

Follow these steps:

1. In your Puppet repo, create a new `hooks` directory:

   ```
   t@mylaptop:~/puppet$ mkdir hooks
   ```

2. Create the `hooks/check_syntax.sh` file with the following contents (based on a script by Puppet Labs):

   ```
   #!/bin/bash
   syntax_errors=0
   error_msg=$(mktemp /tmp/error_msg.XXXXXX)

   git rev-parse --quiet --verify HEAD > /dev/null
   if [ $? -eq 0 ]; then
     against=HEAD
   else
     # Initial commit: diff against an empty tree object
     against=4b825dc642cb6eb9a060e54bf8d69288fbee4904
   fi

   # Get list of new/modified manifest and template files to check
   (in git index)
   for indexfile in $(git diff-index --diff-filter=AM --name-only
   --cached $against | egrep '\.(pp|erb)')
   ```

```
do
  # Don't check empty files
  if [ $(git cat-file -s :0:$indexfile) -gt 0 ]; then
    case $indexfile in
    *.pp )
      # Check puppet manifest syntax
      git cat-file blob :0:$indexfile | puppet parser validate
2>$error_msg ;;
      *.erb )
      # Check ERB template syntax
      git cat-file blob :0:$indexfile | erb -x -T - | ruby -c
2>$error_msg >/dev/null ;;
    esac
    if [ "$?" -ne 0 ]; then
      echo -n "$indexfile: "
      cat $error_msg
      syntax_errors=$((syntax_errors + 1))
    fi
  fi
done
rm -f $error_msg
if [ "$syntax_errors" -ne 0 ]; then
  if [ "$syntax_errors" -gt 1 ]; then
    echo "Error: $syntax_errors syntax errors found, aborting
commit."
  else
    echo "Error: 1 syntax error found, aborting commit."
  fi
  exit 1
fi
```

3. Set execute permission for the `hook` script with the following command:

```
t@mylaptop:~/puppet$ chmod a+x hooks/check_syntax.sh
```

4. Either `symlink` or copy the script to the `pre-commit` hook in your hooks directory:

```
t@mylaptop:~/puppet $ ln -s ../../hooks/check_syntax.sh
.git/hooks/pre-commit
```

The hooks directory is in the root of the git clone, so `../..` will return the symlink from `.git/hooks` to the root of the repository.

How it works...

The `check_syntax.sh` script will prevent you from committing any files with syntax errors when it is used as the pre-commit hook for Git:

```
t@mylaptop $ git commit -m "test commit"
manifests/site.pp: Error: Could not parse for environment production:
Syntax error at 'another' at line 6:5
Error: 1 syntax error found, aborting commit.
```

By adding the hooks directory to your Git repo, anyone who has a checkout can copy the script into their local hooks directory to get this syntax-checking behavior. As a bonus, any improvements you make to the script are already checked into git, so you won't lose them.

Pushing code around with Git

As we have already seen in the decentralized model, Git can be used to transfer files between machines using a combination of `ssh` and `ssh` keys. It can also be useful to have a Git hook do the same on each successful commit to the repository.

There is a hook, called `postcommit`, that can be run after a successful commit to the repository. In this recipe, we'll create a hook that updates the code on our Puppet master with code from our Git repository on the Git server.

Getting ready

Follow these steps to get started:

1. Create an `ssh` key that can access your Puppet user on your Puppet master and install this key into the Git user's account on `git.example.com`:

```
vagrant@git:~$ sudo -iu git
$ ssh-keygen -f ~/.ssh/puppet_rsa
Generating public/private rsa key pair.
Enter passphrase (empty for no passphrase):
Enter same passphrase again:
Your identification has been saved in
/home/git/.ssh/puppet_rsa.
Your public key has been saved in
/home/git/.ssh/puppet_rsa.pub.
The key fingerprint is:
SHA256:4OYZuWnVUf1i5jefNV+M4HeBWDmlmsTaaLdqO2ncIZE git@git
```

```
The key's randomart image is:
+---[RSA 2048]----+
| ..o.  |
| .. +o |
| . ooo.o. |
| . o E=o+.+..|
| = S+o* = +.|
| o *....o +o*|
| * . +... oO|
| . *.. .o|
| ooo |
+----[SHA256]-----+
```

2. Modify the puppet user account to permit logins:

```
[vagrant@puppet ~]$ sudo chsh puppet -s /bin/bash
Changing shell for puppet.
Shell changed.
[vagrant@puppet ~]$ sudo cp /etc/skel/.bash_profile ~puppet
[vagrant@puppet ~]$ sudo cp /etc/skel/.bashrc ~puppet
[vagrant@puppet ~]$ sudo chown puppet:puppet ~puppet/.bash*
```

3. Copy the public key into the `authorized_keys` file of the puppet user on your `puppetmaster`:

```
[vagrant@puppet ~]$ sudo -u puppet -s /bin/bash
[puppet@puppet ~]$ cd ~puppet
[puppet@puppet ~]$ mkdir .ssh
[puppet@puppet ~]$ chmod 700 .ssh
[puppet@puppet ~]$ cd .ssh
[puppet@puppet ~]$ cat puppet_rsa.pub >authorized_keys
[puppet@puppet ~]$ chmod 600 authorized_keys
```

How to do it...

Perform the following steps:

1. Now that the Git user can log in to the Puppet master as the Puppet user, modify the Git user's ssh configuration to use the newly created ssh key by default. Add the following to ~git/.ssh/config:

```
Host puppet.example.com puppet
  Hostname puppet.example.com
  IdentityFile ~/.ssh/puppet_rsa
  User puppet
```

2. Add the Puppet master as a remote location for the Puppet repository on the Git server with the following commands:

```
git@git:~/repos/puppet.git$ git remote add puppetmaster
puppet.example.com:/etc/puppetlabs/code/puppet.git
```

3. On the Puppet master, create an empty Git repository to contain the `puppet git` repository:

```
[puppet@puppet ~]$ cd /etc/puppetlabs/code
[puppet@puppet code]$ git init --bare puppet.git
Initialized empty Git repository in
/etc/puppetlabs/code/puppet.git/
```

4. Back on the Git server, push your `master` branch to the remote server you just created:

```
git@git:~$ cd repos/puppet.git
git@git:~/repos/puppet.git$ git push puppetmaster master
Counting objects: 40, done.
Delta compression using up to 2 threads.
Compressing objects: 100% (27/27), done.
Writing objects: 100% (40/40), 6.23 KiB | 0 bytes/s, done.
Total 40 (delta 3), reused 0 (delta 0)
To puppet.example.com:/etc/puppetlabs/code/puppet.git
 * [new branch]      master -> master
```

5. Move the `production` environment out of the way and clone your local copy of the Git repository in its place:

```
[puppet@puppet ~]$ cd /etc/puppetlabs/code/environments/
[puppet@puppet environments]$ mv production production.orig
[puppet@puppet environments]$ git clone
/etc/puppetlabs/code/puppet.git production
Cloning into 'production'...
done.
```

You will probably have to install git on your puppet server at this point. Use puppet to do it:

```
puppet resource package git ensure=installed.
```

6. At this point, we have a production environment that is based on the Git repository on the Git server. To automate the process, create a `post-receive` file in the hooks directory of the repository on the Git server with the following contents:

```
#!/bin/sh
git push puppetmaster master
ssh puppet@puppet.example.com "cd
/etc/puppetlabs/code/environments/production &amp;& git pull
origin master"
```

7. Make the hook script executable:

```
git@git:~$ cd repos/puppet.git/hooks/
git@git:~/repos/puppet.git/hooks$ chmod 755 post-receive
```

8. Commit a change to the repository from your laptop and verify that the change is propagated to the Puppet master, as follows:

```
t@mylaptop $ echo "# Puppet Cookbook Module" > README.md
t@mylaptop $ git add README.md
t@mylaptop $ git commit -m "README"
[master 9e9d9a0] README
 1 file changed, 1 insertion(+), 3 deletions(-)
t@mylaptop $ git push origin master
Counting objects: 3, done.
Delta compression using up to 8 threads.
Compressing objects: 100% (2/2), done.
Writing objects: 100% (3/3), 367 bytes | 367.00 KiB/s, done.
Total 3 (delta 0), reused 0 (delta 0)
remote: To puppet.example.com:/etc/puppetlabs/code/puppet.git
remote: a68b531..9e9d9a0 master -> master
remote: From /etc/puppetlabs/code/puppet
remote: * branch master -> FETCH_HEAD
remote: Updating a68b531..9e9d9a0
remote: Fast-forward
remote: README.md | 4 +---
remote: 1 file changed, 1 insertion(+), 3 deletions(-)
To git.example.com:repos/puppet.git
   a68b531..9e9d9a0 master -> master
```

How it works...

We create a bare repository on the Puppet master that we then use as a `remote` for the repository on git.example.com (remote repositories must be bare). We then clone that bare repository into the production directory. We add the bare repository on `puppet.example.com` as a remote to the bare repository on git.example.com. We then create a `post-receive` hook in the repository on git.example.com.

The hook issues a Git push to the Puppet master bare repository. We then update the production directory from the updated bare repository on the Puppet master. In the next section, we'll modify the hook to use branches.

Managing environments with Git

Branches are a way of keeping several different tracks of development within a single source repository. Puppet environments are a lot like Git branches. You can have the same code with slight variations between branches, just as you can have different modules for different environments. In this section, we'll show you how to use Git branches to define environments on the Puppet master.

Getting ready

In the previous section, we created a production directory that was based on the master branch; we'll remove that directory now:

```
puppet@puppet:/etc/puppet/environments$ mv production production.master
```

How to do it...

Modify the post-receive hook to accept a branch variable. The hook will use this variable to create a directory on the Puppet master, as follows:

```
#!/bin/sh
read oldrev newrev refname
branch=${refname#*\/*\/}
git push puppetmaster $branch
ssh puppet@puppet.example.com "if [ ! -d
/etc/puppetlabs/code/environments/$branch ]; then git clone
/etc/puppetlabs/code/puppet.git /etc/puppetlabs/code/environments/$branch;
fi; cd
```

```
/etc/puppetlabs/code/environments/$branch; git checkout $branch; git pull"
```

Modify your README file again and push to the repository on `git.example.com`:

```
t@mylaptop $ git push origin master
Counting objects: 3, done.
Delta compression using up to 8 threads.
Compressing objects: 100% (2/2), done.
Writing objects: 100% (3/3), 367 bytes | 367.00 KiB/s, done.
Total 3 (delta 0), reused 0 (delta 0)
remote: To puppet.example.com:/etc/puppetlabs/code/puppet.git
remote: 9e9d9a0..7b7ec43 master -> master
remote: Cloning into '/etc/puppetlabs/code/environments/master'...
remote: done.
remote: Already on 'master'
remote: Already up-to-date.
To git.example.com:repos/puppet.git
   9e9d9a0..7b7ec43 master -> master
```

How it works...

The hook now uses the information sent to it from Git when you do your commit. The third argument to the script is `refname`; the script parses out the branch that is being updated from the reference. We use that branch variable to clone the repository into a new directory and check out the branch.

There's more...

Now, when we want to create a new environment, we can create a new branch in the Git repository. The branch will create a directory on the Puppet master. Each branch of the Git repository represents an environment on the Puppet master:

1. Create the production branch, as shown in the following command line:

   ```
   t@burnaby $ git branch production
   t@burnaby $ git checkout production
   Switched to branch 'production'
   t@burnaby $ echo >> README.md
   t@burnaby $ git add README.md
   t@burnaby $ git commit -m "README"
   [production 5e20247] README
   1 file changed, 1 insertion(+)
   ```

2. Update the production branch and push to the Git server, as follows:

```
t@burnaby $ git push origin production
Counting objects: 3, done.
Delta compression using up to 8 threads.
Compressing objects: 100% (2/2), done.
Writing objects: 100% (3/3), 366 bytes | 366.00 KiB/s, done.
Total 3 (delta 0), reused 0 (delta 0)
remote: To puppet.example.com:/etc/puppetlabs/code/puppet.git
remote: * [new branch] production -> production
remote: error: pathspec 'production' did not match any file(s)
known to git.
remote: From /etc/puppetlabs/code/puppet
remote: cbf08cd..7b7ec43 master -> origin/master
remote: * [new branch] production -> origin/production
remote: Updating 9e9d9a0..7b7ec43
remote: Fast-forward
remote: README.md | 1 +
remote: 1 file changed, 1 insertion(+)
To git.example.com:repos/puppet.git
 * [new branch] production -> production
t@mylaptop puppet$ git branch production
t@mylaptop puppet$ git checkout production Switched to branch
'production'.
t@mylaptop puppet$ vim README
t@mylaptop puppet$git add README
t@mylaptop puppet$ git commit -m "Production Branch"
t@mylaptop puppet$ git push origin production Counting objects:
7, done. Delta compression using up to 4 threads.
Compressing objects: 100% (3/3), done. Writing objects: 100%
(3/3), 372 bytes | 0 bytes/s, done. Total 3 (delta 1), reused 0
(delta 0),remote: To
puppet@puppet.example.com:/etc/puppet/environments/ puppet.git
remote: 11db6e5..832f6a9 production -> production remote:
Cloning into '/etc/puppet/environments/production'... remote:
done. remote: Switched to a new branch 'production' remote:
Branch production set up to track remote branch production from
origin. remote: Already up-to-date. To
git@git.example.com:repos/puppet.git
11db6e5..832f6a9 production -> production
```

Now, whenever we create a new branch, a corresponding directory is created in our environment's directory. A one-to-one mapping is established between environments and branches.

Writing Better Manifests

3

In this chapter, we will cover the following recipes:

- Using arrays of resources
- Using resource defaults
- Using defined types
- Using tags
- Using run stages
- Using roles and profiles
- Using data types in Puppet
- Passing parameters to classes
- Passing parameters from Hiera
- Writing reusable, cross-platform manifests
- Getting information about the environment
- Importing dynamic information
- Passing arguments to shell commands

Introduction

Your Puppet manifests are the living documentation for your entire infrastructure. Keeping them tidy and well-organized is a great way to make it easier to maintain and understand. Puppet gives you a number of tools to do this:

- Arrays
- Defaults
- Defined types
- Dependencies
- Class parameters

We'll see how to use all of these and more. As you read through the chapter, try out the examples and look through your own manifests to see where these features might help you simplify and improve your Puppet code.

Using arrays of resources

Anything that you can do to a resource, you can do to an array of resources. Use this idea to refactor your manifests to make them shorter and clearer.

How to do it...

Here are the steps to refactor using arrays of resources:

1. Identify a class in your manifest where you have several instances of the same kind of resource, for example, packages:

```
package { 'sudo' : ensure      => installed }
package { 'unzip' : ensure     => installed }
package { 'locate' : ensure    => installed }
package { 'lsof' : ensure      => installed }
package { 'cron' : ensure      => installed }
package { 'rubygems' : ensure => installed }
```

2. Group them together and replace them with a single `package` resource using an array:

```
$pkgs = [ 'cron',
          'locate',
          'lsof',
          'rubygems',
          'sudo',
          'unzip' ]
package { $pkgs:
  ensure => installed,
}
```

How it works...

Most of Puppet's resource types can accept an array instead of a single name, and will create one instance for each of the elements in the array. All the parameters you provide for the resource (for example, `ensure => installed`) will be assigned to each of the new resource instances. This shorthand will only work when all the resources have the same attributes.

There's more...

Using an array, you can add or change parameters for all the resources at once. For example, you could add a `hasrestart` option with the following modification:

```
package { $pkgs:
  ensure      => installed,
  hasrestart => true,
}
```

See also

- *The Iterating over multiple items* recipe in `Chapter 1`, *Puppet Language and Style*

Using resource defaults

Resource defaults allow you to specify the default attribute values for a resource. Resource defaults are valid for a given resource type and within the current scope. If you define a resource default in a class, then all resources of that type within the class will be given those defaults. In this example, we'll show you how to specify a resource default for the `File` type.

How to do it...

To show you how to use resource defaults, we'll create an apache module. Within this module, we will specify that all file resources require the httpd package and the default owner and group are the apache user:

1. Create an apache module and create a resource default for the File type:

```
class apache {
  File {
    owner    => 'apache',
    group    => 'apache',
    mode     => '0644',
    require  => Package['httpd']
  }
  package {'httpd': ensure => 'installed'}
}
```

2. Create html files within the /var/www/html directory:

```
$index = @(INDEX)
  <html>
    <body>
      <h1><a href='cookbook.html'>Cookbook! </a></h1>
    </body>
  </html>
  | INDEX
file {'/var/www/html/index.html':
  content => $index,
}
$cookbook = @(COOKBOOK)
  <html>
    <body>
      <h2>PacktPub</h2>
    </body>
  </html>
  | COOKBOOK
file {'/var/www/html/cookbook.html':
  content => $cookbook
}
```

3. Apply the module to a node:

```
t@mylaptop ~ $ sudo /opt/puppetlabs/bin/puppet apply -e
'include apache' --modulepath
/home/thomas/.puppetlabs/etc/code/modules
Notice: Compiled catalog for mylaptop.example.com in
```

```
environment production in 0.54 seconds
Notice:
/Stage[main]/Apache/File[/var/www/html/index.html]/ensure:
defined content as '{md5}05504e959eee487f44e9c0ddfa741829'
Notice:
/Stage[main]/Apache/File[/var/www/html/cookbook.html]/ensure:
defined content as '{md5}e83a49b87d91cf41ee30c0b755f3712e'
Notice: Applied catalog in 0.55 seconds
t@mylaptop ~ $ ls -l /var/www/html
total 8
-rw-r--r--. 1 apache apache 56 Feb 4 21:42 cookbook.html
-rw-r--r--. 1 apache apache 86 Feb 4 21:42 index.html
```

How it works...

The resource default we defined specifies the owner, group, and mode for all file resources within this class (also known as within this scope). We also specify that the httpd package is required before creating these files. This is useful since the package creates the the /var/www/html directory, into which we are going to place these files. Unless you specifically override a resource default, the value for an attribute will be taken from the default.

There's more...

You can specify resource defaults for any resource type. You can also specify resource defaults in site.pp. I find it useful to specify the default action for the Package and Service resources, as follows:

```
Package { ensure => 'installed' }
Service {
  hasrestart => true,
  enable     => true,
  ensure     => true,
}
```

With these defaults, whenever you specify a package, the package will be installed. Whenever you specify a service, the service will be started and enabled to run at boot. These are the usual reasons you specify packages and services; most of the time these defaults will do what you prefer and your code will be cleaner. When you need to disable a service, simply override the defaults.

Using defined types

In the previous example, we saw how to reduce redundant code by grouping identical resources into arrays. However, this technique is limited to resources where all the parameters are the same. When you have a set of resources that have some parameters in common, you need to use a defined type to group them together.

How to do it...

The following steps will show you how to create a definition:

1. Create the following manifest:

```
define tmpfile() {
  file { "/tmp/${name}":
    content => "Hello, world\n",
  }
}
tmpfile { ['a', 'b', 'c']: }
```

2. Run puppet apply:

```
t@mylaptop ~ $ puppet apply tmpfile.pp
Notice: Compiled catalog for mylaptop.example.com in
environment production in 0.02 seconds
Notice: /Stage[main]/Main/Tmpfile[a]/File[/tmp/a]/ensure:
defined content as '{md5}a7966bf58e23583c9a5a4059383ff850'
Notice: /Stage[main]/Main/Tmpfile[b]/File[/tmp/b]/ensure:
defined content as '{md5}a7966bf58e23583c9a5a4059383ff850'
Notice: /Stage[main]/Main/Tmpfile[c]/File[/tmp/c]/ensure:
defined content as '{md5}a7966bf58e23583c9a5a4059383ff850'
Notice: Applied catalog in 0.13 seconds
```

How it works...

You can think of a defined type (introduced with the define keyword) as a cookie-cutter. It describes a pattern that Puppet can use to create lots of similar resources. Any time you declare a tmpfile instance in your manifest, Puppet will insert all the resources contained in the tmpfile definition.

In our example, the definition of `tmpfile` contains a single file resource whose content is `Hello world\n` and whose path is `/tmp/${name}`. If you declared an instance of `tmpfile` with the name `foo`, Puppet will create a file with the `/tmp/foo` path:

```
tmpfile { 'foo': }
```

In other words, `${name}` in the definition will be replaced by the name of any actual instance that Puppet is asked to create. It's almost as though we created a new kind of resource, `tmpfile`, which has one parameter: its name.

Just like with regular resources, we don't have to pass just one title; as in the preceding example, we can provide an array of titles and Puppet will create as many resources as required.

A note on `name`, the `namevar`: every resource you create must have a unique name, the `namevar`. This is different than the title, which is how Puppet refers to the resource internally (although they are often the same).

There's more...

In the example, we created a definition where the only parameter that varies between instances is the name parameter. But we can add whatever parameters we want, so long as we declare them in the definition in parentheses after the name parameter, as follows:

```
define tmpfile (
  String $greeting = "Hello, World!\n"
  ) {
    file { "/tmp/${name}":
      content => $greeting,
  }
}
tmpfile { 'd': greeting => "Good Morning!\n" }
```

In this example, we've specified that the `$greeting` parameter is a String. Puppet will not allow us to try using `tmpfile` without a String:

```
Error: Evaluation Error: Error while evaluating a Resource Statement,
Tmpfile[e]: parameter 'greeting' expects a String value, got Integer at
/home/thomas/tmpfile2.pp:10 on node mylaptop.example.com
```

We also specified a default value for the greeting; if you fail to pass a greeting parameter, the default value will be used. You can declare multiple parameters as a comma-separated list:

```
define mywebapp (
  String $domain = $facts['domain'],
  String $path,
  String $platform,
) {
  notify {"${domain} ${path} ${platform}": }
}

mywebapp { 'mywizzoapp':
  domain   => 'Rails',
  path     => '/var/www/apps/mywizzoapp',
  platform => 'mywizzoapp.com',
}
```

This is a powerful technique for abstracting out everything that's common to certain resources, and keeping it in one place so that you don't repeat yourself. In the preceding example, there might be many individual resources contained within `mywebapp`: packages, config files, source code checkouts, virtual hosts, and so on. But all of them are the same for every instance of `mywebapp` except in the parameters we provide. These might be referenced in a template, for example, to set the domain for a virtual host.

See also

- The *Passing parameters to classes* recipe, in this chapter

Using tags

Sometimes one Puppet class needs to know about another, or at least know whether or not it's present. For example, a class that manages the firewall may need to know whether or not the node is a web server.

Puppet's tagged function will tell you whether a named class or resource is present in the catalog for this node. You can also apply arbitrary tags to a node or class and check for the presence of these tags. Tags are another metaparameter, similar to `require` and `notify`, which we introduced in `Chapter 1`, *Puppet Language and Style*. Metaparameters are used in the compilation of the Puppet catalog but are not attributes of the resource to which they are attached.

How to do it...

To help you find out whether you're running on a particular node or class of nodes, all nodes are automatically tagged with the node name and the names of any classes they include. Here's an example that shows you how to use `tagged` to get this information:

1. Add the following code to your `site.pp` file (replacing `cookbook` with your machine's hostname):

```
node 'cookbook' {
  if tagged('cookbook') {
    notify { 'tagged cookbook': }
  }
}
```

2. Run Puppet:

```
[root@cookbook ~]# puppet agent -t
Info: Using configured environment 'production'
Info: Retrieving pluginfacts
Info: Retrieving plugin
Info: Loading facts
Info: Caching catalog for test.example.com
Info: Applying configuration version '1524111400'
Notice: tagged cookbook
Notice: /Stage[main]/Main/Node[cookbook]/Notify[tagged
cookbook]/message: defined 'message' as 'tagged cookbook'
Notice: Applied catalog in 0.03 seconds
```

Nodes are also automatically tagged with the names of all the classes they include in, addition to several other automatic tags. You can use `tagged` to find out what classes are included on the node. You're not just limited to checking the tags automatically applied by Puppet. You can also add your own. To set an arbitrary `tag` on a node, use the `tag` function, as in the following example:

1. Modify your `site.pp` file, as follows:

```
node 'cookbook' {
  tag('tagging')
  class {'tag_test': }
}
```

2. Add a `tag_test` module with the following `init.pp`:

```
class tag_test {
  if tagged('tagging') {
    notify { 'containing node/class was tagged.': }
  }
}
```

3. Run Puppet:

```
root@cookbook:~# puppet agent -t
Info: Using configured environment 'production'
Info: Retrieving pluginfacts
Info: Retrieving plugin
Info: Caching catalog for cookbook.example.com
Info: Applying configuration version '1517851735'
Notice: containing node/class was tagged.
Notice: /Stage[main]/Tag_test/Notify[containing node/class was
tagged.]/message: defined 'message' as 'containing node/class
was tagged.'
Notice: Applied catalog in 0.30 seconds
```

4. You can also use tags to determine which parts of the manifest to apply. If you use the `--tags` option on the Puppet command line, Puppet will apply only those classes or resources tagged with the specific tags you include. For example, we can define our cookbook class with two classes:

```
node cookbook {
  class {'first_class': }
  class {'second_class': }
}
class first_class {
  notify { 'First Class': }
}
class second_class {
  notify {'Second Class': }
}
```

5. Now, when we run `puppet agent` on the cookbook node, we see both `notify`:

```
root@cookbook:~# puppet agent -t
Info: Using configured environment 'production'
Info: Retrieving pluginfacts
Info: Retrieving plugin
Info: Caching catalog for cookbook.example.com
Info: Applying configuration version '1517851837'
Notice: First Class
```

```
Notice: /Stage[main]/First_class/Notify[First Class]/message:
defined 'message' as 'First Class'
Notice: Second Class
Notice: /Stage[main]/Second_class/Notify[Second Class]/message:
defined 'message' as 'Second Class'
Notice: Applied catalog in 0.27 seconds
```

6. Apply only the `first_class` add `--tags` function to the command line:

```
root@cookbook:~# puppet agent -t --tags first_class
Info: Using configured environment 'production'
Info: Retrieving pluginfacts
Info: Retrieving plugin
Info: Caching catalog for cookbook.example.com
Info: Applying configuration version '1517851867'
Notice: First Class
Notice: /Stage[main]/First_class/Notify[First Class]/message:
defined 'message' as 'First Class'
Info: Stage[main]: Unscheduling all events on Stage[main]
Notice: Applied catalog in 0.30 seconds
```

There's more...

You can use tags to create a collection of resources, and then make the collection a dependency for some other resource. For example, say some service depends on a config file that is built from a number of file snippets, as in the following example:

```
class firewall::service {
  service { 'firewall':
    ...
  }
  File <| tag == 'firewall-snippet' |> ~> Service['firewall']
}
class myapp {
  file { '/etc/firewall.d/myapp.conf':
    tag => 'firewall-snippet',
    ...
  }
}
```

Here, we've specified that the firewall service should be notified if any file resource tagged `firewall-snippet` is updated. All we need to do to add a firewall config snippet for any particular application or service is to tag it firewall-snippet, and Puppet will do the rest.

Although we could add a notify => `Service["firewall"]` function to each snippet resource if our definition of the firewall service were ever to change, we would have to hunt down and update all the snippets accordingly. The tag lets us encapsulate the logic in one place, making future maintenance and refactoring much easier.

What's <| `tag == 'firewall-snippet'` |> `syntax`? This is called a resource collector, and it's a way of specifying a group of resources by searching for some piece of data about them; in this case, the value of a tag. You can find out more about resource collectors and the <| |> operator (sometimes known as the spaceship operator) on the Puppet Labs website: `http://docs.puppetlabs.com/puppet/3/reference/ lang_collectors.html`.

What does ~> mean? This is a chaining arrow with notification. The resource(s) on the left must come before the resource(s) on the right. If any resources on the left update, then they notify the resources on the right.

 More information on resource relationships may be found on the puppet website: `https://puppet.com/docs/puppet/5.0/lang_relationships. html`.

Using run stages

A common requirement is to apply a certain group of resources before other groups (for example, installing a package repository or a custom Ruby version), or after others (for example, deploying an application once its dependencies are installed). Puppet's run stages feature allows you to do this.

By default, all resources in your manifest are applied in a single stage named `main`. If you need a resource to be applied before all others, you can assign it to a new run stage that is specified to come before main. Similarly, you could define a run stage that comes after `main`. In fact, you can define as many run stages as you need and tell Puppet which order they should be applied in.

In this example, we'll use stages to ensure one class is applied first and another last.

How to do it...

Here are the steps to create an example using run stages:

1. Create the `modules/admin/manifests/stages.pp` file with the following contents:

```
class admin::stages {
  stage { 'first': before => Stage['main'] }
  stage { 'last': require => Stage['main'] }

  class { 'admin::me_last': stage => 'last', }
  class { 'admin::me_first': stage => 'first', }
}
```

2. Create the `admin::me_first` and `admin::me_last` classes, as follows:

```
class admin::me_first {
  notify { 'This will be done first': }
}
class admin::me_last {
  notify { 'This will be done last': }
}
```

3. Modify your `site.pp` file, as follows:

```
node 'cookbook' {
  class {'first_class': }
  class {'second_class': }
  include admin::stages
}
```

4. Run Puppet:

```
root@cookbook:~# puppet agent -t
Info: Using configured environment 'production'
Info: Retrieving pluginfacts
Info: Retrieving plugin
Info: Caching catalog for cookbook.example.com
Info: Applying configuration version '1517854357'
Notice: This will be done first
Notice: /Stage[first]/Admin::Me_first/Notify[This will be done
first]/message: defined 'message' as 'This will be done first'
Notice: First Class
Notice: /Stage[main]/First_class/Notify[First Class]/message:
defined 'message' as 'First Class'
Notice: Second Class
```

```
Notice: /Stage[main]/Second_class/Notify[Second Class]/message:
defined 'message' as 'Second Class'
Notice: This will be done last
Notice: /Stage[last]/Admin::Me_last/Notify[This will be done
last]/message: defined 'message' as 'This will be done last'
Notice: Applied catalog in 0.25 seconds
```

How it works...

Let's examine this code in detail to see what's happening. First, we declare the first and last run stages, as follows:

```
stage { 'first':
  before => Stage['main']
}
stage { 'last':
  require => Stage['main']
}
```

For the first stage, we've specified that it should come before main. That is, every resource marked as being in the first stage will be applied before any resource in the main stage (the default stage).

The last stage requires the main stage, so no resource in the last stage can be applied until after every resource in the main stage.

We then declare some classes that we'll later assign to these run stages:

```
class admin::me_first {
  notify { 'This will be done first': }
}
class admin::me_last {
  notify { 'This will be done last': }
}
```

We can now put it all together and include these classes on the node, specifying the run stages for each as we do so:

```
class { 'me_first':
  stage => 'first',
}
class { 'me_last':
  stage => 'last',
}
```

Note that, in the class declarations for `me_first` and `me_last`, we didn't have to specify that they take a stage parameter. The stage parameter is another metaparameter, which means it can be applied to any class or resource without having to be explicitly declared. When we ran `puppet agent` on our `Puppet` node, the notify from the `me_first` class was applied before the notifies from `first_class` and `second_class`. The notify from `me_last` was applied after the main stage, so it comes after the two notifies from `first_class` and `second_class`. If you run puppet agent multiple times, you will see that the notifies from `first_class` and `second_class` may not always appear in the same order, but the `me_first` class will always come first and the `me_last` class will always come last.

There's more...

You can define as many run stages as you like and set up any ordering for them. This can greatly simplify a complicated manifest that would otherwise require lots of explicit dependencies between resources. Beware of accidentally introducing dependency cycles, though; when you assign something to a run stage, you're automatically making it dependent on everything in prior stages.

You may like to define your stages in the `site.pp` file instead so that, at the top level of the manifest, it's easy to see which stages are available.

Gary Larizza has written a helpful introduction to using run stages, with some real-world examples, on his website: `http://garylarizza.com/blog/2011/03/11/using-run-stages-with-puppet/`.

A caveat: many people don't like to use run stages, feeling that Puppet already provides sufficient resource-ordering control, and that using run stages indiscriminately can make your code very hard to follow. The use of run stages should be kept to a minimum wherever possible. There are a few key examples where the use of stages creates less complexity. The most notable is when a resource modifies the system used to install packages on the system. It helps to have a package management stage that comes before the main stage. When packages are defined in the main (default) stage, your manifests can count on the updated package management configuration information being present. For instance, for a Yum-based system, you would create a `yumrepos` stage that comes before `main`. You can specify this dependency using chaining arrows, as shown in the following code snippet:

```
stage {'yumrepos': }
Stage['yumrepos'] -> Stage['main']
```

We can then create a class that creates a Yum repository (`yumrepo`) resource and assign it to the yumrepos stage, as follows:

```
class yums {
  notify {'always before the rest': }
  yumrepo {'testrepo':
    baseurl => 'file:///var/yum',
    ensure => 'present',
  }
}
class {'yums':
  stage => 'yumrepos',
}
```

For Apt-based systems, the same example would be a stage where Apt sources are defined. The key with stages is to keep their definitions in your `site.pp` file, where they are highly visible and to use them sparingly where you can guarantee that you will not introduce dependency cycles.

See also

- The *Using tags* recipe, in this chapter
- The *Drawing dependency graphs* recipe in `Chapter 10`, *Monitoring, Reporting, and Troubleshooting*

Using roles and profiles

Well-organized Puppet manifests are easy to read; the purpose of a module should be evident in its name. The purpose of a node should be defined in a single class. This single class should include all classes that are required to perform that purpose. Craig Dunn wrote a post about such a classification system, which he dubbed "roles and profiles" (`http://www. craigdunn.org/2012/05/239/`). In this model, roles are the single purpose of a node; a node may only have one role, a role may contain more than one profile, and a profile contains all the resources related to a single service. In this example, we will create a web server role that uses several profiles.

How to do it...

We'll create two modules to store our roles and profiles. Roles will contain one or more profiles. Each role or profile will be defined as a subclass, such as profile::base:

1. Decide on a naming strategy for your roles and profiles. In our example, we will create two modules, roles and profiles, that will contain our roles and profiles, respectively:

```
t@t510 $ puppet module generate thomas-profiles --skip-
interview
Notice: Generating module at /home/thomas/puppet/profiles...
Notice: Populating templates...
...
t@mylaptop $ puppet module generate thomas-roles --skip-
interview
Notice: Generating module at /home/thomas/puppet/roles...
Notice: Populating templates...
...
```

2. Begin defining the constituent parts of our webserver role as profiles. To keep this example simple, we will create two profiles. First, a base profile to include our basic server configuration classes. Second, an apache class to install and configure the Apache web server (httpd), as follows:profiles/manifests/base.pp

```
class profiles::base {
  include base
}
```

The other file is profiles/manifests/apache.pp:

```
class profiles::apache {
  $apache = $::osfamily ? {
    'RedHat' => 'httpd',
    'Debian' => 'apache2',
  }
  service { $apache:
    enable => true,
    ensure => true,
  }
  package { $apache:
    ensure => 'installed',
  }
}
```

3. Define a `roles::webserver` class for our webserver role as follows:
   `roles/manifests/webserver.pp`

   ```
   class roles::webserver {
     include profiles::apache
     include profiles::base
   }
   ```

4. Apply the `roles::webserver` class to a node. In a centralized installation, you would use either an **External Node Classifier** (**ENC**) to apply the class to the node, or you would use Hiera to define the role:

   ```
   node 'webtest' {
     include roles::webserver
   }
   ```

How it works...

Breaking down the parts of the web server configuration into different profiles allows us to apply those parts independently. We created a base profile that we can expand to include all the resources we would like applied to all nodes. Our `roles::webserver` class simply includes the `base` and `apache` classes.

There's more...

As we'll see in the next section, we can pass parameters to classes to alter how they work. In our `roles::webserver` class, we can use the class instantiation syntax instead of `include`, and override it with parameters in the classes. For instance, to pass a parameter to the `base` class, we would use the following:

```
class {'profiles::base':
  parameter => 'newvalue'
}
```

This replaces our previous use:

```
include profiles::base
```

In previous versions of this book, node and class inheritance were used to achieve a similar goal, code reuse. Node inheritance is deprecated in Puppet Version 3.7 and higher. Node and class inheritance should be avoided. Using roles and profiles achieves the same level of readability and is much easier to follow.

Using data types in Puppet

In previous releases of Puppet, variables were not typed. A variable could hold any sort of value. Although this makes writing code somewhat easier, it leads to many problems. Variables that expect an array could be passed a string; variables that expect an integer may be passed a String. Type mismatch can have very bad affects so, to combat this problem, several helper functions were created in `stdlib` to validate the type of a variable. The validation functions were named for the data type they validated and included `validate_array`, `validate_hash`, `validate_numeric`, and `validate_string`. All these functions have been deprecated in Puppet 5 and replaced with the `assert_type` function. The `assert_type` function can be used to ensure that a variable is of any given type. Puppet5 also enforces types when they are assigned to class parameters, as we'll see in the next section.

How to do it...

In this example, we'll create a password variable and ensure that it is at least eight characters long:

1. Create a password manifest, as follows:

```
$password = "pass"
$valid_password = assert_type(String[8],$password)

notify {"v=${valid_password}": }
```

2. Next, use `puppet apply` on the manifest:

```
t@mylaptop $ puppet apply password.pp
Error: Evaluation Error: Error while evaluating a Function
Call, assert_type(): expects a String[8, default] value, got
String at /home/thomas/password.pp:2:19 on node
mylaptop.example.com
```

3. Our password was not long enough, so change the password to an eight-character password and rerun `puppet apply`:

```
t@mylaptop $ puppet apply password.pp
Notice: Compiled catalog for mylaptop.example.com in
environment production in 0.01 seconds
Notice: v=password
```

```
Notice: /Stage[main]/Main/Notify[v=password]/message: defined
'message' as 'v=password'
Notice: Applied catalog in 0.02 seconds
```

There's more...

The following types are available in Puppet5:

- String
- Integer, float, and numeric
- Boolean
- Array
- Hash
- Regexp (a regular expression matcher)
- Undef
- Default (the default of a case statement, for example)

More information on types is available on the Puppet website at https://puppet.com/docs/puppet/latest/lang_data_type.html.

In addition to these data types, there are several abstract data types built upon the code data types. The abstract data types can be used to ensure that variables have very specific values. For example, when specifying a port to use for a package, you can use the enum type to enforce that the port be one of a selection of String values, as shown here:

```
$state = 'install'
$pkg = assert_type(Enum['installed','absent'], $state)
```

When we run puppet apply on this manifest, we return an error:

```
t@mylaptop $ puppet apply enum.pp
Error: Evaluation Error: Error while evaluating a Function Call,
assert_type(): expects a match for Enum['absent', 'installed'], got
'install' at /home/thomas/enum.pp:2:8 on node mylaptop.example.com
```

There are a few abstract data types. Variant is another useful one, if you want to accept a String or an array of String, you can define your variable as follows:

```
$pkgs = ['ssh','gcc']
assert_type(Variant[Array[String],String],$pkgs)
```

For more information on abstract data types, see the Puppet website at `https://puppet.com/docs/puppet/latest/lang_data_abstract.html`.

Passing parameters to classes

Sometimes it's very useful to parameterize some aspect of a class. For example, you might need to manage different versions of a gem package and, rather than making separate classes for each that differ only in the version number, you can pass in the version number as a parameter.

How to do it...

In this example, we'll create a definition that accepts parameters:

1. Declare the parameter as a part of the class definition:

```
class eventmachine(
  String $version
  ) {
  package { 'eventmachine':
    provider => gem,
    ensure   => $version,
  }
}
```

2. Use the following syntax to include the class on a node:

```
class { 'eventmachine':
  version => '1.0.3',
}
```

How it works...

The class definition class `eventmachine ($version) {` is just like a normal class definition except it specifies that the class takes one parameter: `$version`. Inside the class, we've defined a package resource:

```
package { 'eventmachine':
  provider => gem,
  ensure   => $version,
}
```

This is a gem package, and we're requesting to install the `$version` version.

Include the class on a node, but instead of the usual `include` syntax, `include eventmachine`, we use the class declaration syntax as follows:

```
class { 'eventmachine': version => '1.0.3', }
```

This has the same effect but also sets a value for the parameter version as `1.0.3`.

There's more...

You can specify multiple parameters for a `class` as follows:

```
class mysql(
  Variant[String, Array[String]] $package,
  String $socket,
  Integer $port
  ) {
  ...
}
```

Then, supply them in the same way:

```
class { 'mysql':
  package => 'percona-server-server-5.5',
  socket  => '/var/run/mysqld/mysqld.sock',
  port    => 3306,
}
```

Specifying default values

You can also give default values for some of your parameters. When you include the class without setting a parameter, the default value will be used. For instance, if we created a MySQL class with three parameters, we could provide default values for any of the parameters, as shown in the code snippet:

```
class mysql(
  Variant[String, Array[String]] $package,
  String $socket,
  Integer $port=3306
  ) {
```

Or we can provide them for all:

```
class mysql(
   Variant[String, Array[String]] package = 'percona-server-server-5.5',
   String socket                  = '/var/run/mysqld/mysqld.sock',
   Integer port                   = 3306
   ) {
```

Defaults allow you to use a default value and override that default when you need to. Unlike a definition, only one instance of a parameterized class can exist on a node. When you need to have several different instances of the resource, use `define` instead.

Passing parameters from Hiera

Like the parameter defaults we introduced in the previous `chapter` *Puppet Infrastructure* , Hiera may be used to provide default values to classes. Automatic parameter lookup via Hiera has been on by default since version 3 of Puppet.

Getting ready

Configure hiera as we did in `Chapter` 2, *Puppet Infrastructure*. Create a global or common YAML file; this will serve as the default for all values.

How to do it...

1. We'll create a class with parameters and no default values. Create the directory `modules/mysql/manifests` and then create `modules/mysql/manifests/init.pp` with the following content:

```
class mysql (
  Integer $port,
  String $socket,
  Variant[String,Array[String]] $package
  ) {
    notify {"Port: ${port} Socket: ${socket} Package:
${package}": }
  }
```

2. Update your `common.yaml` file in Hiera with the default values for the `mysql` class:

```
---
mysql::port: 3306
mysql::package: 'mysql-server'
mysql::socket: '/var/lib/mysql/mysql.sock'
```

3. Apply the class to a node; you can add the `mysql` class to your default node for now:

```
node default {
  class {'mysql': }
}
```

4. Run `puppet agent` and verify the output:

```
[root@testnode ~]# puppet agent -t
...
Notice: Port: 3306 Socket: /var/lib/mysql/mysql.sock Package:
mysql-server
Notice: /Stage[main]/Mysql/Notify[Port: 3306 Socket:
/var/lib/mysql/mysql.sock Package: mysql-server]/message:
defined 'message' as 'Port: 3306 Socket:
/var/lib/mysql/mysql.sock Package: mysql-server'
Notice: Applied catalog in 0.05 seconds
```

How it works...

When we instantiate the MySQL class in our manifest, we provided no values for any of the attributes. Puppet knows to look for a value in Hiera that matches `class_name::parameter_name:` or `::class_name::parameter_name:`.

When Puppet finds a value, it uses it as the parameter for the class. If Puppet fails to find a value in Hiera and no default is defined, a catalog failure will result in the following command line:

```
Error: Could not retrieve catalog from remote server: Error 500 on SERVER:
Server Error: Evaluation Error: Error while evaluating a Function Call,
Class[Mysql]: expects a value for parameter 'port' at
/etc/puppetlabs/code/environments/production/manifests/site.pp:21:3 on node
testnode.example.com
```

There's more...

You can define a Hiera hierarchy and supply different values for parameters based on facts. You could, for instance, have `%{::facts.os.family}` in your hierarchy and have different YAML files based on the `facts.os.family` fact (that is, RedHat, Suse, and Debian).

Writing reusable, cross-platform manifests

Every system administrator dreams of a unified, homogeneous infrastructure of identical machines all running the same version of the same OS. As in other areas of life, however, the reality is often messy and doesn't conform to the plan.

You are probably responsible for a bunch of assorted servers of varying age and architecture running different kernels from different OS distributions, often scattered across different data centers and ISPs.

This situation should strike terror into the hearts of sysadmins of the `ssh` in a `for loop` persuasion because executing the same commands on every server can have different, unpredictable, and even dangerous results.

We should certainly strive to bring older servers up-to-date and get working as far as possible on a single reference platform to make administration simpler, cheaper, and more reliable. But until you get there, Puppet makes coping with heterogeneous environments slightly easier.

How to do it...

Here are some examples of how to make your manifests more portable:

1. Where you need to apply the same manifest to servers with different OS distributions, the main differences will probably be the names of packages and services and the location of config files. Try to capture all these differences into a single class by using selectors to set global variables:

```
$ssh_service = $::operatingsystem? {
  /Ubuntu|Debian/ => 'ssh',
  default         => 'sshd',
}
```

You needn't worry about the differences in any other part of the manifest; when you refer to something, use the variable with confidence that it will point to the right thing in each environment:

```
service { $ssh_service:
  ensure => running,
}
```

2. Often we need to cope with mixed architectures; this can affect the paths to shared libraries, and also may require different versions of packages. Again, try to encapsulate all the required settings in a single architecture class that sets global variables:

```
$libdir = $::architecture ? {
  amd64   => '/usr/lib64',
  default => '/usr/lib',
}
```

Then you can use these wherever an architecture-dependent value is required in your manifests or even in templates:

```
; php.ini [PHP]
; Directory in which the loadable extensions (modules) reside.
extension_dir = <%= @libdir %>/php/modules
```

How it works...

The advantage of this approach (which could be called top-down) is that you only need to make your choices once. The alternative, bottom-up approach would be to have a selector or case statement everywhere a setting is used:

```
service { $::operatingsystem? {
  /Ubuntu|Debian/ => 'ssh',
  default         => 'sshd' }:
  ensure          => running, }
```

This not only results in lots of duplication, but makes the code harder to read. And when a new operating system is added to the mix, you'll need to make changes throughout the whole manifest, instead of just in one place.

There's more...

If you are writing a module for public distribution (for example, on Puppet Forge), making your module as cross-platform as possible will make it more valuable to the community. As far as you can, test it on many different distributions, platforms, and architectures, and add the appropriate variables so that it works everywhere.

If you use a public module and adapt it to your own environment, consider updating the public version with your changes if you think they might be helpful to other people.

Even if you are not thinking of publishing a module, bear in mind that it may be in production use for a long time and may have to adapt to many changes in the environment. If it's designed to cope with this from the start, it'll make life easier for you or whoever ends up maintaining your code.

See also

- The *Using public modules* recipe in `Chapter 8`, *External Tools and the Puppet Ecosystem*
- The *Importing configuration data with Hiera* recipe in `Chapter 8`, *External Tools and the Puppet Ecosystem*

Getting information about the environment

Often in a Puppet manifest, you need to know some local information about the machine you're on. Facter is the tool that accompanies Puppet to provide a standard way of getting information (facts) from the environment about things such as the following:

- Operating system
- Memory size
- Architecture
- Processor count

To see a complete list of the facts available on your system, run the following code:

```
$ sudo facter
aio_agent_version => 5.3.3
augeas => {
```

```
    version => "1.8.1"
}
...
```

While it can be handy to get this information from the command line, the real power of Facter lies in being able to access these facts in your Puppet manifests.

Some modules define their own facts; to see any facts that have been defined locally, add the –p (pluginsync) option to `facter`, as follows:

```
$ sudo facter -p
```

This is deprecated in Puppet5. To access facts defined in puppet, use the `puppet facts` face instead:

```
$ puppet facts
```

puppet facts will return all the facts for a node and redirect the output to a pager or a file to inspect the results.

How to do it...

Here's an example of using Facter facts in a manifest:

1. Reference a Facter fact in your manifest like any other variable. Facts are global variables in Puppet, so they should be prefixed with a double colon (::), as in the following code snippet:

```
$funfacts = @("FACTS")
   This is ${::facts['os']['name']}
   version ${::facts['os']['release']['full']},
   on ${::facts['os']['architecture']} architecture,
   kernel version ${::kernelversion}
   | FACTS

notify {'funfacts':
   message => $funfacts
}
```

2. When Puppet runs, it will fill in the appropriate values for the current node:

```
Notice: Compiled catalog for mylaptop.example.com in
environment production in 0.01 seconds
Notice: This is Fedora
version 27,
on x86_64 architecture,
kernel version 4.14.11
```

How it works...

Facter provides a standard way for manifests to get information about the nodes to which they are applied. When you refer to a fact in a manifest, Puppet will query Facter to get the current value and insert it into the manifest. Facter facts are top-scope variables.

Always refer to them with leading double colons to ensure that you are using the facter value and not a local variable: `$::hostname` NOT `$hostname`. In Puppet5, I prefer to use the facts hash instead of referring to facts directly. `$::facts['hostname']` cannot be overridden by a variable, it must come from a fact.

There's more...

You can also use facts in **EPP** templates. For example, you might want to insert the node's hostname into a file or change a configuration setting for an application based on the memory size of the node. When you use fact names in templates, remember that they don't need a dollar sign because this is Ruby, not Puppet:

```
$KLogPath <%=
  case $::kernelversion
    {/^2/: { '/var/run/rsyslog/kmsg' }
    default: { '/proc/kmsg' }
  } %>
```

Variable references in epp templates are always fully scoped. To access variables defined in the class where you called the epp function, use the full path to that class. For example, to reference the `mysql::port` variable we defined earlier in the `mysql` modules, use the following:

```
MySQL Port = <%= $::mysql::port %>
```

See also

- The *Creating custom Facter facts* recipe in Chapter 8, *External Tools and the Puppet Ecosystem*

Importing dynamic information

Even though some system administrators like to wall themselves off from the rest of the office using piles of old printers, we all need to exchange information with other departments from time to time. For example, you may want to insert data into your Puppet manifests that is derived from some outside source. The generate function is ideal for this. Functions are executed on the machine compiling the catalog (the master for centralized deployments); an example such as the one shown here will only work in a masterless configuration.

Getting ready

Follow these steps to prepare to run the example:

1. Create the /usr/local/bin/message.rb script with the following contents:

   ```
   #!/opt/puppetlabs/puppet/bin/ruby
   puts "This runs on the master if you are centralized"
   ```

2. Make the script executable:

   ```
   $ sudo chmod a+x /usr/local/bin/message.rb
   ```

How to do it...

This example calls the external script we created previously and gets its output:

1. Create a message.pp manifest containing the following:

   ```
   $message = generate('/usr/local/bin/message.rb')
   notify { $message: }
   ```

2. Run Puppet:

```
Notice: Compiled catalog for mylaptop.example.com in
environment production in 0.04 seconds
Notice: This runs on the master if you are centralized

Notice: /Stage[main]/Main/Notify[This runs on the master if you
are centralized
]/message: defined 'message' as "This runs on the master if you
are centralized\n"
Notice: Applied catalog in 0.02 seconds
```

How it works...

The generate function runs the specified script or program and returns the result, in this case, a cheerful message from Ruby.

This isn't terribly useful as it stands, but you get the idea. Anything a script can do print, fetch, or calculate, for example, the results of a database query can be brought into your manifest using generate. You can also, of course, run standard UNIX utilities, such as cat and grep.

There's more...

If you need to pass arguments to the executable called by generate, add them as extra arguments to the function call:

```
$message = generate('/bin/cat', '/etc/motd')
```

Puppet will try to protect you from malicious shell calls by restricting the characters you can use in a call to generate, so shell pipes and redirection aren't allowed, for example. The simplest and safest thing to do is to put all your logic into a script and then call that script.

See also

- The *Creating custom Facter facts* recipe in Chapter 8, *External Tools and the Puppet Ecosystem*
- The *Importing configuration data with Hiera* recipe in Chapter 8, *External Tools and the Puppet Ecosystem*

Passing arguments to shell commands

If you want to insert values into a command line (to be run by an `exec` resource, for example), they often need to be quoted, especially if they contain spaces. The `shellquote` function will take any number of arguments, including arrays, and quote each of the arguments and return them all as a space-separated string that you can pass to commands.

In this example, we would like to set up an exec resource that will rename a file; but both the source and the target name contain spaces, so they need to be correctly quoted in the command line.

How to do it...

Here's an example of using the `shellquote` function:

1. Create a `shellquote.pp` manifest with the following command:

```
$source = 'Hello Jerry'
$target = 'Hello... Newman'
$argstring = shellquote($source, $target)
$command = "/bin/mv ${argstring}"
notify { $command: }
```

2. Run Puppet:

```
t@mylaptop ~ $ puppet apply shellquote.pp
Notice: Compiled catalog for mylaptop.example.com in
environment production in 0.02 seconds
Notice: /bin/mv "Hello Jerry" "Hello... Newman"
Notice: /Stage[main]/Main/Notify[/bin/mv "Hello Jerry"
"Hello... Newman"]/message: defined 'message' as '/bin/mv
"Hello Jerry" "Hello... Newman"'
Notice: Applied catalog in 0.02 seconds
```

How it works...

First, we define the $source and $target variables, which are the two filenames we want to use in the command line:

```
$source = 'Hello Jerry'
$target = 'Hello... Newman'
```

Then we call shellquote to concatenate these variables into a quoted, space-separated string, as follows:

```
$argstring = shellquote($source, $target)
```

Then we put together the final command line:

```
$command = "/bin/mv ${argstring}"
```

The result will be as follows:

```
/bin/mv "Hello Jerry" "Hello... Newman"
```

This command line can now be run with an exec resource. What would happen if we didn't use shellquote? See the following:

```
$source = 'Hello Jerry'
$target = 'Hello... Newman'
$command = "/bin/mv ${source} ${target}"
notify { $command: }
Notice: /bin/mv Hello Jerry Hello... Newman
```

This won't work because mv expects space-separated arguments, so it will interpret this as a request to move the Hello, Jerry, and Hello... files into a directory named Newman, which probably isn't what we want.

4
Working with Files and Packages

In this chapter, we will cover the following recipes:

- Making quick edits to config files
- Editing INI-style files with `puppetlabs-inifile`
- Using Augeas to reliably edit config files
- Building config files using snippets
- Using ERB templates
- Using array iterations in templates
- Using EPP templates
- Using GnuPG to encrypt secrets
- Comparing package versions

Introduction

In this chapter, we'll learn how to make small edits to files, how to make larger changes in a structured way using the Augeas tool, how to construct files from concatenated snippets, and how to generate files from templates. We'll also learn how to install packages from additional repositories, and how to manage those repositories. In addition, we'll see how to store and decrypt secret data with Puppet.

Making quick edits to config files

When you need to have Puppet change a particular setting in a config file, it's common to simply deploy the whole file with Puppet. This isn't always possible, though, especially if it's a file that several different parts of your Puppet manifest may need to modify.

What would be useful is a simple recipe to add a line to a config file if it's not already present, for example, adding a module name to /etc/modules to tell the kernel to load that module at boot. There are several ways to do this; the simplest is to use the file_line type provided by the puppetlabs-stdlib module. In this example, we install the stdlib module and use this type to append a line to a text file.

Getting ready

Install the puppetlabs-stdlib module using puppet:

```
t@mylaptop ~ $ puppet module install puppetlabs-stdlib
Notice: Preparing to install into /home/thomas/.puppetlabs/etc/code/modules
...
Notice: Downloading from https://forgeapi.puppet.com ...
Notice: Installing -- do not interrupt ...
/home/thomas/.puppetlabs/etc/code/modules
└── puppetlabs-stdlib (v4.24.0)
```

This installs the module from the forge into my user's puppet directory. To install it into the system directory, run the command as root or use sudo. For the purpose of this example, we'll continue working as our own user.

How to do it...

Using the file_line resource type, we can verfiy that a line exists or is absent in a config file. Using file_line, we can quickly make edits to files without controlling the entire file:

1. Create a manifest named oneline.pp that will use file_line on a file in /tmp:

```
file {'/tmp/cookbook':
  ensure => 'file',
}
file_line {'cookbook-hello':
  path => '/tmp/cookbook',
  line => 'Hello World!',
```

```
        require => File['/tmp/cookbook'],
    }
```

2. Run `puppet apply` on the `oneline.pp` manifest:

```
t@mylaptop ~ $ puppet apply oneline.pp
Notice: Compiled catalog for mylaptop.example.com in
environment production in 0.02 seconds
Notice: /Stage[main]/Main/File[/tmp/cookbook]/ensure: created
Notice: /Stage[main]/Main/File_line[cookbook-hello]/ensure:
created
Notice: Applied catalog in 0.02 seconds
```

3. Verify that `/tmp/cookbook` contains the line we defined:

```
t@mylaptop ~ $ cat /tmp/cookbook
Hello World!
t@mylaptop ~ $
```

How it works...

We installed the `puppetlabs-stdlib` module into the `default` module path for Puppet, so when we ran `puppet apply`, Puppet knew where to find the `file_line` type definition. Puppet then created the `/tmp/cookbook` file if it didn't exist. The line `Hello World!` was not found in the file, so Puppet added the line to the file.

There's more...

We can define more instances of `file_line` and add more lines to the file; we can have multiple resources modifying a single file:

1. Modify the `oneline.pp` file and add another `file_line` resource:

```
file {'/tmp/cookbook':
  ensure => 'file',
}
file_line {'cookbook-hello':
  path => '/tmp/cookbook',
  line => 'Hello World!',
  require => File['/tmp/cookbook'],
}
file_line {'cookbook-goodbye':
  path => '/tmp/cookbook',
```

```
    line => 'So long, and thanks for all the fish.',
    require => File['/tmp/cookbook'],
  }
```

2. Now apply the manifest again and verify whether the new line is appended to the file:

```
t@mylaptop ~ $ puppet apply oneline.pp
Notice: Compiled catalog for mylaptop.example.com in
environment production in 0.02 seconds
Notice: /Stage[main]/Main/File_line[cookbook-goodbye]/ensure:
created
Notice: Applied catalog in 0.02 seconds
t@mylaptop ~ $ cat /tmp/cookbook
Hello World!
So long, and thanks for all the fish.
```

3. The `file_line` type also supports pattern-matching and line-removal, as we'll show you in the following example:

```
file {'/tmp/cookbook':
  ensure => 'file',
}
file_line {'cookbook-remove':
  ensure => 'absent',
  path => '/tmp/cookbook',
  line => 'Hello World!',
  require => File['/tmp/cookbook'],
}
file_line {'cookbook-match':
  path => '/tmp/cookbook',
  line => 'Oh freddled gruntbuggly, thanks for all the fish.',
  match => 'fish.$',
  require => File['/tmp/cookbook'],
}
```

4. Verify the contents of /tmp/cookbook before your Puppet runs:

```
t@mylaptop ~ $ cat /tmp/cookbook
Hello World!
So long, and thanks for all the fish.
```

5. Apply the updated manifest:

```
t@mylaptop ~ $ puppet apply oneline3.pp
Notice: Compiled catalog for mylaptop.example.com in
environment production in 0.02 seconds
Notice: /Stage[main]/Main/File_line[cookbook-remove]/ensure:
removed
Notice: /Stage[main]/Main/File_line[cookbook-match]/ensure:
created
Notice: Applied catalog in 0.02 seconds
t@mylaptop ~ $ cat /tmp/cookbook
Oh freddled gruntbuggly, thanks for all the fish.
```

Editing files with `file_line` works well if the file is unstructured. Structured files may have similar lines in different sections that have different meanings. In the next section, we'll show you how to deal with one particular type of structured file: a file using the INI syntax.

Editing INI-style files with puppetlabs-inifile

INI files are used throughout the system, Puppet uses the INI syntax for the `puppet.conf` file. The `puppetlabs-inifile` module creates two types: `ini_setting` and `ini_subsetting`.

Getting ready

Install the module from the forge as follows:

```
t@mylaptop ~ $ puppet module install puppetlabs-inifile
Notice: Preparing to install into /home/thomas/.puppetlabs/etc/code/modules
...
Notice: Downloading from https://forgeapi.puppet.com ...
Notice: Installing -- do not interrupt ...
/home/thomas/.puppetlabs/etc/code/modules
└── puppetlabs-inifile (v2.2.0)
```

How to do it...

In this example, we will create a /tmp/server.conf file and ensure that the server_true setting is set in that file:

1. Create an initest.pp manifest with the following contents:

```
ini_setting {'server_true':
  path    => '/tmp/server.conf',
  section => 'main',
  setting => 'server',
  value   => 'true',
}
```

2. Apply the manifest:

```
t@mylaptop ~ $ puppet apply initest.pp
Notice: Compiled catalog for mylaptop.example.com in
environment production in 0.05 seconds
Notice: /Stage[main]/Main/Ini_setting[server_true]/ensure:
created
Notice: Applied catalog in 0.02 seconds
```

3. Verify the contents of the /tmp/server.conf file:

```
t@mylaptop ~ $ cat /tmp/server.conf
[main]
server = true
```

How it works...

The inifile module defines two types: ini_setting and ini_subsetting. Our manifest defines an ini_setting resource that creates a server setting within the main section of the INI file. In our case, the file didn't exist, so Puppet first created the file, then created the main section, and finally added the setting to the main section.

There's more...

Using `ini_subsetting`, you can have several resources added to a setting. For instance, our `server.conf` file has a server's line; we could have each node append its own hostname to a server's line:

1. Add the following to the end of the `initest.pp` file:

```
ini_subsetting {'server_name':
  path        => '/tmp/server.conf',
  section     => 'main',
  setting     => 'server_host',
  subsetting  => "$hostname",
}
```

2. Apply the manifest:

```
t@mylaptop ~ $ puppet apply initest2.pp
Notice: Compiled catalog for mylaptop.example.com in
environment production in 0.05 seconds
Notice: /Stage[main]/Main/Ini_subsetting[server_name]/ensure:
created
Notice: Applied catalog in 0.03 seconds
t@mylaptop ~ $ cat /tmp/server.conf
[main]
server = true
server_host = mylaptop
```

3. Temporarily change your hostname and rerun Puppet:

```
t@mylaptop ~ $ sudo hostname inihost
[sudo] password for thomas:
t@mylaptop ~ $ puppet apply initest2.pp
Notice: Compiled catalog for inihost.example.com in environment
production in 0.05 seconds
Notice: /Stage[main]/Main/Ini_subsetting[server_name]/ensure:
created
Notice: Applied catalog in 0.02 seconds
t@mylaptop ~ $ cat /tmp/server.conf
[main]
server = true
server_host = mylaptop inihost
```

When working with the INI syntax files, using the `inifile` module is an excellent choice.

If your configuration files are not in INI syntax, another tool, Augeas, can be used. In the following section, we will use Augeas to modify files.

Using Augeas to reliably edit config files

Sometimes it seems like every application has its own subtly different config file format, and writing regular expressions to parse and modify all of them can be a tiresome business.

Thankfully, Augeas is here to help. Augeas is a system that aims to simplify working with different config file formats by presenting them all as a simple tree of values. Puppet's Augeas support allows you to create `augeas` resources that can make the required config changes intelligently and automatically.

How to do it...

Follow these steps to create an example Augeas resource:

1. Modify your `base` module as follows:

```
class base {
  augeas { 'enable-ip-forwarding':
    incl    => '/etc/sysctl.conf',
    lens    => 'Sysctl.lns',
    changes => ['set net.ipv4.ip_forward 1'],
  }
}
```

2. Run Puppet:

```
[root@cookbook ~]# puppet agent -t
Info: Using configured environment 'production'
Info: Retrieving pluginfacts
Info: Retrieving plugin
Info: Caching catalog for cookbook.example.com
Info: Applying configuration version '1518670471'
Notice: Augeas[enable-ip-forwarding](provider=augeas):
--- /etc/sysctl.conf 2016-03-31 17:39:49.000000000 +0000
+++ /etc/sysctl.conf.augnew 2018-02-15 04:54:32.413264392 +0000
@@ -2,3 +2,4 @@
 # To override those settings, enter new settings here, or in
an /etc/sysctl.d/<name>.conf file
```

```
#
# For more information, see sysctl.conf(5) and sysctl.d(5).
+net.ipv4.ip_forward = 1

Notice: /Stage[main]/Base/Augeas[enable-ip-forwarding]/returns:
executed successfully
Notice: Applied catalog in 0.12 seconds
```

3. Verify that the setting has been correctly applied:

```
[root@cookbook ~]# sysctl -p |grep ip_forward
net.ipv4.ip_forward = 1
```

How it works...

We declare an `augeas` resource named `enable-ip-forwarding`:

```
augeas { 'enable-ip-forwarding':
```

We specify that we want to make changes in the `/etc/sysctl.conf` file:

```
incl => '/etc/sysctl.conf',
```

Next, we specify the lens to use on this file. Augeas uses files called lenses to translate a configuration file into an object representation. Augeas is included in the all-in-one `puppet agent` package and includes several lenses, located in `/opt/puppetlabs/puppet/share/augeas/lenses/dist` by default. When specifying the lens in an `augeas` resource, the name of the lens is capitalized and has the `.lns` suffix. In this case, we will specify the `sysctl` lens, as follows:

```
lens => 'Sysctl.lns',
```

The `changes` parameter specifies the changes we want to make. Its value is an array, because we can supply several changes at once. In this example, there is only change, so the value is an array of one element:

```
changes => ['set net.ipv4.ip_forward 1'],
```

In general, Augeas changes take the following form:

```
set <parameter> <value>
```

In this case, the setting will be translated into a line similar to this in `/etc/sysctl.conf`:

```
net.ipv4.ip_forward=1
```

There's more...

I've chosen /etc/sysctl.conf as the example because it can contain a wide variety of kernel settings and you may want to change these settings for all sorts of different purposes and in different Puppet classes. You might want to enable IP-forwarding, as in the example, for a router class, but you might also want to tune the value of net.core.somaxconn for a load-balancer class.

This means that simply puppetizing the /etc/sysctl.conf file and distributing it as a text file won't work, because you might have several different and conflicting versions depending on the setting you want to modify. Augeas is the right solution here because you can define augeas resources in different places, which modify the same file, and they won't conflict.

For more information about using Puppet and Augeas, see the page on the Puppet labs website: http://projects.puppetlabs.com/projects/1/ wiki/Puppet_Augeas.

Another project that uses Augeas is Augeasproviders. Augeasproviders uses Augeas to define several types. One of these types is sysctl; using this type you can make sysctl changes without knowing how to write the changes in Augeas. More information is available on the forge at https://forge.puppetlabs.com/domcleal/augeasproviders.

Learning how to use Augeas can be a little confusing at first. Augeas provides a command-line tool, augtool, that can be used to get acquainted with making changes in Augeas.

Building config files using snippets

Sometimes you can't deploy a whole config file in one piece, yet making line-by-line edits isn't enough. Often, you need to build a config file from various bits of configuration managed by different classes. You may run into a situation where local information needs to be imported into the file as well. In this example, we'll build a config file using a local file as well as snippets defined in our manifests.

Getting ready

Although it's possible to create our own system to build files from pieces, we'll use the `puppetlabs-supported concat` module. We will start by installing the `concat` module. In a previous example we installed the module to our local machine; in this example, we'll modify the Puppet server configuration and download the module to the Puppet server:

1. In your Git repository, create an `environment.conf` file with the following contents:

   ```
   modulepath = public:modules
   manifest = manifests/site.pp
   ```

2. Create a `public` directory and download the module into that directory, as follows:

   ```
   t@mylaptop $ mkdir public
   t@mylaptop $ cd public
   /home/thomas/puppet/public
   t@mylaptop $ puppet module install puppetlabs-concat --
   modulepath=.
   Notice: Preparing to install into /home/thomas/puppet/public
   . . .
   Notice: Downloading from https://forgeapi.puppet.com ...
   Notice: Installing -- do not interrupt ...
   /home/thomas/puppet/public
   └──┬ puppetlabs-concat (v4.1.1)
      └── puppetlabs-stdlib (v4.24.0)
   ```

3. Now, add the new modules to our Git repository:

   ```
   t@mylaptop $ git add .
   t@mylaptop $ git commit -m 'adding concat'

   [production 131bb18] adding concat
    582 files changed, 33414 insertions(+)
    create mode 100644 public/concat/CHANGELOG.md
    create mode 100644 public/concat/CONTRIBUTING.md
    create mode 100644 public/concat/Gemfile
   . . .
   ```

4. Then, push them to our Git server:

```
t@mylaptop $ git push origin production Counting objects: 631,
done.
Delta compression using up to 8 threads. Compressing objects:
100% (610/610), done.
Writing objects: 100% (631/631), 346.21 KiB | 7.87 MiB/s, done.
Total 631 (delta 167), reused 0 (delta 0)
remote: Resolving deltas: 100% (167/167), completed with 1
local object. remote: To
puppet.example.com:/etc/puppetlabs/code/puppet.git
remote: 5e20247..131bb18 production -> production remote:
Switched to a new branch 'production'
...
remote: Fast-forward
remote: public/concat/CHANGELOG.md | 390 +++
remote: public/concat/CONTRIBUTING.md | 271 +++
remote: public/concat/Gemfile | 157 ++
remote: public/concat/LICENSE | 202 ++
```

How to do it...

Refer to the following steps:

1. Now that we have the `concat` module available on our server, we can create a `concat` container resource in our `base` module:

```
concat {'hosts.allow':
  path => '/etc/hosts.allow',
  mode => '0644',
}
```

2. Create a `concat::fragment` module for the header of the new file:

```
concat::fragment {'hosts.allow header':
  target  => 'hosts.allow',
  content => "# File managed by puppet\n",
  order   => '01'
}
```

3. Create a `concat::fragment` that includes a local file:

```
concat::fragment {'hosts.allow local':
  target => 'hosts.allow',
  source => '/etc/hosts.allow.local',
  order  => '10',
}
```

4. Create a `concat::fragment` module that will go at the end of the file:

```
concat::fragment {'hosts.allow tftp':
  target  => 'hosts.allow',
  content => "in.ftpd: .example.com\n",
  order   => '50',
}
```

5. On the node, create `/etc/hosts.allow.local` with the following contents:

in.tftpd: .example.com

Without this file in place on the node (cookbook), you will receive an error when you run Puppet, since the file is required by the `hosts.allow local concat::fragment` resource:

```
Error:
/Stage[main]/Base/Concat[hosts.allow]/Concat_file[hosts.a
llow]: Failed to generate additional resources using
'eval_generate': undefined method `join' for
"/etc/hosts.allow.local":String.
```

6. Copy the code to the Puppet master by checking in your changes to the `base/manifests/init.pp` manifest:

```
t@mylaptop $ git add manifests/init.pp
t@mylaptop $ git commit -m 'adding concat resource'
[production dace061] adding concat resource
 1 file changed, 23 insertions(+)
t@mylaptop $ git push origin production
Counting objects: 6, done.
Delta compression using up to 8 threads.
Compressing objects: 100% (5/5), done.
Writing objects: 100% (6/6), 700 bytes | 700.00 KiB/s, done.
Total 6 (delta 3), reused 0 (delta 0)
remote: To puppet.example.com:/etc/puppetlabs/code/puppet.git
remote: 131bb18..dace061 production -> production
```

7. Run `puppet agent` on the cookbook node to have the file created:

```
[root@cookbook ~]# puppet agent -t
...
Info: Caching catalog for cookbook.example.com
Info: Applying configuration version '1518740229'
Notice:
/Stage[main]/Base/Concat[hosts.allow]/File[/etc/hosts.allow]/co
ntent:
--- /etc/hosts.allow 2013-06-07 14:31:32.000000000 +0000
+++ /tmp/puppet-file20180216-8258-1xxgbot 2018-02-16
00:17:24.797415488 +0000
@@ -1,10 +1,3 @@
-#
-# hosts.allow This file contains access rules which are used
to
-# allow or deny connections to network services that
-# either use the tcp_wrappers library or that have been
-# started through a tcp_wrappers-enabled xinetd.
-#
-# See 'man 5 hosts_options' and 'man 5 hosts_access'
-# for information on rule syntax.
-# See 'man tcpd' for information on tcp_wrappers
-#
+# File managed by puppet
+in.tftpd: .example.com
+in.ftpd: .example.com

Info: Computing checksum on file /etc/hosts.allow
Info:
/Stage[main]/Base/Concat[hosts.allow]/File[/etc/hosts.allow]:
Filebucketed /etc/hosts.allow to puppet with sum
3fb7d181e3e605ca91541c0d82753616
Notice:
/Stage[main]/Base/Concat[hosts.allow]/File[/etc/hosts.allow]/co
ntent: content changed '{md5}3fb7d181e3e605ca91541c0d82753616'
to '{md5}593f6e35731ac9f7a3f97d09533cadd7'
Notice: Applied catalog in 0.11 seconds
```

8. Verify that the contents of the new file are as follows:

```
[root@cookbook ~]# cat /etc/hosts.allow
# File managed by puppet
in.tftpd: .example.com
in.ftpd: .example.com
```

How it works...

The concat resource defines a container that will hold all the subsequent `concat::fragment` resources. Each `concat::fragment` resource references the concat resource as the target. Each `concat::fragment` also includes an `order` attribute. The `order` attribute is used to specify the order in which the fragments are added to the final file. Our `/etc/hosts.allow` file is built with the header line, the contents of the local file, and the `in.tftpd` line we defined.

Using ERB templates

While you can deploy config files easily with Puppet as simple text files, templates are much more powerful. A template file can do calculations, execute Ruby code, or reference the values of variables from your Puppet manifests. Anywhere you might deploy a text file using Puppet, you can use a template instead.

In the simplest case, a template can just be a static text file. More usefully, you can insert variables into it using the ERB (embedded Ruby) syntax. For example:

```
<%= @name %>, this is a very large drink.
```

If the template is used in a context where the variable $name contains Zaphod Beeblebrox, the template will evaluate to:

```
Zaphod Beeblebrox, this is a very large drink.
```

This simple technique is very useful for generating lots of files that only differ in the values of one or two variables, such as virtual hosts, and for inserting values into a script, such as database names and passwords.

How to do it...

In this example, we'll use an ERB template to insert a password into a backup script:

1. Create the `modules/admin/templates/backup-mysql.sh.erb` file with the following contents:

```
#!/bin/sh
/usr/bin/mysqldump -uroot \
  -p<%= @mysql_password %> \
  --all-databases | \
  /bin/gzip > /backup/mysql/all-databases.sql.gz
```

2. Modify your `site.pp` file as follows:

```
node 'cookbook' {
 $mysql_password = 'secret'
 file { '/usr/local/bin/backup-mysql':
   content => template('admin/backup-mysql.sh.erb'),
   mode    => '0755',
 }
}
```

3. Run Puppet:

```
[root@cookbook ~]# puppet agent -t
...
Info: Caching catalog for cookbook.example.com
Info: Applying configuration version '1518740630'
Notice:
/Stage[main]/Main/Node[cookbook]/File[/usr/local/bin/backup-
mysql]/ensure: defined content as
'{md5}35fe7a37fab0d2b51dd0a7f9818c5161'
Notice: Applied catalog in 0.02 seconds
```

4. Check whether Puppet has correctly inserted the password into the template:

```
[root@cookbook ~]# cat /usr/local/bin/backup-mysql
#!/bin/sh /usr/bin/mysqldump -uroot \
  -pTopSecret \
  --all-databases | \
  /bin/gzip > /backup/mysql/all-databases.sql.gz
```

How it works...

Wherever a variable is referenced in the template, for example `<%= @mysql_password %>`, Puppet will replace it with the corresponding value (`TopSecret`, in this example).

There's more...

In the example, we only used one variable in the template, but you can have as many as you like. These can also be facts:

```
ServerName <%= @fqdn %>
```

Or they can be Ruby expressions:

```
MAILTO=<%= @emails.join(',') %>
```

Or they can be any Ruby code you want:

```
ServerAdmin <%= @sitedomain == 'coldcomfort.com' ? 'seth@coldcomfort.com' :
'flora@poste.com' %>
```

See also

- The *Using GnuPG to encrypt secrets* recipe in this chapter
- `https://docs.puppetlabs.com/guides/templating.html`

Using array iterations in templates

In the previous example, we saw that you can use Ruby to interpolate different values in templates depending on the result of an expression. But you're not limited to getting one value at a time. You can put lots of them in a Puppet array and then have the template generate some content for each element of the array using a loop.

How to do it...

Follow these steps to build an example of iterating over arrays:

1. Modify your `site.pp` file as follows:

```
node 'cookbook' {
  $ipaddresses = ['192.168.0.1','158.43.128.1', '10.0.75.207' ]
  file { '/tmp/addresslist.txt':
    content => template('base/addresslist.erb')
  }
}
```

2. Create a `modules/base/templates/addresslist.erb` file with the following contents:

```
<% @ipaddresses.each do |ip| -%>
IP address <%= ip %> is present
<% end -%>
```

3. Update the code on your Puppet master and run `puppet agent` on the cookbook:

```
[root@cookbook ~]# puppet agent -t
...
Info: Caching catalog for cookbook.example.com
Info: Applying configuration version '1518741106'
Notice:
/Stage[main]/Main/Node[cookbook]/File[/tmp/addresslist.txt]/ens
ure: defined content as '{md5}e3a34b5c67ef2dc715a3431f5835c119'
```

4. Check the contents of the generated file:

```
[root@cookbook ~]# cat /tmp/addresslist.txt
IP address 192.168.0.1 is present
IP address 158.43.128.1 is present
IP address 10.0.75.207 is present
```

How it works...

In the first line of the template, we reference the ipaddresses array and call its each method:

```
<% @ipaddresses.each do |ip| -%>
```

In Ruby, this creates a loop that will execute once for each element of the array. Each time around the loop, the ip variable will be set to the value of the current element. In our example, the ipaddresses array contains three elements, so the following line will be executed three times, once for each element:

```
IP address <%= ip %> is present.
```

This will result in three output lines:

```
IP address 192.168.0.1 is present
IP address 158.43.128.1 is present
IP address 10.0.75.207 is present
```

The final line ends the loop:

```
<% end -%>
```

Note that the first and last lines end with -%>, instead of just %>, as we saw before. The effect of - is to suppress the new line that would otherwise be generated on each pass through the loop, giving us unwanted blank lines in the file.

There's more...

Templates can also iterate over hashes, or arrays of hashes:

```
$ifaces = [
  {
    name => 'eth0',
    ip => '192.168.0.1'
  }, {
    name => 'eth1',
    ip => '158.43.128.1'
  }, {
    name => 'eth2',
    ip => '10.0.75.207'
  } ]

$content = @(HASH)
  <% @ifaces.each do |iface| -%>
  Interface <%= iface['name'] %> has the address <%= iface['ip'] %>.
  <% end -%>
  | HASH
file {'/tmp/hash':
  content => inline_template($content),
}
```

This results in the following:

```
Interface eth0 has the address 192.168.0.1.
Interface eth1 has the address 158.43.128.1.
Interface eth2 has the address 10.0.75.207.
```

See also

- The *Using ERB templates* recipe in this chapter

Using EPP templates

EPP templates are the replacement for ERB templates, which will be deprecated in a future release of Puppet. EPP templates use the Puppet syntax and are not compiled through Ruby. Two new functions are defined to call EPP templates: `epp` and `inline_epp`. These functions are the EPP equivalents of the ERB `template` and `inline_template` functions, respectively. The main difference from **EPP** templates is that variables are referenced using the Puppet notation, `$variable`, instead of `@variable`. All variables are fully scoped in EPP templates; there is no need to use the scope function as with ERB templates.

How to do it...

We'll create an EPP template and use `puppet apply` to compile the template:

1. Create an EPP template in `epp-test.epp` with the following content:

   ```
   This is <%= $message %>.
   ```

2. Create an `epp.pp` manifest, which uses the `epp` and `inline_epp` functions:

   ```
   $message = "the message"
   file {'/tmp/epp-test':
     content => epp('/home/thomas/puppet/epp-test.epp')
   }
   notify {"message":
     message => inline_epp('Also prints <%= $message %>')
   }
   ```

3. Apply the manifest:

```
t@mylaptop $ puppet apply epp.pp
Notice: Compiled catalog for mylaptop.example.com in
environment production in 0.02 seconds
Notice: /Stage[main]/Main/File[/tmp/epp-test]/ensure: defined
content as '{md5}999ccc2507d79d50fae0775d69b63b8c'
Notice: Also prints the message
Notice: /Stage[main]/Main/Notify[message]/message: defined
'message' as 'Also prints the message'
Notice: Applied catalog in 0.02 seconds
```

4. Verify that the template worked as intended:

```
t@mylaptop $ cat /tmp/epp-test
This is the message.
```

How it works...

The `epp` and `inline_epp` functions are used to invoke EPP templates. EPP templates allow the Puppet syntax to be used within a template, making it easier to build a configuration file with Puppet variables used throughout the file.

There's more...

Both `epp` and `inline_epp` allow for variables to be overridden within the function call. A second parameter to the function call can be used to specify values for variables used within the scope of the function call. For example, we can override the value of `$message` with the following code:

```
$message = 'the message'
file {'/tmp/epp-test':
  content => epp('/home/tuphill/puppet/epp-test.epp', {'message' =>
"override $message"} )
}
notify {'message':
  message => inline_epp('Also prints <%= $message %>', {'message' =>
"inline override $message"})
}
```

Now when we run Puppet and verify the output, we see that the value of $message has been overridden:

```
Notice: Compiled catalog for burnaby.strangled.net in environment
production in 0.02 seconds
Notice: /Stage[main]/Main/File[/tmp/epp-test]/content: content changed
'{md5}15184a663d3d90f366cd28d470c4c92e' to
'{md5}bbc60fc4b0a4b35196ee0b799d30a3c0'
Notice: Also prints inline override the message
Notice: /Stage[main]/Main/Notify[message]/message: defined 'message' as
'Also prints inline override the message'
Notice: Applied catalog in 0.03 seconds
```

Using GnuPG to encrypt secrets

We often need Puppet to have access to secret information, such as passwords or crypto keys, so it can configure systems properly. But how do you avoid putting such secrets directly into your Puppet code, where they're visible to anyone who has read access to your repository?

It's a common requirement for third-party developers and contractors to be able to make changes via Puppet, but they definitely shouldn't see any confidential information. Similarly, if you're using a distributed Puppet setup such as that described in Chapter 2, *Puppet Infrastructure*, every machine has a copy of the whole repo, including secrets for other machines that it doesn't need and shouldn't have. How can we prevent this?

One answer is to encrypt the secrets using the GnuPG tool, so that any secret information in the Puppet repo is undecipherable (for all practical purposes) without the appropriate key. Then we distribute the key securely to the people or machines that need it.

Getting ready

First, you'll need an encryption key, so follow these steps to generate one. If you already have a GnuPG key that you'd like to use, go on to the next section. To complete this section, you will need to install the gpg command:

1. Use `puppet resource` to install `gpg`:

```
t@mylaptop $ sudo /opt/puppetlabs/bin/puppet resource package
gnupg ensure=installed
package { 'gnupg':
  ensure => '1.4.22-3.fc27',
}
```

You may need to use `gnupg2` as the package name, depending on your target OS.

2. Run the following command. Answer the prompts as shown, but substitute your name and email address for mine. When prompted for a passphrase, just hit *Enter*:

```
t@mylaptop ~ $ gpg --gen-key
gpg (GnuPG) 1.4.22; Copyright (C) 2015 Free Software
Foundation, Inc.
This is free software: you are free to change and redistribute
it.
There is NO WARRANTY, to the extent permitted by law.

gpg: keyring `/home/thomas/.gnupg/secring.gpg' created
Please select what kind of key you want:
    (1) RSA and RSA (default)
    (2) DSA and Elgamal
    (3) DSA (sign only)
    (4) RSA (sign only)
Your selection? 1
RSA keys may be between 1024 and 4096 bits long.
What keysize do you want? (2048) <enter>
Requested keysize is 2048 bits
Please specify how long the key should be valid.
        0 = key does not expire
      <n> = key expires in n days
      <n>w = key expires in n weeks
      <n>m = key expires in n months
      <n>y = key expires in n years
Key is valid for? (0) <enter>
Key does not expire at all
Is this correct? (y/N) y
You need a user ID to identify your key; the software
constructs the user ID
from the Real Name, Comment and Email Address in this form:
    "Heinrich Heine (Der Dichter) <heinrichh@duesseldorf.de>"
```

```
Real name: Thomas Uphill
Email address: thomas@narrabilis.com
Comment: <enter>
You selected this USER-ID:
    "Thomas Uphill <thomas@narrabilis.com>"

Change (N)ame, (C)omment, (E)mail or (O)kay/(Q)uit? O
You need a Passphrase to protect your secret key.
```

You don't want a `passphrase`—this is probably a bad idea! I will do it anyway. You can change your passphrase at any time, using this program with the `--edit-key` option.

```
gpg: key 560A024B marked as ultimately trusted
public and secret key created and signed:
gpg: checking the trustdb
gpg: 3 marginal(s) needed, 1 complete(s) needed, PGP trust
model
gpg: depth: 0 valid: 1 signed: 0 trust: 0-, 0q, 0n, 0m, 0f, 1u
pub 2048R/560A024B 2018-02-16
      Key fingerprint = 2F5C 7154 8EB7 F3BD 8061 B2C9 8991 C7FB
560A 024B
uid Thomas Uphill <thomas@narrabilis.com>
sub 2048R/59ADD062 2018-02-16
```

You may see a message similar to this if your system is not configured with a source of randomness: We need to generate a lot of random bytes. It is a good idea to perform some other action (type on the keyboard, move the mouse, utilize disks) during the prime generation; this gives the random number generator a better chance to gain enough entropy. In this case, install and start a random-number-generator daemon, such as `haveged` or `rng-tools`.

3. Copy the `gpg` key you just created into the Puppet user's account on your Puppet master:

```
t@burnaby ~ $ scp -r .gnupg puppet@puppet.example.com:
secring.gpg 100% 2498 3.4MB/s 00:00
pubring.gpg~ 100% 1196 4.1MB/s 00:00
trustdb.gpg 100% 1280 5.0MB/s 00:00
pubring.gpg 100% 1196 6.1MB/s 00:00
random_seed 100% 600 2.4MB/s 00:00
gpg.conf 100% 9188 28.3MB/s 00:00
```

How to do it...

With your encryption key installed on the Puppet user's keyring (the key-generation process described in the previous section will do this for you), you're ready to set up Puppet to decrypt secrets:

1. Create the following directory:

   ```
   t@cookbook:~/puppet$ mkdir -p
   modules/admin/lib/puppet/parser/functions
   ```

2. Create `/admin/lib/puppet/parser/functions/secret.rb` file modules with the following contents:

   ```
   module Puppet::Parser::Functions
     newfunction(:secret, :type => :rvalue) do |args|
       `gpg --no-tty -d #{args[0]}`
     end
   end
   ```

3. Create the `secret_message` file with the following contents:

   ```
   For a moment, nothing happened.
   Then, after a second or so, nothing continued to happen.
   ```

4. Encrypt this file with the following command (use the email address you supplied when creating the GnuPG key):

   ```
   t@mylaptop ~ $ gpg -e -r thomas@narrabilis.com secret_message
   ```

5. Move the resulting encrypted file into your Puppet repo:

   ```
   t@mylaptop:~/puppet$ mv secret_message.gpg modules/admin/files/
   ```

6. Remove the original (plaintext) file:

   ```
   t@mylaptop:~/puppet$ rm secret_message
   ```

7. Modify your `site.pp` file, as follows:

```
node 'cookbook' {
  $message =
secret('/etc/puppetlabs/code/environments/production/modules/ad
min/files/secret_message.gpg')
  notify { "The secret message is: ${message}": }
}
```

8. Run Puppet:

```
[root@cookbook ~]# puppet agent -t
Info: Caching catalog for cookbook.example.com
Info: Applying configuration version '1412145910'
Info: Loading facts
Info: Caching catalog for cookbook.example.com
Info: Applying configuration version '1518823829'
Notice: /Stage[main]/Main/Node[cookbook]/Notify[The secret
message is: For a moment, nothing happened.
Then, after a second or so, nothing continued to happen.
]/message: defined 'message' as "The secret message is: For a
moment, nothing happened. \nThen, after a second or so, nothing
continued to happen.\n"
Notice: Applied catalog in 0.26 seconds
```

How it works...

First, we've created a custom function to allow Puppet to decrypt secret files using GnuPG:

```
module Puppet::Parser::Functions
  newfunction(:secret, :type => :rvalue) do |args|
    'gpg --no-tty -d #{args[0]}'
  end
end
```

The preceding code creates a function named secret that takes a file path as an argument and returns decrypted text. It doesn't manage encryption keys, so you need to ensure that the Puppet user has the necessary key installed. You can check this with the following command (run it as the Puppet user):

```
puppet@puppet:~ $ gpg --list-secret-keys
/opt/puppetlabs/server/data/puppetserver/.gnupg/secring.gpg
-----------------------------------------------------------
sec 2048R/560A024B 2018-02-16
uid Thomas Uphill <thomas@narrabilis.com>
ssb 2048R/59ADD062 2018-02-16
```

Having set up the secret function and the required key, we now encrypt a message to this key:

```
tuphill@mylaptop ~/puppet $ gpg -e -r thomas@narrabilis.com secret_message
```

This creates an encrypted file that can only be read by someone with access to the secret key (or Puppet running on a machine that has the secret key).

We then call the secret function to decrypt this file and get the contents:

```
$message = secret('
/etc/puppetlabs/code/environments/production/modules/admin/files/secret_mes
sage.gpg')
```

There's more...

You should use the secret function, or something like it, to protect any confidential data in your Puppet repo: passwords, AWS credentials, license keys, even other secret keys such as SSL host keys.

You may decide to use a single key, which you push to machines as they're built, perhaps as part of a bootstrap process similar to that described in the *Bootstrapping Puppet with Rake* recipe in Chapter 2, *Puppet Infrastructure*. For even greater security, you might want to create a new key for each machine, or group of machines, and encrypt a given secret only for the machines that need it.

For example, your web servers might need a certain secret that you don't want to be accessible on any other machine. You could create a key for the web servers, and encrypt data only for this key.

See also

- The *Importing configuration data with Hiera* recipe in Chapter 8, *External Tools and the Puppet Ecosystem*

Comparing package versions

Package version numbers are odd things. They look like decimal numbers, but they're not; a version number is often in the form of 2.6.4, for example. If you need to compare one version number with another, you can't do a straightforward string comparison: 2.6.4 would be interpreted as greater than 2.6.12. And a numeric comparison won't work because they're not valid numbers.

Puppet's versioncmp function comes to the rescue. If you pass two things that look like version numbers, it will compare them and return a value indicating which is greater:

```
versioncmp( A, B )
```

This function returns:

- 0 if A and B are equal
- 1 if A is greater than B
- -1 if A is less than B

How to do it...

Here's an example using the versioncmp function:

1. Create a versioncmp.pp manifest, as follows:

```
$app_version = '1.2.2'
$min_version = '1.2.10'
if versioncmp($app_version, $min_version) >= 0 {
  notify { 'Version OK': }
} else {
  notify { 'Upgrade needed': }
}
```

2. Run Puppet:

```
t@mylaptop $ puppet apply versioncmp.pp
Notice: Compiled catalog for mylaptop.example.com in
environment production in 0.03 seconds
Notice: Upgrade needed
Notice: /Stage[main]/Main/Notify[Upgrade needed]/message:
defined 'message' as 'Upgrade needed'
Notice: Applied catalog in 0.15 seconds
```

3. Change the value of $app_version, as follows:

```
$app_version = '1.2.14'
```

4. Run Puppet again:

```
t@mylaptop $ puppet apply versioncmp2.pp
Notice: Compiled catalog for mylaptop.example.com in
environment production in 0.03 seconds
Notice: Version OK
Notice: /Stage[main]/Main/Notify[Version OK]/message: defined
'message' as 'Version OK'
Notice: Applied catalog in 0.11 seconds
```

How it works...

We've specified that the minimum acceptable version ($min_version) is 1.2.10. So, in the first example, we want to compare it with the $app_version of 1.2.2. A simple alphabetic comparison of these two strings (in Ruby, for example) would give the wrong result, but versioncmp correctly determines that 1.2.2 is less than 1.2.10 and alerts us that we need to upgrade.

In the second example, $app_version is now 1.2.14, which versioncmp correctly recognizes as greater than $min_version, so we get the Version OK message.

5
Users and Virtual Resources

In this chapter, we will cover the following recipes:

- Using virtual resources
- Managing users with virtual resources
- Managing users' SSH access
- Managing users' customization files
- Using exported resources

Introduction

Users can be a real pain. I don't mean the people, though doubtless that's sometimes true. But keeping UNIX user accounts and file permissions in sync across a network of machines, some of them running different operating systems, can be very challenging without some kind of centralized configuration management.

Each new developer who joins the organization needs an account on every machine, along with `sudo` privileges and group memberships, and needs his/her SSH key authorized for a bunch of different accounts. The system administrator who has to take care of this manually will be at the job all day, while the system administrator who uses Puppet will be done in minutes, and can head out for an early lunch.

In this chapter, we'll look at some handy patterns and techniques to manage users and their associated resources. Users are also one of the most common applications for virtual resources, so we'll find out all about those. In the final section, we'll introduce exported resources, which are useful for sharing resources across multiple machines.

Using virtual resources

Virtual resources in Puppet might seem complicated and confusing but, in fact, they're very simple. They're exactly like regular resources, but they don't actually take effect until they're realized (in the sense of "made real"); a regular resource, on the other hand, can only be declared once per node (so two classes can't declare the same resource, for example). A virtual resource can be realized as many times as you like.

This comes in handy when you need to move applications and services between machines. If two applications that use the same resource end up sharing a machine, they will cause a conflict unless you make the resource virtual.

To clarify this, let's look at a typical situation where virtual resources might come in handy.

You are responsible for two popular web applications: WordPress and Drupal. Both are web apps running on Apache, so they both require the Apache package to be installed. The definition for `wordpress` might look something like the following:

```
class wordpress {
  package {'httpd':
    ensure => 'installed',
  }
  service {'httpd':
    ensure => 'running',
    enable => true,
  }
}
```

The definition for `drupal` might look like this:

```
class drupal {
  package {'httpd':
    ensure => 'installed',
  }
  service {'httpd':
    ensure => 'running',
    enable => true,
  }
}
```

All is well until you need to consolidate both apps onto a single server:

```
node 'bigbox' {
  include wordpress
  include drupal
}
```

Now Puppet will complain because you tried to define two resources with the same name: httpd.

You could remove the duplicate Apache package definition from one of the classes, but then nodes without the class including Apache would fail. You can get around this problem by putting the Apache package in its own class and then using `include apache` everywhere it's needed; Puppet doesn't mind you including the same class multiple times. In reality, putting Apache in its own class solves most problems but, in general, this method has the disadvantage that every potentially conflicting resource must have its own class.

Virtual resources can be used to solve this problem. A virtual resource is just like a normal resource, except that it starts with the @ character:

```
@package { 'httpd':
  ensure => installed
}
```

You can think of it as being like a placeholder resource; you want to define it but you aren't sure you are going to use it yet. Puppet will read and remember virtual resource definitions, but won't actually create the resource until you realize the resource.

To create the resource, use the `realize` function:

```
realize(Package['httpd'])
```

You can call realize as many times as you want on the resource and it won't result in a conflict. So virtual resources are the way to go when several different classes all require the same resource, and they may need to coexist on the same node.

How to do it...

Here's how to build the example using virtual resources:

1. Create a `virtual` module with the following contents:

```
class virtual {
  @paclass virtual {
  @package {'httpd':
    ensure  => installed
  }
  @service {'httpd':
    ensure  => running,
    enable  => true,
```

```
        require => Package['httpd']
   }
}
```

2. Create the `httpd` module with the following contents:

```
package {'httpd':
   ensure   => installed
}
@service {'httpd':
   ensure   => running,
   enable   => true,
   require => Package['httpd']
}
}
```

3. Create the `drupal` module with the following contents:

```
class drupal {
  include virtual
  realize(Package['httpd'])
  realize(Service['httpd'])
}
```

4. Create the `wordpress` module with the following contents:

```
class wordpress {
  include virtual
  realize(Package['httpd'])
  realize(Service['httpd'])
}
```

5. Modify your `site.pp` file, as follows:

```
node 'bignode' {
  include drupal
  include wordpress
}
```

6. Run Puppet:

```
[root@bignode ~]# puppet agent -t
Info: Using configured environment 'production'
Info: Retrieving pluginfacts
Info: Retrieving plugin
Info: Retrieving locales
Info: Caching catalog for bignode.example.com
Info: Applying configuration version '1518763667'
Notice: /Stage[main]/Virtual/Package[httpd]/ensure: created
Notice: /Stage[main]/Virtual/Service[httpd]/ensure: ensure
changed 'stopped' to 'running'
Info: /Stage[main]/Virtual/Service[httpd]: Unscheduling refresh
on Service[httpd]
Info: Creating state file
/opt/puppetlabs/puppet/cache/state/state.yaml
Notice: Applied catalog in 12.03 seconds
```

How it works...

You define the package and service as `virtual` resources in one place: the `virtual` class. All nodes can include this class and you can put all your virtual services and packages in it. None of the packages will actually be installed on a node or the services started until you call realize:

```
class virtual {
  @package { 'httpd':
    ensure => installed
  }
}
```

Every class that needs the Apache package can call realize on this `virtual` resource:

```
class drupal {
  include virtual
  realize(Package['httpd'])
  realize(Service['httpd'])
}
```

Puppet knows, because you made the resource `virtual`, that you intended to have multiple references to the same package, and didn't just accidentally create two resources with the same name. So it does the right thing.

There's more...

To realize virtual resources, you can also use the collection spaceship syntax:

```
Package <| title = 'httpd' |>
```

The advantage of this syntax is that you're not restricted to the resource name; you could also use a tag, for example:

```
Package <| tag = 'web' |>
```

Alternatively, you can just specify all instances of the resource type by leaving the query section blank:

```
Package <|  |>
```

> In general, this sort of blank realization will probably cause problems. It is better to use tags to only realize the resources you need.

Managing users with virtual resources

Users are a great example of a resource that may need to be realized by multiple classes. Consider the following situation. To simplify the administration of a large number of machines, you defined classes for two kinds of user: `developers` and `sysadmins`. All machines need to include `sysadmins`, but only some machines need access to developers:

```
node 'server' {
  include user::sysadmins
}
node 'webserver' {
  include user::sysadmins
  include user::developers
}
```

However, some users may be members of both groups. If each group simply declares its members as regular user resources, this will lead to a conflict when a node includes both developers and `sysadmins`, as in the webserver example.

To avoid this conflict, a common pattern is to make all users virtual resources, defined in a single `user::virtual` class that every machine includes, and then realize the users where they are needed. This way, there will be no conflict if a user is a member of multiple groups.

How to do it...

Follow these steps to create a `user::virtual` class:

1. Create the `modules/user/manifests/virtual.pp` file with the following contents:

```
class user::virtual {
  @user { 'thomas': ensure => present }
  @user { 'theresa': ensure => present }
  @user { 'josko': ensure => present }
  @user { 'nate': ensure => present }
}
```

2. Create the `modules/user/manifests/developers.pp` file with the following contents:

```
class user::developers {
  realize(User['theresa'])
  realize(User['nate'])
}
```

3. Create the `modules/user/manifests/sysadmins.pp` file with the following contents:

```
class user::sysadmins {
  realize(User['thomas'])
  realize(User['theresa'])
  realize(User['josko'])
}
```

4. Modify your `site.pp` file as follows:

```
node 'cookbook' {
  include user::virtual
  include user::sysadmins
  include user::developers
}
```

5. Run Puppet:

```
[root@cookbook ~]# puppet agent -t
Info: Caching catalog for cookbook.example.com
Info: Applying configuration version '1520441337'
Notice: /Stage[main]/User::Virtual/User[thomas]/ensure: created
Notice: /Stage[main]/User::Virtual/User[theresa]/ensure:
created
Notice: /Stage[main]/User::Virtual/User[josko]/ensure: created
Notice: /Stage[main]/User::Virtual/User[nate]/ensure: created
Notice: Applied catalog in 0.14 seconds
```

How it works...

When we include the `user::virtual` class, all the users are declared as virtual resources (because we included the @ symbol):

```
@user { 'thomas': ensure  => present }
@user { 'theresa': ensure => present }
@user { 'josko': ensure   => present }
@user { 'nate': ensure    => present }
```

That is to say, the resources exist in Puppet's catalog; they can be referred to by, and linked with, other resources and they are in every respect identical to regular resources, except that Puppet doesn't actually create the corresponding users on the machine.

In order for that to happen, we need to call `realize` on the virtual resources. When we include the `user::sysadmins` class, we get the following code:

```
realize(User['thomas'])
realize(User['theresa'])
realize(User['josko'])
```

Calling realize on a virtual resource tells Puppet: I'd like to use that resource now. This is what it does, as we can see from the run output:

```
Notice: /Stage[main]/User::Virtual/User[theresa]/ensure: created
```

However, Theresa is in both the developers and sysadmins classes! Won't that mean we end up calling realize twice on the same resource?

```
realize(User['theresa'])
...
realize(User['theresa'])
```

Yes, it does, and that's fine. You're explicitly allowed to realize resources multiple times, and there will be no conflict. So long as some class, somewhere, calls realize on Theresa's account, it will be created. Unrealized resources are simply discarded during catalog compilation.

There's more...

When you use this pattern to manage your own users, every node should include the `user::virtual` class as a part of your basic housekeeping configuration. This class will declare all users (as virtual) in your organization or site. This should also include any users who exist only to run applications or services (such as Apache, www-data, or deploy, for example). Then, you can realize them as needed on individual nodes or in specific classes.

For production use, you'll probably also want to specify a UID and GID for each user or group, so that these numeric identifiers are synchronized across your network. You can do this using the `uid` and `gid` parameters for the user resource.

If you don't specify a user's UID, for example, you'll just get the next ID number available on a given machine, so the same user on different machines will have a different UID. This can lead to permission problems when using shared storage, or moving files between machines.

A common pattern when defining users as virtual resources is to assign tags to the users based on their assigned roles within your organization. You can then use the collector syntax instead of realize to collect users with specific tags applied.

For example, see the following code snippet:

```
@user { 'thomas':
  ensure => present,
  tag    => 'sysadmin'
}
@user { 'theresa':
  ensure => present,
  tag    => 'sysadmin'
}
```

```
@user { 'josko':
  ensure => present,
  tag     => 'dev'
}
User <| tag == 'sysadmin' |>
```

In the previous example, only `thomas` and `theresa` users would be included.

See also

- The *Using virtual resources* recipe in this chapter
- The *Managing users' customization files* recipe in this chapter

Managing users' SSH access

A sensible approach to access control for servers is to use named user accounts with passphrase-protected SSH keys, rather than having users share an account with a widely-known password. Puppet makes this easy to manage thanks to the built-in `ssh_authorized_key` type.

To combine this with virtual users, as described in the previous section, you can create a define, which includes both `user` and `ssh_authorized_key`. This will also come in handy when adding customization files and other resources to each user.

How to do it...

Follow these steps to extend your virtual users' class to include SSH access:

1. Create a new `ssh_user` module to contain our `ssh_user` definition. Create the `modules/ssh_user/manifests/init.pp` file as follows:

```
define ssh_user(
  String $key,
  Enum['ssh-rsa','ssh-ed25519'] $keytype
  ) {
  user { $name:
    ensure  => present,
  }
  file { "/home/${name}":
    ensure  => directory,
```

```
      mode     => '0700',
      owner    => $name,
      require  => User["$name"]
    }
    file { "/home/${name}/.ssh":
      ensure   => directory,
      mode     => '0700',
      owner    => "$name",
      require  => File["/home/${name}"],
    }
    ssh_authorized_key { "${name}_key":
      key      => $key,
      type     => "$keytype",
      user     => $name,
      require  => File["/home/${name}/.ssh"],
    }
  }
}
```

2. Modify your `modules/user/manifests/virtual.pp` file, comment out the previous definition for user `thomas`, and replace it with the following:

```
@ssh_user { 'thomas':
  key      => 'AAAA3NzaC1yc2E.../5fijRh+OJBJ',
  keytype => 'ssh-ed25519'
}
```

3. Modify your `modules/user/manifests/sysadmins.pp` file as follows:

```
class user::sysadmins {
 realize(Ssh_user['thomas'])
   ...
}
```

4. Run Puppet:

```
[root@cookbook ~]# puppet agent -t
Info: Using configured environment 'production'
Info: Retrieving pluginfacts
Info: Retrieving plugin
Info: Loading facts
Info: Caching catalog for cookbook.example.com
Info: Applying configuration version '1520454705'
Notice:
/Stage[main]/User::Virtual/Ssh_user[thomas]/File[/home/thomas]/
ensure: created
Notice:
/Stage[main]/User::Virtual/Ssh_user[thomas]/File[/home/thomas/.
```

```
ssh]/ensure: created
Notice:
/Stage[main]/User::Virtual/Ssh_user[thomas]/Ssh_authorized_key[
thomas_key]/ensure: created
Notice: Applied catalog in 0.06 seconds
You have new mail in /var/spool/mail/root
```

How it works...

For each user in our `user::virtual` class, we need to create:

- The user account itself
- The user's `home` directory and `.ssh` directory
- The user's `.ssh/authorized_keys` file

We could declare separate resources to implement all of these for each user, but it's much easier to create a definition instead, which wraps them into a single resource:

1. By creating a new module for our definition, we can refer to define from anywhere (in any scope):

   ```
   define ssh_user(
     String $key,
     Enum['ssh-rsa','ssh-ed25519'] $keytype
     ) {
   ...
   ```

2. After we create the user, we can then create the `home` directory; we need the user first so that, when we assign ownership, we can use the username, `owner => $name`:

   ```
   file { "/home/${name}":
     ensure  => directory,
     mode    => '0700',
     owner   => $name,
     require => User["$name"]
   }
   ```

   Puppet can create the user's `home` directory using the `managehome` attribute to the user resource. Relying on this mechanism is problematic in practice, as it does not account for users that were created outside Puppet without home directories.

3. Next, we need to ensure that the `.ssh` directory exists within the `home` directory of the user. We require the `home` directory, `File["/home/${name}"]`, since that needs to exist before we create this subdirectory. This implies that the user already exists because the `home` directory required the user:

```
file { "/home/${name}/.ssh":
 ensure  => directory,
 mode    => '0700',
 owner   => "$name",
 require => File["/home/${name}"],
 }
```

4. Finally, we create the `ssh_authorized_key` resource, again requiring the containing folder (`File["/home/${name}/.ssh"]`). We use the `$key` and `$keytype` variables to assign the key and type parameters to the `ssh_authorized_key` type, as follows:

```
ssh_authorized_key { "${name}_key":
 key     => $key,
 type    => "$keytype",
 user    => $name,
 require => File["/home/${name}/.ssh"],
 }
```

5. We passed the `$key` and `$keytype` variables when we defined the `ssh_user` resource for `thomas`:

```
@ssh_user { 'thomas':
 key     => 'AAAA3NzaC1yc2E.../5fijRh+OJBJ',
 keytype => 'ssh-ed25519'
 }
```

The value for the key in the preceding code snippet is the `ssh` key's public key value; it is usually stored in an `id_rsa.pub` file.

6. Now, with everything defined, we just need to call `realize` on `thomas` for all these resources to take effect:

```
realize(Ssh_user['thomas'])
```

7. Notice that, this time, the virtual resource we're realizing is not simply the user resource, as before, but the `ssh_user` defined type we created, which includes the user and the related resources needed to set up the SSH access:

```
Notice:
/Stage[main]/User::Virtual/Ssh_user[thomas]/File[/home/thomas]/
ensure: created
Notice:
/Stage[main]/User::Virtual/Ssh_user[thomas]/File[/home/thomas/.
ssh]/ensure: created
Notice:
/Stage[main]/User::Virtual/Ssh_user[thomas]/Ssh_authorized_key[
thomas_key]/ensure: created
```

There's more...

Of course, you can add whatever resources you like to the `ssh_user` definition to have Puppet automatically create them for new users. We'll see an example of this in the next recipe, *Managing users' customization files*.

Managing users' customization files

Users tend to customize their shell environments, terminal colors, aliases, and so forth. This is usually achieved by a number of `dotfiles` in their `home` directory, for example, `.bash_profile` or `.vimrc`.

You can use Puppet to synchronize and update each user's `dotfiles` across a number of machines by extending the virtual user setup we have developed throughout this chapter. We'll start a new module, `dmin_user`, and use the file type's `recurse` attribute to copy files into each user's `home` directory.

How to do it...

Here's what you need to do:

1. Create the `admin_user` defined type (`define admin_user`) in the `modules/admin_user/manifests/init.pp` file, as follows:

```
define admin_user (
  String $key,
```

```
Enum['ssh-rsa','ssh-ed25519'] $keytype,
String $dotfiles = false,
) {
user { $name:
  ensure => present,
}
file { "/home/${name}/.ssh":
  ensure     => directory,
  mode       => '0700',
  owner      => "$name",
  require    => File["/home/${name}"],
}
ssh_authorized_key { "${name}_key":
  key        => $key,
  type       => "$keytype",
  user       => $name,
  require    => File["/home/${name}/.ssh"],
}
# dotfiles
if $dotfiles == false {
  # just create the directory
  file { "/home/${name}":
    ensure  => 'directory',
    mode    => '0700',
    owner   => $name,
    group   => $name,
    require => User["$name"] }
} else {
  # copy in all the files in the subdirectory
  file { "/home/${name}":
    recurse => true,
    mode    => '0700',
    owner   => $name,
    group   => $name,
    source  => "puppet:///modules/admin_user/${name}",
    require => User["$name"]
  }
}
}
```

2. Modify the `modules/user/manifests/sysadmins.pp` file as follows:

```
class user::sysadmins {
  realize(Admin_user['thomas'])
}
```

3. Alter the definition of `thomas` in `modules/user/manifests/virtual.pp` as follows:

```
@ssh_user { 'thomas':
  key      => 'AAAA3NzaC1yc2E.../5fijRh+OJBJ',
  keytype  => 'ssh-ed25519',
  dotfiles => true
}
```

4. Create a subdirectory in the `admin_user` module for the file for `thomas`:

```
$ mkdir -p modules/admin_user/files/thomas
```

5. Create `dotfiles` for `thomas` in the directory you just created:

```
$ echo "alias vi=vim" > modules/admin_user/files/thomas/.bashrc
$ echo "set tabstop=2" > modules/admin_user/files/thomas/.vimrc
```

6. Run Puppet:

```
[root@cookbook ~]# puppet agent -t
...
Notice:
/Stage[main]/User::Virtual/Admin_user[thomas]/File[/home/thomas
/.bashrc]/ensure: defined content as
'{md5}033c3484e4b276e0641becc3aa268a3a'
Notice:
/Stage[main]/User::Virtual/Admin_user[thomas]/File[/home/thomas
/.vimrc]/ensure: defined content as
'{md5}cb2af2d35b18b5ac2539057bd429d3ae'
```

How it works...

We created a new `admin_user` definition, which defines the `home` directory recursively if `$dotfiles` is not false (the default value):

```
if $dotfiles == false {
  # just create the directory
  file { "/home/${name}": ensure => 'directory',
    mode    => '0700',
    owner   => $name,
    group   => $name,
    require => User["$name"] }
} else {
  # copy in all the files in the subdirectory
  file { "/home/${name}":
```

```
        recurse => true,
        mode    => '0700',
        owner   => $name,
        group   => $name,
        source  => "puppet:///modules/admin_user/${name}",
        require => User["$name"]
    }
}
```

We created a directory to hold the user's `dotfiles` within the `admin_user` module; all the files within that directory will be copied into the user's `home` directory:

```
Notice:
/Stage[main]/User::Virtual/Admin_user[thomas]/File[/home/thomas/.bashrc]/en
sure: defined content as '{md5}033c3484e4b276e0641becc3aa268a3a'
Notice:
/Stage[main]/User::Virtual/Admin_user[thomas]/File[/home/thomas/.vimrc]/ens
ure: defined content as '{md5}cb2af2d35b18b5ac2539057bd429d3ae'
```

Using the `recurse` option allows us to add as many `dotfiles` as we want for each user without having to modify the definition of the user.

There's more...

We could specify that the `source` attribute of the `home` directory is a directory where users can place their own `dotfiles`. This way, each user could modify their own `dotfiles` and have them transferred to all the nodes in the network without our involvement.

See also

- The *Managing users with virtual resources* recipe in this chapter

Using exported resources

So far, all our recipes have dealt with a single machine. It is possible with Puppet to have resources from one node affect another node. This interaction is managed with exported resources. Exported resources are just like any resource you might define for a node but, instead of applying to the node on which they were created, they are exported for use by all nodes in the environment. Exported resources can be thought of as virtual resources that go one step further and exist beyond the node on which they were defined.

There are two actions with exported resources. When an exported resource is created, it is said to be defined. When all the exported resources are harvested, they are said to be collected. Defining exported resources is similar to virtual resources; the resource in question has two @ symbols prepended. For example, to define a `file` resource as external, use `@@file`. Collecting resources is done with the spaceship operator, `<<| |>>`; this is thought to look like a spaceship. To collect the exported file resource (`@@file`), you would use `File <<| |>>`.

There are many examples that use exported resources, the most common one involves SSH host keys. Using exported resources, it is possible to have every machine that is running Puppet share their SSH host keys with the other connected nodes. The idea here is that each machine exports its own host key and then collects all the keys from the other machines. In our example, we will create two classes; first, a class that exports the SSH host key from every node. We will include this class in our base class. The second class will be a collector class, which collects the SSH host keys. We will apply this class to our Jumpboxes or SSH login servers.

 Jumpboxes are machines that have special firewall rules to allow them to log in to different locations.

Getting ready

To use exported resources, you will need to enable `storeconfigs` on your Puppet masters. It is possible to use exported resources with a masterless (decentralized) deployment; however, we will assume you are using a centralized model for this example. In Chapter 2, *Puppet Infrastructure*, we configured PuppetDB using the `puppetdb` module from the Forge. It is possible to use other backends if you desire; however, all of these except `puppetdb` are deprecated. More information is available at `http://projects.puppetlabs.com/projects/puppet/wiki/Using_Stored_Configuration`.

Ensure your Puppet masters are configured to use PuppetDB as a `storeconfigs` container.

How to do it...

We'll create an `ssh_host` class to export the ssh keys of a host and ensure that it is included in our base class.

1. Create the first class, `base::ssh_host`, which we will include in our base class:

```
class base::ssh_host {
  @@sshkey{ "$::fqdn":
    ensure       => 'present',
    host_aliases => ["$::hostname","$::ipaddress"],
    key          => ${::ssh['rsa']['key']},
    type         => 'rsa',
  }
}
```

2. Remember to include this class from inside the `base` class definition:

```
class base {
  ...
  include base::ssh_host
}
```

3. Create a definition for `jumpbox`, either in a class or within the node definition for `jumpbox`:

```
node 'jumpbox' {
  Sshkey <<| |>>
}
```

4. Run Puppet on a few nodes to create the exported resources. In my case, I ran Puppet on my Puppet server (`puppet.example.com`) and my cookbook node (`cookbook`). Finally, run Puppet on `jumpbox` to verify that the SSH host keys for our other nodes are collected:

```
[root@jumpbox ~]# puppet agent -t
...
Info: Caching catalog for jumpbox.example.com
Info: Applying configuration version '1520459518'
Notice:
/Stage[main]/Main/Node[jumpbox]/Sshkey[puppet.example.com]/ensu
re: created
Notice:
/Stage[main]/Main/Node[jumpbox]/Sshkey[cookbook.example.com]/en
sure: created
```

How it works...

We created an `sshkey` resource for the node using the `facter` facts for the fully-qualified `fqdn`, `hostname`, `ipaddress`, and `$facts['ssh']['rsa']['key']` domain names. We use `fqdn` as the title for our exported resource because each exported resource must have a unique name. We can assume that the `fqdn` of a node will be unique within our organization (although sometimes they may not be, Puppet can be good at finding out such things when you least expect it). We then go on to define aliases by which our node may be known. We use the `hostname` variable for one alias and the main IP address of the machine as the other. If you had other naming conventions for your nodes, you could include other aliases here. We assume that hosts are using RSA keys, so we use the `$facts['ssh']['rsa']['key']` variable in our definition. In a large installation, you would wrap this definition in tests to ensure that the RSA keys existed. You would also use `ED25519` keys if they existed as well.

With the `sshkey` resource defined and exported, we then created a `jumpbox` node definition. In this definition, we used the `Sshkey <<| |>>` spaceship syntax to collect all defined exported `sshkey` resources.

There's more...

When defining exported resources, you can add tag attributes to the resource to create subsets of exported resources. For example, if you had a development and production area on your network, you could create different groups of `sshkey` resources for each area, as shown in the following code snippet:

```
@@sshkey{"$::fqdn":
  host_aliases => ["$::hostname","$::ipaddress"],
  key          => $facts['ssh']['rsa']['key'],
  type         => 'rsa',
  tag          => "$::environment",
}
```

You could then modify `jumpbox` to only collect resources for production, for example, as follows:

```
Sshkey <<| tag == 'production' |>>
```

Two important things to remember when working with exported resources: first, every resource must have a unique name across your installation. Using the FQDN within the title is usually enough to keep your definitions unique. Second, any resource can be made virtual. Even defined types that you created may be exported. Exported resources can be used to achieve some fairly complex configurations that automatically adjust when machines change.

A word of caution when working with an extremely large number of nodes (more than 5,000): exported resources can take a long time to collect and apply, particularly if each exported resource creates a file.

Managing Resources and Files

6

In this chapter, we will cover the following recipes:

- Distributing cron jobs efficiently
- Scheduling when resources are to be applied
- Using host resources
- Using exported host resources
- Using multiple file sources
- Distributing and merging directory trees
- Cleaning up old files
- Auditing resources
- Temporarily disabling resources

Introduction

In the previous chapter, we introduced virtual and exported resources. Virtual and exported resources are ways to manage how resources are applied to a node. In this chapter, we will deal with when and how to apply resources. In some cases, you may only wish to apply a resource in the off hours, while in others, you may wish to only audit the resource without making any changes. In other cases, you may wish to apply completely different resources based on which node is using the code. As we will see, Puppet has the flexibility to deal with all these scenarios.

Distributing cron jobs efficiently

When you have many servers executing the same cron job, it's usually a good idea not to run them all at the same time. If all of the jobs access a common server (for example, when running backups), it may put too much load on that server, and even if they don't, all the servers will be busy at the same time, which may affect their capacity to provide other services.

How to do it...

Here's how to have Puppet schedule the same job at a different time for each machine:

1. Modify your `site.pp` file as follows:

```
node 'cookbook' {
  cron { 'run-backup':
    ensure  => present,
    command => '/usr/local/bin/backup',
    hour    => split($facts['ipaddress'],'\.')[3] % 24,
    minute  => '00',
  }
}
```

2. Run Puppet:

```
[root@cookbook ~]# puppet agent -t
...
Notice: /Stage[main]/Main/Node[cookbook]/Cron[run-
backup]/ensure: created
```

3. Check `crontab` to see how the job has been configured:

```
# HEADER: This file was autogenerated at 2018-03-15 19:13:55
+0000 by puppet.
# HEADER: While it can still be managed manually, it is
definitely not recommended.
# HEADER: Note particularly that the comments starting with
'Puppet Name' should
# HEADER: not be deleted, as doing so could cause duplicate
cron jobs.
# Puppet Name: run-backup
0 15 * * * /usr/local/bin/backup
```

How it works...

We want to distribute the hour of the `cronjob` runs across all our nodes. We are attempting to distribute the jobs as evenly as we can, so we choose something that is consistent on a node but varies between nodes. In this example, we use the last octet of the IP address. The last octet is a number from 1-254. We use the modulo operator (`%`) to transform this into a number from 0-23. This way, the values will be distributed across the nodes and will not change per node (unless the IP address changes). To calculate the number, we use the `split` function to generate an array of octets. We then refer to the last octet, `[3]` (computer scientists start at `0`).

Another option here is to use the `fqdn_rand()` function, which works in much the same way as our example.

There's more...

If you have several cron jobs per machine and you want to run them a certain number of hours apart, add this number to the value we just calculated before taking the modulus. Let's say we want to run the `dump_database` job at some arbitrary time and the `run_backup` job an hour later, this can be done using the following code snippet:

```
cron { 'dump-database':
  ensure  => present,
  command => '/usr/local/bin/dump_database',
  hour    => split($facts['ipaddress'],'\.')[3] + 1 % 24,
  minute  => '00',
}
```

The two jobs will end up with different hour values for each machine Puppet runs on, but `run_backup` will always be one hour after `dump_database`.

Most cron implementations have directories for hourly, daily, weekly, and monthly tasks. The /etc/cron.hourly, /etc/cron.daily, /etc/cron.weekly, and /etc/cron.monthly directories exist on both our Debian and Enterprise Linux machines. These directories hold executables, which will be run on the referenced schedule (hourly, daily, weekly, or monthly). I find it better to describe all of the jobs in these folders and push the jobs as file resources. An admin on the box searching for your script will be able to find it with grep in these directories. To use the same trick here, we would push a cron task into /etc/cron. hourly and then verify that the hour is the correct hour for the task to run at:

1. Create a cron class in modules/cron/init.pp:

   ```
   class cron {
     file { '/etc/cron.hourly/run-backup':
       content => epp('cron/backup.epp'),
       mode    => '0755',
     }
   }
   ```

2. Include the cron class in your cookbook node in site.pp:

   ```
   node cookbook {
     include cron
   }
   ```

3. Create a template in modules/cron/templates/backup.epp to hold the cron task:

   ```
   #!/bin/bash
   runhour=<%= split($facts["ipaddress"],"\.")[3] % 24 %>
   hour=$(date +%H)
   if [ "$runhour" -ne "$hour" ]; then
    exit 0
   fi
   exec /usr/local/bin/dump_database
   ```

4. Run Puppet:

   ```
   [root@cookbook ~]# puppet agent -t
   . . .
   Notice: /Stage[main]/Cron/File[/etc/cron.hourly/run-
   backup]/ensure: defined content as '{md5}155dc47d262fdd64e32993
   81d523750a'
   ```

5. Verify that the script has the same value we calculated before, `15`:

```
[root@cookbook ~]# cat /etc/cron.hourly/run-backup
#!/bin/bash
runhour=15
hour=$(date +%H)
if [ "$runhour" -ne "$hour" ]; then
 exit 0
fi
exec /usr/local/bin/dump_database
```

Now, this job will run every hour but only when the hour, returned by `$(date +%H)`, is equal to `15` will the rest of the script run. Creating your cron jobs as file resources in a large organization makes it easier for your fellow administrators to find them. When you have a very large number of machines, it can be advantageous to add another random wait at the beginning of your job. You would need to modify the line before `echo run-backup` and add the following:

```
MAXWAIT=600
sleep $((RANDOM%MAXWAIT))
```

 The double parentheses, `((`, and `RANDOM` are a bash shell built-in. The preceding code may not work in other shells.

This will sleep for a maximum of 600 seconds, but will sleep for a different amount each time it runs (assuming your random number generator is working). This sort of random wait is useful when you have thousands of machines all running the same task and you need to stagger the runs as much as possible.

See also

- The *Running Puppet from cron* recipe in `Chapter 2`, *Puppet Infrastructure*

Scheduling when resources are to be applied

So far, we have looked at what Puppet can do, and the order that it does things in, but not when it does them. One way to control this is to use the `schedule` metaparameter. When you need to limit the number of times a resource is applied within a specified period, `schedule` can help. For example:

```
exec { "/usr/bin/apt-get update":
  schedule => daily,
}
```

The most important thing to understand about `schedule` is that it can only stop a resource being applied. It doesn't guarantee that the resource will be applied with a certain frequency. For example, the `exec` resource shown in the preceding code snippet has `schedule => daily,` but this just represents an upper limit on the number of times the `exec` resource can run per day. It won't be applied more than once a day. If you don't run Puppet at all, the resource won't be applied at all. Using the hourly schedule, for instance, is meaningless on a machine configured to run the agent every four hours (via the `runinterval` configuration setting).

That being said, `schedule` is best used to restrict resources from running when they shouldn't, or don't need to; for example, you might want to make sure that `apt-get` update isn't run more than once an hour. There are some built-in schedules available for you to use:

- Hourly
- Daily
- Weekly
- Monthly
- Never

However, you can modify these and create your own custom schedules, using the `schedule` resource. We'll see how to do this in the following example. Let's say we want to make sure that an `exec` resource representing a maintenance job won't run during office hours, when it might interfere with production.

How to do it...

In this example, we'll create a custom `schedule` resource and assign this to the resource:

1. Modify your `site.pp` file as follows:

```
schedule { 'outside-office-hours':
  period => daily,
  range  => ['17:00-23:59','00:00-09:00'],
  repeat => 1,
}

node 'cookbook' {
  notify { 'Doing some maintenance':
    schedule => 'outside-office-hours',
  }
}
```

2. Run Puppet. What you'll see will depend on the time of the day. If it's currently outside the office-hours period you defined, Puppet will apply the resource as follows:

```
[root@cookbook ~]# date
Thu Mar 15 20:59:28 UTC 2018
[root@cookbook ~]# puppet agent -t
...
Notice: Doing some maintenance
Notice: /Stage[main]/Main/Node[cookbook]/Notify[Doing some
maintenance]/message: defined 'message' as 'Doing some
maintenance'
```

3. If the time is within the office-hours period, Puppet will do nothing:

```
[root@cookbook ~]# date
Thu Mar 15 09:30:04 UTC 2018
[root@cookbook ~]# puppet agent -t
...
Info: Caching catalog for cookbook.example.com
Info: Applying configuration version '1521147639'
Notice: Applied catalog in 0.07 seconds
```

How it works...

A schedule consists of three bits of information:

- The period (hourly, daily, weekly, or monthly)
- The range (defaults to the whole period, but can be a smaller part of it)
- The repeat count (how often the resource is allowed to be applied within the range; the default is 1, or once per period)

Our custom schedule, named outside-office-hours, supplies these three parameters:

```
schedule { 'outside-office-hours':
  period => daily,
  range => ['17:00-23:59','00:00-09:00'],
  repeat => 1,
}
```

The period is daily, and the range is defined as an array of two time intervals:

- 17:00-23:59
- 00:00-09:00

The outside-office-hours schedule is now available for us to use with any resource, just as though it were built into Puppet, such as the daily or hourly schedules. In our example, we assign this schedule to the exec resource using the schedule metaparameter:

```
notify { 'Doing some maintenance':
  schedule => 'outside-office-hours',
}
```

Without this schedule parameter, the resource would be applied every time Puppet runs. With it, Puppet will check the following parameters to decide whether or not to apply the resource:

- Whether the time is in the permitted range
- Whether the resource has already been run the maximum permitted number of times in this period

For example, let's consider what happens if Puppet runs at 4 p.m., 5 p.m., and 6 p.m. on a given day:

- 4 p.m.: It's outside the permitted time range, so Puppet will do nothing
- 5 p.m.: It's inside the permitted time range, and the resource hasn't been run yet in this period, so Puppet will apply the resource
- 6 p.m.: It's inside the permitted time range, but the resource has already been run the maximum number of times in this period, so Puppet will do nothing

And so on, until the next day.

There's more...

The `repeat` parameter governs how many times the resource will be applied, given the other constraints of the schedule. For example, to apply a resource no more than six times an hour, use a `schedule` as follows:

```
period => hourly,
repeat => 6,
```

Remember that this won't guarantee that the job is run six times an hour. It just sets an upper limit; no matter how often Puppet runs or anything else happens, the job won't be run if it has already run six times in that hour. If Puppet only runs once a day, the job will just be run once. So `schedule` is best used to make sure that things don't happen at certain times (or don't exceed a given frequency).

Using host resources

It's not always practical or convenient to use DNS to map your machine names to IP addresses, especially in cloud infrastructures, where those addresses may change all the time. However, if you use entries in the `/etc/hosts` file instead, you then have the problem of how to distribute those entries to all machines and keep them up to date.

Here's a better way to do it: Puppet's `host` resource type controls a single `/etc/hosts` entry, and you can use this to easily map a hostname to an IP address across your whole network. For example, if all your machines need to know the address of the main database server, you can manage it with a `host` resource.

How to do it...

Follow these steps to create an example host resource:

1. Modify your `site.pp` file as follows:

```
node 'cookbook' {
  host { 'packtpub.com':
    ensure => present,
    ip     => '83.166.169.231',
  }
}
```

2. Run Puppet:

```
[root@cookbook ~]# puppet agent -t
...
/Stage[main]/Main/Node[cookbook]/Host[packtpub.com]/ensure:
created
```

3. Verify that the entry has been added:

```
[root@cookbook ~]# grep packtpub /etc/hosts
83.166.169.231 packtpub.com
```

How it works...

Puppet will check the target file (usually `/etc/hosts`) to see whether the host entry already exists, and if not, add it. If an entry for that hostname already exists with a different address, Puppet will change the address to match the manifest.

There's more...

Organizing your host resources into classes can be helpful. For example, you could put the host resources for all your DB servers into one class called `admin::dbhosts`, which is included by all web servers.

Where machines may need to be defined in multiple classes (for example, a database server might also be a repository server), virtual resources can solve this problem. For example, you could define all your hosts as virtual in a single class:

```
class admin::allhosts {
  @host { 'db1.packtpub.com':
    tag => 'database'
    ...
  }
}
```

You could then realize the hosts you need in the various classes:

```
class admin::dbhosts {
  Host <| tag=='database' |>
}
class admin::webhosts {
  Host <| tag=='web' |>
}
```

Using exported host resources

In the previous example, we used the spaceship syntax to collect virtual host resources for hosts of type database or hosts of type web. You can use the same trick with exported resources. The advantage of using exported resources is that as you add more database servers, the collector syntax will automatically pull in the newly created exported host entries for those servers. This makes your /etc/hosts entries more dynamic.

Getting ready

We will be using exported resources. If you haven't already done so, set up puppetdb and enable storeconfigs to use puppetdb as outlined in Chapter 2, *Puppet Infrastructure*.

How to do it...

In this example, we will configure database servers and clients to communicate with each other. We'll make use of exported resources to do the configuration:

1. Create a new database module, db:

   ```
   t@mylaptop ~/puppet/modules $ mkdir -p db/manifests/
   ```

2. Create a new class for your database servers, `db::server`:

```
class db::server {
  @@host {"$::fqdn":
    host_aliases => $::hostname,
    ip => $::ipaddress,
    tag => 'db::server',
  }
  # rest of db class
}
```

3. Create a new class for your database clients:

```
class db::client {
  Host <<| tag == 'db::server' |>>
}
```

4. Apply the database server module to some nodes; in `site.pp`, for example:

```
node 'dbserver1.example.com' {
  class {'db::server': }
}
node 'dbserver2.example.com' {
  class {'db::server': }
}
```

5. Run Puppet on the nodes with the `database::server` module to create the exported resources.

6. Apply the database client module to `cookbook`:

```
node 'cookbook' {
  class {'db::client': }
}
```

7. Run Puppet:

```
[root@cookbook ~]# puppet agent -t
...
Info: Caching catalog for cookbook.example.com
Info: Applying configuration version '1521170400'
Notice:
/Stage[main]/Db::Client/Host[dbserver1.example.com]/ensure:
created
```

```
Info: Computing checksum on file /etc/hosts
Notice:
/Stage[main]/Db::Client/Host[dbserver2.example.com]/ensure:
created
Notice: Applied catalog in 0.11 seconds
```

8. Verify the host entries in /etc/hosts:

```
[root@cookbook ~]# grep dbserver /etc/hosts
192.168.50.30 dbserver1.example.com dbserver1
192.168.50.40 dbserver2.example.com dbserver2
```

How it works...

In the db::server class, we create an exported host resource:

```
@@host {"$::fqdn":
  host_aliases => $::hostname,
  ip           => $::ipaddress,
  tag          => 'db::server',
}
```

This resource uses the fully qualified domain name ($::fqdn) of the node on which it is applied. We also use the short hostname ($::hostname) as an alias of the node. Aliases are printed after fqdn in /etc/hosts. We use the node's $::ipaddress as the IP address for the host entry. Finally, we add a tag to the resource so that we can collect based on that tag later.

The important thing to remember here is that if the IP address should change for the host, the exported resource will be updated, and nodes that collect the exported resource will update their host records accordingly.

We created a collector in db::client, which only collects exported host resources that have been tagged with db::server:Host <<| tag == 'db::server' |>>.

We applied the db::server class to a couple of nodes, dbserver1 and dbserver2, which we then collected on the cookbook string by applying the db::client class. The host entries were placed in /etc/hosts (the default file). We can see that the host entry contains both the fqdn and the short hostname for dbserver1 and dbserver2.

There's more...

Using exported resources in this manner is very useful. Another similar system would be to create an NFS server class, which creates exported resources for the mount points that it exports (via NFS). You can then use tags to have clients collect the appropriate mount points from the server. In the previous example, we made use of a tag to aid our collection of exported resources. It is worth noting that there are several tags automatically added to resources when they are created, one of which is the scope where the resource was created.

Using multiple file sources

A neat feature of Puppet's file resource is that you can specify multiple values for the source parameter. Puppet will search them in order. If the first source isn't found, it moves on to the next, and so on. You can use this to specify a default substitute if the particular file isn't present, or even a series of increasingly generic substitutes.

How to do it...

This example demonstrates using multiple file sources:

1. Create a new `greeting` module as follows:

```
class greeting {
  file { '/tmp/greeting':
    source => [
      'puppet:///modules/greeting/hello.txt',
      'puppet:///modules/greeting/universal.txt'],
  }
}
```

2. Create the `modules/greeting/files/hello.txt` file with the following content:

```
Hello, world.
```

3. Create the `modules/greeting/files/universal.txt` file with the following content:

```
Bah-weep-Graaaaagnah wheep ni ni bong
```

4. Add the class to a node:

```
node cookbook {
  class {'greeting': }
}
```

5. Run Puppet:

```
[root@cookbook ~]# puppet agent -t
...
Notice: /Stage[main]/Greeting/File[/tmp/greeting]/ensure:
defined content as '{md5}54098b367d2e87b078671fad4afb9dbb'
[root@cookbook ~]# cat /tmp/greeting
Hello, world.
```

6. Check the contents of the /tmp/greeting file:

```
[root@cookbook ~]# cat /tmp/greeting
Hello, world.
```

7. Remove the hello.txt file from your Puppet repository and rerun the agent:

```
[root@cookbook ~]# puppet agent -t
...
/Stage[main]/Greeting/File[/tmp/greeting]/content:
--- /tmp/greeting 2018-03-15 17:43:49.000691243 +0000
+++ /tmp/puppet-file20180315-14570-1cgedrz 2018-03-15
17:43:56.280695516 +0000
@@ -1 +1 @@
-Hello, world.
+Bah-weep-Graaaaagnah wheep ni ni bong
```

How it works...

On the first Puppet run, it searches for the available file sources in the order given:

```
source => [
  'puppet:///modules/greeting/hello.txt',
  'puppet:///modules/greeting/universal.txt' ],
```

The hello.txt file is first in the list, and is present, so Puppet uses that as the source for /tmp/greeting:

```
Hello, world.
```

On the second Puppet run, `hello.txt` is missing, so Puppet goes on to look for the next file, `universal.txt`. This is present, so it becomes the source for `/tmp/greeting`:

```
Bah-weep-Graaaaagnah wheep ni ni bong
```

There's more...

You can use this trick anywhere you have a file resource. A common example is a service that is deployed on all nodes, such as `rsyslog`. The `rsyslog` configuration is the same on every host except for the `rsyslog` server. Create a `rsyslog` class with a file resource for the `rsyslog` configuration file:

```
class rsyslog {
  file { '/etc/rsyslog.conf': source => [
    "puppet:///modules/rsyslog/rsyslog.conf.${::hostname}",
    'puppet:///modules/rsyslog/rsyslog.conf' ],
}
```

Then, you put the default configuration in `rsyslog.conf`. For your `rsyslog` server, `logger`, create `rsyslog.conf.logger`. The `rsyslog.conf.logger` file will be used before `rsyslog. conf`, because it is listed first in the array of sources.

See also

- The *Passing parameters to classes* recipe in Chapter 3, *Writing Better Manifests*

Distributing and merging directory trees

As we saw in Chapter 5, , the file resource has a `recurse` parameter, which allows Puppet to transfer entire directory trees. We used this parameter to copy an admin user's dotfiles into their home directory. In this section, we'll show you how to use `recurse` and another parameter, `sourceselect`, to extend our previous example.

How to do it...

Modify the `admin` user example as follows:

1. Remove the `$dotfiles` parameter and remove the condition based on `$dotfiles`. Add a second source to the home directory file resource:

```
define admin_user (
String $key,
  Enum['ssh-rsa','ssh-ed25519'] $keytype,
) {
  $username = $name
  user { $username:
    ensure => present,
  }
  file { "/home/${username}/.ssh":
    ensure  => directory,
    mode    => '0700',
    owner   => $username,
    group   => $username,
    require => File["/home/${username}"],
  }
  ssh_authorized_key { "${username}_key":
    key     => $key,
    type    => "$keytype",
    user    => $username,
    require => File["/home/${username}/.ssh"],
  }
  # copy in all the files in the subdirectory
  file { "/home/${username}":
    recurse => true,
    mode    => '0700',
    owner   => $username,
    group   => $username,
    source  => [
      "puppet:///modules/admin_user/${username}",
      'puppet:///modules/admin_user/base' ],
    sourceselect => 'all',
    require      => User["$username"],
  }
}
```

2. Create a `base` directory and copy all the system default files from `/etc/skel`:

```
t@mylaptop ~/puppet/modules/admin_user/files $ cp -a /etc/skel
base
```

3. Create a new `admin_user`— one that will not have a directory defined:

```
node 'cookbook' {
  admin_user {'steven':
    key => 'AAAAB3N...', keytype => 'ssh-rsa', }
}
```

4. Run Puppet:

```
[root@cookbook ~]# puppet agent -t
...
/Stage[main]/Main/Node[cookbook]/Admin_user[steven]/User[steven
]/ensure: created
Notice:
/Stage[main]/Main/Node[cookbook]/Admin_user[steven]/File[/home/
steven]/ensure: created
Notice:
/Stage[main]/Main/Node[cookbook]/Admin_user[steven]/File[/home/
steven/.bash_logout]/ensure: defined content as
'{md5}6a5bc1cc5f80a48b540bc09d082b5855'
Notice:
/Stage[main]/Main/Node[cookbook]/Admin_user[steven]/File[/home/
steven/.bash_profile]/ensure: defined content as
'{md5}f939eb71a81a9da364410b799e817202'
Notice:
/Stage[main]/Main/Node[cookbook]/Admin_user[steven]/File[/home/
steven/.bashrc]/ensure: defined content as
'{md5}2f8222b4f275c4f18e69c34f66d2631b'
Notice:
/Stage[main]/Main/Node[cookbook]/Admin_user[steven]/File[/home/
steven/.ssh]/ensure: created
Notice:
/Stage[main]/Main/Node[cookbook]/Admin_user[steven]/Ssh_authori
zed_key[steven_key]/ensure: created
Notice: Applied catalog in 0.49 seconds
```

How it works...

If a file resource has the `recurse` parameter set on it, and it is a directory, Puppet will deploy not only the directory itself, but all its contents (including subdirectories and their contents). As we saw in the previous example, when a file has more than one source, the first source file found is used to satisfy the request. This applies to directories as well.

There's more...

By specifying the `sourceselect` parameter as `all`, the contents of all the source directories will be combined. For example, add `thomas admin_user` back into your node definition in `site.pp` for `cookbook`:

```
admin_user {'thomas':
  key     => 'ABBA...',
  keytype => 'rsa', }
```

Now run Puppet again on `cookbook`:

```
[root@cookbook thomas]# puppet agent -t
Notice:
/Stage[main]/User::Virtual/Admin_user[thomas]/File[/home/thomas/.bash_logou
t]/ensure: defined content as '{md5}6a5bc1cc5f80a48b540bc09d082b5855'
Notice:
/Stage[main]/User::Virtual/Admin_user[thomas]/File[/home/thomas/.bash_profi
le]/ensure: defined content as '{md5}f939eb71a81a9da364410b799e817202'
```

Because we previously applied `thomas admin_user` to `cookbook`, the user already existed. The two files defined in the `thomas` directory on the Puppet server were already in the home directory, so only the additional files, `.bash_logout` and `.bash_profile`, were created. Using these two parameters together, you can have default files that can be overridden easily.

Sometimes, you want to deploy files to an existing directory but remove any files that aren't managed by Puppet. A good example would be if you are using `mcollective` in your environment. The directory holding client credentials should only have certificates that come from Puppet.

The `purge` parameter will do this for you. Define the directory as a resource in Puppet:

```
file { '/etc/mcollective/ssl/clients':
  purge   => true,
  recurse => true,
}
```

The combination of `recurse` and `purge` will remove all files and subdirectories in `/etc/mcollective/ssl/clients` that are not deployed by Puppet. You can then deploy your own files to that location by placing them in the appropriate directory on the Puppet server.

If there are subdirectories that contain files you don't want to purge, just define the subdirectory as a Puppet resource, and it will be left alone:

```
file { '/etc/mcollective/ssl/clients':
  purge   => true,
  recurse => true,
}
file { '/etc/mcollective/ssl/clients/local':
  ensure  => directory,
  require => File['/etc/mcollective/ssl/clients'],
}
```

Be aware that, at least in current implementations of Puppet, recursive file copies can be quite slow and place a heavy memory load on the server. If the data doesn't change very often, it might be better to deploy and unpack a `tar` file instead. This can be done with a file resource for the `tar` file and an `exec`, which requires the file resource and unpacks the archive. Recursive directories are less of a problem when filled with small files. Puppet is not a very efficient file server, so creating large `tar` files and distributing them with Puppet is not a good idea either. If you need to copy large files around, using the Operating System's packager is a better solution.

Cleaning up old files

Puppet's `tidy` resource will help you clean up old or out-of-date files, reducing disk usage. For example, if you have Puppet reporting enabled, as described in the section on generating reports, you might want to regularly delete old report files.

How to do it...

Let's get started:

1. Modify your `site.pp` file as follows:

```
node 'cookbook' {
  tidy { '/var/log/audit':
    age     => '2w',
    recurse => true,
  }
}
```

2. Run Puppet:

```
[root@cookbook ~]# puppet agent -t
Notice:
/Stage[main]/Main/Node[cookbook]/File[/var/log/audit/audit.log.
1]/ensure: removed
```

How it works...

Puppet searches the specified path for any files matching the age parameter; in this case, 2w (two weeks). It also searches subdirectories (recurse => true).

Any files matching your criteria will be deleted.

There's more...

You can specify file ages in seconds, minutes, hours, days, or weeks by using a single character to specify the time unit, as follows:

- 60s
- 180m
- 24h
- 30d
- 4w

You can specify that files greater than a given size should be removed, as follows:

```
size => '100m',
```

This removes files of 100 megabytes and over. For kilobytes, use k, and for bytes, use b.

 Note that if you specify both age and size parameters, they are treated as independent criteria. For example, if you specify the following, Puppet will remove all files that are either at least one day old, or at least 512 KB in size:
```
age  => "1d",
size => "512k",
```

Auditing resources

Dry run mode, using the --noop switch, is a simple way to audit any changes to a machine under Puppet's control. However, Puppet also has a dedicated audit feature, which can report changes to resources or specific attributes.

How to do it...

Here's an example showing Puppet's auditing capabilities:

1. Modify your site.pp file as follows:

```
node 'cookbook' {
  file { '/etc/passwd':
    audit => [ owner, mode ],
  }
}
```

2. Run Puppet:

```
[root@cookbook ~]# puppet agent -t
...
Warning: /File[/etc/passwd]/audit: The `audit` metaparameter is
deprecated and will be ignored in a future release.
   (at
/etc/puppetlabs/code/environments/production/manifests/site.pp:
53)
```

```
Notice: /Stage[main]/Main/Node[cookbook]/Tidy[/var/log]:
Tidying 0 files
Info: Applying configuration version '1521221789'
Notice:
/Stage[main]/Main/Node[cookbook]/File[/etc/passwd]/owner: audit
change: newly-recorded value 0
Notice:
/Stage[main]/Main/Node[cookbook]/File[/etc/passwd]/mode: audit
change: newly-recorded value 0644
```

 The deprecation warning should be removed in future releases of Puppet5. The decision to deprecate `audit` was reverted in `https://tickets.puppetlabs.com/browse/PUP-893`.

How it works...

The `audit` metaparameter tells Puppet that you want to record and monitor certain things about the resource. The value can be a list of the parameters that you want to audit.

In this case, when Puppet runs, it will now record the owner and mode of the `/etc/passwd` file. In future runs, Puppet will spot whether either of these has changed. For example, try running the following:

```
[root@cookbook ~]# chmod 666 /etc/passwd
```

Puppet will pick up this change and log it on the next run:

```
Notice: /Stage[main]/Main/Node[cookbook]/File[/etc/passwd]/mode: audit
change: previously recorded value '0644' has been changed to '0666'
```

There's more...

This feature is very useful for auditing large networks for any changes to machines, either malicious or accidental. It's also very handy to keep an eye on things that aren't managed by Puppet, for example, application code on production servers.

 You can read more about Puppet's auditing capability at `http://puppet.com/blog/all-about-auditing-puppet/`.

If you just want to audit everything about a resource, use `all`:

```
file { '/etc/passwd':
  audit => all,
}
```

See also

- The *Doing a dry run* recipe in Chapter 10, *Monitoring, Reporting, and Troubleshooting*

Temporarily disabling resources

Sometimes, you want to disable a resource for a time so that it doesn't interfere with other work. For example, you might want to tweak a configuration file on the server until you have the exact settings you want, before checking it into Puppet. You don't want Puppet to overwrite it with an old version in the meantime, so you can set the `noop` metaparameter on the resource:

```
noop => true,
```

How to do it...

This example shows you how to use the `noop` metaparameter:

1. Modify your `site.pp` file as follows:

```
node 'cookbook' {
  file { '/etc/resolv.conf':
    content => "nameserver 127.0.0.1\n",
    noop    => true,
  }
}
```

2. Run Puppet:

```
[root@cookbook ~]# puppet agent -t
...
Notice:
/Stage[main]/Main/Node[cookbook]/File[/etc/resolv.conf]/content
:
```

```
--- /etc/resolv.conf 2018-03-15 16:12:55.727454381 +0000
+++ /tmp/puppet-file20180316-24960-1ioes0p 2018-03-16
07:57:56.690184900 +0000
@@ -1,3 +1 @@
-# Generated by NetworkManager
-search strangled.net example.com
-nameserver 10.0.2.3
+nameserver 127.0.0.1

Notice:
/Stage[main]/Main/Node[cookbook]/File[/etc/resolv.conf]/content
: current_value '{md5}7855b539f68427e8d999a6a6b1ce7adb', should
be '{md5}949343428bded6a653a85910f6bdb48e' (noop)
```

How it works...

The `noop` metaparameter is set to `true`, so for this particular resource, it's as if you had to run Puppet with the `--noop` flag. Puppet noted that the resource would have been applied, but otherwise did nothing.

The nice thing about running the agent in test mode (`-t`) is that Puppet gave a diff of what it would have done if the `noop` was not present (you can tell Puppet to show the diffs without using `-t` with `--show_diff`; `-t` implies many different settings):

```
--- /etc/resolv.conf 2018-03-15 16:12:55.727454381 +0000
+++ /tmp/puppet-file20180316-24960-1ioes0p 2018-03-16 07:57:56.690184900
+0000
@@ -1,3 +1 @@
-# Generated by NetworkManager
-search strangled.net example.com
-nameserver 10.0.2.3
+nameserver 127.0.0.1
```

This can be very useful when debugging a template; you can work on your changes and then see what they would look like on the node without actually applying them. Using the diff, you can see whether your updated template produces the correct output.

Managing Applications

7

In this chapter, we will cover the following recipes:

- Using public modules
- Managing Apache servers
- Creating Apache virtual hosts
- Creating NGINX virtual hosts
- Managing MariaDB
- Creating databases and users

Introduction

Without applications, a server is just a very expensive space heater. In this chapter, I'll present some recipes to manage some specific software with Puppet: MariaDB, Apache, NGINX, and Ruby. I hope the recipes will be useful to you in themselves. However, the patterns and techniques they use are applicable to almost any software, so you can adapt them to your own purposes without much difficulty. One thing that these applications have in common is: they are common. Most Puppet installations will have to deal with a web server, either Apache or NGINX. Most, if not all, will have databases and some of those will have MariaDB. When everyone has to deal with a problem, community solutions are generally better tested and more thorough than homegrown solutions. We'll use modules from the Puppet Forge in this chapter to manage these applications.

When you are writing your own `Apache` or `NGINX` modules from scratch, you'll have to pay attention to the nuances of the distributions you support. Some distributions call the Apache package `httpd`, while others use `apache2`; the same can be said for MySQL. In addition, Debian-based distributions use an enabled folder method to enable custom sites in Apache, which are virtual sites, whereas RPM-based distributions do not (for more information on virtual sites, visit `http://httpd.apache.org/docs/2.4/vhosts/`).

Using public modules

When you write a Puppet module to manage some software or service, you don't have to start from scratch. Community-contributed modules are available at the Puppet Forge site for many popular applications. Sometimes, a community module will be exactly what you need, and you can download and start using it straight away. In most cases, you will need to make some modifications to suit your particular needs and environment.

Like all community efforts, there are some excellent and some less-than-excellent modules on the Forge. You should read the README section of the module and decide whether the module is going to work in your installation. At the very least, ensure that your distribution is supported. puppetlabs has introduced a set of modules that are supported, that is, if you are an enterprise customer, they will support your use of the module in your installation. Additionally, most Forge modules deal with multiple operating systems, distributions, and a great number of use cases. In many cases, not using a Forge module is like reinventing the wheel. One caveat, though, is that Forge modules may be more complex than your local modules. You should read the code and get a sense of what the module is doing. Knowing how the module works will help you debug it later.

How to do it...

In this example, we'll use the puppet module command to find and install the useful stdlib module, which contains many utility functions to help you develop Puppet code. It is one of the aforementioned supported modules by puppetlabs. I'll download the module into my user's home directory and manually install it in the Git repository:

1. Run the following command:

   ```
   t@mylaptop $ puppet module search puppetlabs-stdlib
   Notice: Searching https://forgeapi.puppet.com ...
   NAME DESCRIPTION AUTHOR KEYWORDS
   puppetlabs-stdlib Standard libr... @puppetlabs stdlib
   trlinkin-validate_multi Validate that... @trlinkin dsl
   puppet-extlib extlib provid... @puppet stdlib
   ```

2. We verified that we have the right module, so we'll install it with module install:

   ```
   t@mylaptop ~ $ puppet module install puppetlabs-stdlib
   Notice: Preparing to install into
   ```

```
/home/thomas/.puppetlabs/etc/code/modules ...
Notice: Downloading from https://forgeapi.puppet.com ...
Notice: Installing -- do not interrupt ...
/home/thomas/.puppetlabs/etc/code/modules
└──── puppetlabs-stdlib (v4.25.0)
```

3. The module is now ready to use in your manifests; most good modules come with a `README.md` or `README` file to show you how to do this.

How it works...

You can search for modules that match the package or software you're interested in with the `puppet module search` command. To install a specific module, use `puppet module install`. You can add the `-i` option to tell Puppet where to find your module directory. You can browse the site to see what's available at `http://forge.puppet.com`. More information on supported modules is available at `https://forge.puppet.com/supported`. The current list of supported modules is available at `https://forge.puppetlabs.com/modules?endorsements=supported`.

There's more...

Modules on the Forge include a `metadata.json` file, which describes the module and which operating systems the module supports. This file also includes a list of modules that are required by the module. This file was previously named `Modulefile` and was not in JSON format; the old `Modulefile` format was deprecated in version 3.6. As we will see in our next section, when installing a module from the Forge, the required dependencies will automatically be installed as well. Not all publicly-available modules are on the Puppet Forge. Some other great places to look at on GitHub are as follows:

- `https://github.com/camptocamp`
- `https://github.com/example42`

Though not a collection of modules as such, the Puppet Cookbook website has many useful and illuminating code examples, patterns, and tips, maintained by the admirable Dean Wilson: `http://www.puppetcookbook.com/`

Managing Apache servers

Apache is the world's favorite web server, so it's highly likely that part of your Puppetly duties will include installing and managing Apache.

How to do it...

We'll install and use the `puppetlabs-apache` module to install and start Apache. This time, when we run the `puppet module install` command, we'll use the `-i` option to tell Puppet to install the module in our Git repository's module's directory:

1. Install the module using `puppet module install`:

```
t@mylaptop $ puppet module install -i modules puppetlabs-apache
Notice: Preparing to install into /home/thomas/puppet/modules
...
Notice: Downloading from https://forgeapi.puppet.com ...
Notice: Installing -- do not interrupt ...
/home/thomas/puppet/modules
└─┬ puppetlabs-apache (v3.1.0)
  ├── puppetlabs-concat (v4.2.1)
  └── puppetlabs-stdlib (v4.25.0)
```

2. Add the modules to your Git repository and push them out:

```
t@mylaptop $ git add modules
t@mylaptop $ git commit -m 'adding modules to repo'
[production 66f2ed5] adding modules to repo
 1052 files changed, 80823 insertions(+)
 create mode 100644 modules/apache/CHANGELOG.md
...
t@mylaptop $ git push origin production
...
remote: create mode 100644 modules/stdlib/types/windowspath.pp
To git.example.com:repos/puppet.git
 04178ab..66f2ed5 production -> production
```

3. Create a web server node definition in `site.pp`:

```
node webserver {
  class {'apache': }
}
```

4. Run Puppet to apply the default Apache module configuration:

```
[root@webserver ~]# puppet agent -t
Info: Caching certificate for webserver.example.com Info:
Caching certificate for webserver.example.com
Info: Using configured environment 'production' Info:
Retrieving pluginfacts
Info: Retrieving plugin Notice:
/File[/opt/puppetlabs/puppet/cache/lib/facter/apache_version.rb
]/ensure: defin
ed content as '{md5}2562993ee2b268e532b48cffc56bdaa0' Notice:
/File[/opt/puppetlabs/puppet/cache/lib/puppet/functions/apache]
/ensure: created
...
Info: Concat[15-default.conf]: Scheduling refresh of
Class[Apache::Service]
Info: Class[Apache::Service]: Scheduling refresh of
Service[httpd]
Notice: /Stage[main]/Apache::Service/Service[httpd]/ensure:
ensure changed 'stopped' to 'running'
Info: /Stage[main]/Apache::Service/Service[httpd]: Unscheduling
refresh on Service[httpd]
Notice: Applied catalog in 3.06 seconds
```

5. Verify that you can reach webserver.example.com:

```
[root@webserver ~]# curl http://webserver.example.com
<!DOCTYPE HTML PUBLIC "-//W3C//DTD HTML 3.2 Final//EN">
<html>
 <head>
  <title>Index of /</title>
 </head>
 <body>
<h1>Index of /</h1>
  <table>
   <tr><th valign="top"><img src="/icons/blank.gif"
alt="[ICO]"></th><th><a href="?C=N;O=D">Name</a></th><th><a
href="?C=M;O=A">Last modified</a></th><th><a
href="?C=S;O=A">Size</a></th><th><a
href="?C=D;O=A">Description</a></th></tr>
   <tr><th colspan="5"><hr></th></tr>
   <tr><th colspan="5"><hr></th></tr>
  </table>
</body></html>
```

How it works...

Installing the `puppetlabs-apache` module from the Forge causes both `puppetlabs-concat` and `puppetlabs-stdlib` to be installed into our modules directory. The `concat` module is used to stitch snippets of files together in a specific order. It is used by the Apache module to create the main Apache configuration files.

We then defined a web server node and applied the `apache` class to that node. We used all the default values and let the Apache module configure our server to be an Apache web server.

The Apache module then rewrote all our Apache configurations. By default, the module purges all the configuration files from the Apache directory (`/etc/apache2` or `/etc/httpd`, depending on the distribution). The module can configure many different distributions and handle the nuances of each distribution. As a user of the module, you don't need to know how your distribution deals with the Apache module configuration.

After purging and rewriting the configuration files, the module ensures that the `apache2` service is running (`httpd` on the test box based on **Enterprise Linux (EL)**).

We then tested the webserver using cURL. There was nothing returned but an empty index page. This is the expected behavior. Normally, when we install Apache on a server, there are some files that display a default page (`welcome.conf` on EL-based systems); since the module purged those configurations, we only see an empty page.

In a production environment, you would modify the defaults applied by the Apache module; the suggested configuration from the README is as follows:

```
class { 'apache':
  default_mods => false,
  default_confd_files => false,
}
```

Creating Apache virtual hosts

Apache virtual hosts are created with the `apache` module with
the `apache::vhost` defined type. We will create a new `vhost` on our Apache webserver
called `navajo`, after one of the Apache tribes.

How to do it...

Follow these steps to create Apache virtual hosts:

1. Create a `navajo apache::vhost` definition as follows:

```
apache::vhost { 'navajo.example.com':
  port => '80',
  docroot => '/var/www/navajo',
}
```

2. Create an index file for the new `vhost`:

```
$navajo = @(NAVAJO)
  <html>
    <head>
      <title>navajo.example.com</title>
    </head>
    <body>http://en.wikipedia. org/wiki/Navajo_people
    </body>
  </html>
  | NAVAJO
file {'/var/www/navajo/index.html':
  content => $navajo,
  mode => '0644',
  require => Apache::Vhost['navajo.example.com']
}
```

3. Run Puppet to create the new `vhost`:

```
[root@webserver ~]# puppet agent -t
Info: Caching catalog for webserver.example.com
...
Notice:
/Stage[main]/Main/Node[webserver]/Apache::Vhost[navajo.example.
com]/File[/var/www/navajo]/ensure: created
Notice:
/Stage[main]/Main/Node[webserver]/Apache::Vhost[navajo.example.
com]/Concat[25-
navajo.example.com.conf]/File[/etc/httpd/conf.d/25-
navajo.example.com.conf]/ensure: defined content as
'{md5}c2c851756828cc876e0cadb159d573fa'
Info: Concat[25-navajo.example.com.conf]: Scheduling refresh of
Class[Apache::Service]
Info: Class[Apache::Service]: Scheduling refresh of
Service[httpd]
```

4. Verify that you can reach the new virtual host:

```
[root@webserver ~]# curl http://navajo.example.com
<html>
 <head>
 <title>navajo.example.com</title>
 </head>
 <body>http://en.wikipedia. org/wiki/Navajo_people
 </body>
</html>
```

You will need navajo.example.com to resolve to your host; you can create a host entry with the following snippet:

host { 'navajo.example.com': ip => '127.0.0.1' }

Alternatively, you can specify how to reach navajo.example.com when issuing the curl command, as follows:

curl -H 'Host: navajo.example.com' http://127.0.0.1

How it works...

The apache::vhost defined type creates a virtual host configuration file for Apache, 25-navajo.example.com.conf. The file is created with a template; 25 at the beginning of the filename is the priority level of this virtual host. When Apache first starts, it reads through its configuration directory and starts executing files in alphabetical order. Files that begin with numbers are read before files that start with letters. In this way, the Apache module ensures that the virtual hosts are read in a specific order, which can be specified when you define the virtual host. The contents of this file are as follows:

```
# ********************************
# Vhost template in module puppetlabs-apache
# Managed by Puppet
# ********************************
<VirtualHost *:80>
 ServerName navajo.example.com
## Vhost docroot
 DocumentRoot "/var/www/navajo"
## Directories, there should at least be a declaration for /var/www/navajo
<Directory "/var/www/navajo">
 Options Indexes FollowSymLinks MultiViews
 AllowOverride None
 Require all granted
```

```
    </Directory>
  ## Logging
  ErrorLog "/var/log/httpd/navajo.example.com_error.log"
  ServerSignature Off
  CustomLog "/var/log/httpd/navajo.example.com_access.log" combined
</VirtualHost>
```

As you can see, the default file has created log files and set up directory access permissions and options, in addition to specifying the listen port and `DocumentRoot`.

The `vhost` definition creates the `DocumentRoot` directory, specified as `root` to the `apache::virtual` definition. The directory is created before the virtual host configuration file; after that file has been created, a `notify` trigger is sent to the Apache process to restart.

Our manifest included a file that required the `Apache::Vhost['navajo.example.com']` resource; our file was then created after the directory and the virtual host configuration file.

When we run cURL on the new website, we see the contents of the index file that we created.

There's more...

Both the defined type and the template take into account a multitude of possible configuration scenarios for virtual hosts. It is highly unlikely that you will find a setting that is not covered by this module. You should look at the definition for `apache::virtual` and the sheer number of possible arguments.

The module also takes care of several settings for you. For instance, if we change the listen port on our navajo virtual host from `80` to `8080`, the module will make the following changes in `/etc/httpd/conf.d/ports.conf`:

```
-Listen 80
+Listen 8080
-NameVirtualHost *:80
+NameVirtualHost *:8080
```

And it will make these changes in our virtual host file:

```
-<VirtualHost *:80>
+<VirtualHost *:8080>
```

After a `puppet` run on our web server, we would now be able to `curl` on port 8080 and see the same results:

```
[root@webserver ~]# curl http://navajo.example.com:8080
<html>
 <head>
 <title>navajo.example.com</title>
 </head>
 <body>http://en.wikipedia. org/wiki/Navajo_people
 </body>
</html>
```

And when we use `curl` to connect to `najavo.example.com` on `port 80`, we see the following:

```
[root@webserver ~]# curl http://navajo.example.com
<!DOCTYPE HTML PUBLIC "-//W3C//DTD HTML 3.2 Final//EN">
<html>
 <head>
  <title>Index of /</title>
 </head>
 <body>
<h1>Index of /</h1>
  <table>
   <tr><th valign="top"><img src="/icons/blank.gif" alt="[ICO]"></th><th><a
href="?C=N;O=D">Name</a></th><th><a href="?C=M;O=A">Last
modified</a></th><th><a href="?C=S;O=A">Size</a></th><th><a
href="?C=D;O=A">Description</a></th></tr>
   <tr><th colspan="5"><hr></th></tr>
   <tr><th colspan="5"><hr></th></tr>
</table>
</body></html>
```

As we can see, the virtual host is no longer listening on port 80 and we receive the default empty directory listing we saw in our earlier example.

Creating NGINX virtual hosts

NGINX is a fast, lightweight web server that is preferred over Apache in many contexts, especially where high performance is important. NGINX is configured slightly differently than Apache; like Apache though, there is a Forge module that can be used to configure NGINX for us. Unlike Apache, however, the module that is suggested for use is not supplied by puppetlabs, but by James Fryman. This module uses some interesting tricks to configure itself. Previous versions of this module used R.I. Pienaar's `module_data` `package`. This package is used to configure `hieradata` within a module. It's used to supply default values to the `nginx` module. I wouldn't recommend starting out with this module at this point, but it is a good example of where module configuration may be headed in the future. Giving modules the ability to modify hieradata may prove useful.

How to do it...

In this example, we'll use a Forge module to configure NGINX. We'll download the module and use it to configure `virtualhosts`:

1. Download the `puppet-nginx` module from the Forge:

```
t@mylaptop $ puppet module install -i modules puppet-nginx
Notice: Preparing to install into /home/thomas/puppet/modules
...
Notice: Created target directory /home/thomas/puppet/modules
Notice: Downloading from https://forgeapi.puppet.com ...
Notice: Installing -- do not interrupt ...
/home/thomas/puppet/modules
└─┬ puppet-nginx (v0.11.0)
  ├── puppetlabs-concat (v4.2.1)
[/home/thomas/.puppetlabs/etc/code/modules]
  └── puppetlabs-stdlib (v4.25.0)
[/home/thomas/.puppetlabs/etc/code/modules]
```

2. Replace the definition for webserver with an `nginx` configuration:

```
node webserver {
  service {'httpd': ensure => false }
  class {'nginx': }
  nginx::resource::server{ 'mescalero.example.com':
    www_root => '/var/www/mescalero',
  }
  file {'/var/www/mescalero':
    ensure => 'directory',
    mode => '0755',
    require =>
Nginx::Resource::Server['mescalero.example.com'],
  }
  $mescalero = @(MESCALERO)
    <html>
      <head>
        <title>mescalero.example.com</title>
      </head>
      <body>
        http:// en.wikipedia.org/wiki/Mescalero
      </body>
    </html>
    | MESCALERO
  file {'/var/www/mescalero/index.html':
    content => $mescalero,
    mode => '0644',
    require => File['/var/www/mescalero'],
  }
}
```

3. Run `puppet agent` on your `webserver` node:

```
[root@webserver ~]# puppet agent -t
...
Info: Caching catalog for webserver.example.com [87/1835]
Info: Applying configuration version '1522256325'
Notice:
/Stage[main]/Main/Node[webserver]/Service[httpd]/ensure: ensure
changed 'running' to 'stopped'
Notice: /Stage[main]/Nginx::Package::Redhat/Yumrepo[nginx-
release]/ensure: created
Info: Yumrepo[nginx-release] (provider=inifile): changing mode
of /etc/yum.repos.d/nginx-release.repo from 600 to 6$
4
Notice:
/Stage[main]/Nginx::Package::Redhat/Package[nginx]/ensure:
```

```
created
Info: Class[Nginx::Package]: Scheduling refresh of
Class[Nginx::Service]
Notice:
/Stage[main]/Nginx::Config/File[/etc/nginx/conf.stream.d]/ensur
e: created
Notice:
/Stage[main]/Nginx::Config/File[/etc/nginx/conf.mail.d]/ensure:
created
...
Notice:
/Stage[main]/Nginx::Config/File[/etc/nginx/nginx.conf]/content:
--- /etc/nginx/nginx.conf 2017-10-17 13:21:13.000000000 +0000
+++ /tmp/puppet-file20180328-19387-1bx1j5k 2018-03-28
17:00:01.290886282 +0000
@@ -1,32 +1,64 @@
+# MANAGED BY PUPPET
+user nginx;
...
Notice:
/Stage[main]/Main/Node[webserver]/Nginx::Resource::Server[mesca
lero.example.com]/Concat[/etc/nginx/sites-av
ailable/mescalero.example.com.conf]/File[/etc/nginx/sites-
available/mescalero.example.com.conf]/ensure: defined con
tent as '{md5}69f8354a0f61a5175e3c2e6ee195262a'
Info: Concat[/etc/nginx/sites-
available/mescalero.example.com.conf]: Scheduling refresh of
Class[Nginx::Service]
Notice:
/Stage[main]/Main/Node[webserver]/Nginx::Resource::Server[mesca
lero.example.com]/File[mescalero.example.com
.conf symlink]/ensure: created
Info:
/Stage[main]/Main/Node[webserver]/Nginx::Resource::Server[mesca
lero.example.com]/File[mescalero.example.com.c
onf symlink]: Scheduling refresh of Class[Nginx::Service]
Info: Class[Nginx::Service]: Scheduling refresh of
Service[nginx]
Notice: /Stage[main]/Nginx::Service/Service[nginx]/ensure:
ensure changed 'stopped' to 'running'
Info: /Stage[main]/Nginx::Service/Service[nginx]: Unscheduling
refresh on Service[nginx]
Notice:
/Stage[main]/Main/Node[webserver]/File[/var/www/mescalero]/ensu
re: created
Notice:
/Stage[main]/Main/Node[webserver]/File[/var/www/mescalero/index
.html]/ensu
```

```
re: defined content as '{md5}cb3f
6427eb6923b58fa159916ef296f6'
Notice: Applied catalog in 18.53 seconds
```

4. Verify that you can reach the new `virtualhost`:

```
[root@webserver ~]# curl -H 'Host: mescalero.example.com'
http://127.0.0.1
<html>
 <head>
 <title>mescalero.example.com</title>
 </head>
 <body>
 http:// en.wikipedia.org/wiki/Mescalero
 </body>
</html>
```

How it works...

Installing the `puppet-nginx` module causes the `concat` and `stdlib` modules to be installed (we already had a copy of `stdlib`, so all this did was verify we had it). We run Puppet on our master to have the plugins created by these modules added to our running master. The `stdlib` and `concat` have facter and Puppet plugins that need to be installed for the NGINX module to work properly.

With the plugins synchronized, we can then run the Puppet agent on our web server. As a precaution, we add a resource to stop Apache if it was previously started (we can't have NGINX and Apache both listening on port `80`). After the puppet agent runs, we verified that NGINX was running and the virtual host was configured.

There's more...

This module had a lot of interesting things like the `apache` modules, the `NGINX` module can be used to create very complex configurations. One interesting option is the ability to configured `NGINX` as a proxy server in only a few lines of code. I suggest looking at the `README.md` of the module or the module page on the forge at `https://forge.puppet.com/puppet/nginx`

In the next section, we'll use a supported module to configure and manage MySQL installations.

Managing MariaDB

MySQL is a very widely used database server, and you'll probably need to install and configure a MySQL server at some point. On January 27, 2010, Oracle bought Sun Microsystems. Sun Microsystems originally developed MySQL. When Oracle took over, the project was forked into MariaDB. MariaDB was made to keep the MySQL server open source and maintained. When we use the `puppetlabs-mysql` module, we will actually be installing MariaDB. The `puppetlabs-mysql` module can simplify your MariaDB deployments.

How to do it...

Follow these steps to create the example:

1. Install the `puppetlabs-mysql` module:

```
t@burnaby $ puppet module install -i modules puppetlabs-mysql
Notice: Preparing to install into /home/thomas/puppet/modules
...
Notice: Downloading from https://forgeapi.puppet.com ...
Notice: Installing -- do not interrupt ...
/home/thomas/puppet/modules
└──┬ puppetlabs-mysql (v5.3.0)
   ├── puppet-staging (v3.1.0)
   ├── puppetlabs-stdlib (v4.25.0)
   └── puppetlabs-translate (v1.1.0)
```

2. Create a new node definition for your MySQL server:

```
node dbserver {
  class { 'mysql::server':
      root_password => 'PacktPub',
    override_options => {
            'mysqld' => {
  'max_connections' => '1024'
      }
    }
  }
}
```

3. Run Puppet to install the database server and apply the new root password:

```
Info: Applying configuration version '1522263661'
Notice: /Stage[main]/Mysql::Server::Config/File[mysql-config-
file]/ensure: defined content as
'{md5}15d890f0648fc49e43fcffc6ed7bd2d8'
Notice: /Stage[main]/Mysql::Server::Install/Package[mysql-
server]/ensure: created
Notice:
/Stage[main]/Mysql::Server::Installdb/Mysql_datadir[/var/lib/my
sql]/ensure: created
Notice:
/Stage[main]/Mysql::Server::Service/Service[mysqld]/ensure:
ensure changed 'stopped' to 'running'
Info: /Stage[main]/Mysql::Server::Service/Service[mysqld]:
Unscheduling refresh on Service[mysqld]
Notice:
/Stage[main]/Mysql::Server::Root_password/Mysql_user[root@local
host]/password_hash: defined 'password_hash' as
'*6ABB0D4A7D1381BAEE4D078354557D495ACFC059'
Notice:
/Stage[main]/Mysql::Server::Root_password/File[/root/.my.cnf]/e
nsure: defined content as
'{md5}a65d0eb64218eebf5eeed997de0e72a8'
Info: Creating state file
/opt/puppetlabs/puppet/cache/state/state.yaml
Notice: Applied catalog in 16.42 seconds
```

4. Verify that you can connect to the database:

```
[root@dbserver ~]# mysql
Welcome to the MariaDB monitor. Commands end with ; or \g.
Your MariaDB connection id is 10
Server version: 5.5.56-MariaDB MariaDB Server

Copyright (c) 2000, 2017, Oracle, MariaDB Corporation Ab and
others.

Type 'help;' or '\h' for help. Type '\c' to clear the current
input statement.

MariaDB [(none)]> \q
Bye
```

How it works...

The MySQL module installs the MariaDB server and ensures that the server is running. It then configures the root password for MariaDB. The module does a lot of other things for you as well. It creates a `.my.cnf` file with the root user password. When we run the `mysql client`, the `.my.cnf` file sets all the defaults, so we do not need to supply any arguments.

There's more...

In the next section, we'll show you how to create databases and users.

Creating databases and users

Managing a database means more than ensuring the service is running; a database server is nothing without databases. Databases need users and privileges. Privileges are handled with GRANT statements. We will use the `puppetlabs-mysql` package to create a database and a user with access to that database. We'll create a MariaDB user, `drupal`, and a database, called `drupal`. We'll create a `nodes` table within the `drupal` database and place data into that table.

How to do it...

Follow these steps to create the databases and users:

1. Create a database definition within your `dbserver` class:

```
mysql::db { 'drupal':
  host     => 'localhost',
  user     => 'drupal',
  password => 'Cookbook',
  sql      => '/root/drupal.sql',
  require  => File['/root/drupal.sql']
}
$drupal = @(DRUPAL)
  CREATE TABLE users (
    id INT PRIMARY KEY AUTO_INCREMENT,
    title VARCHAR(255),
    body TEXT);
  INSERT INTO users (id, title, body) VALUES (1,'First
Node','Contents of first Node');
```

```
    INSERT INTO users (id, title, body) VALUES (2,'Second
Node','Contents of second Node');
  | DRUPAL
file { '/root/drupal.sql':
  ensure  => present,
  content => $drupal,
}
```

2. Allow the Drupal user to modify the nodes table:

```
mysql_grant { 'drupal@localhost/drupal.nodes':
  ensure     => 'present',
  options    => ['GRANT'],
  privileges => ['ALL'],
  table      => 'drupal.nodes',
  user       => 'drupal@localhost',
}
```

3. Run Puppet to have the user, database, and GRANT created:

```
[root@dbserver ~]# puppet agent -t
Info: Using configured environment 'production'
Info: Retrieving pluginfacts
Info: Retrieving plugin
Info: Loading facts
Info: Caching catalog for dbserver.example.com
Info: Applying configuration version '1522266120'
Notice:
/Stage[main]/Main/Node[dbserver]/File[/root/drupal.sql]/ensure:
defined content as '{md5}f0f695b4b093cd225da626ae207f425a'
Notice:
/Stage[main]/Main/Node[dbserver]/Mysql::Db[drupal]/Mysql_databa
se[drupal]/ensure: created
Info:
/Stage[main]/Main/Node[dbserver]/Mysql::Db[drupal]/Mysql_databa
se[drupal]: Scheduling refresh of Exec[drupal-import]
Notice:
/Stage[main]/Main/Node[dbserver]/Mysql::Db[drupal]/Mysql_user[d
rupal@localhost]/ensure: created
Notice:
/Stage[main]/Main/Node[dbserver]/Mysql_grant[drupal@localhost/d
rupal.nodes]/ensure: created
Notice:
/Stage[main]/Main/Node[dbserver]/Mysql::Db[drupal]/Mysql_grant[
drupal@localhost/drupal.*]/ensure: created
```

```
Notice:
/Stage[main]/Main/Node[dbserver]/Mysql::Db[drupal]/Exec[drupal-
import]: Triggered 'refresh' from 1 event
Notice: Applied catalog in 0.32 seconds
```

4. Verify that the database and table have been created:

```
[root@dbserver ~]# mysql -u drupal -pCookbook drupal
Reading table information for completion of table and column
names
You can turn off this feature to get a quicker startup with -A

Welcome to the MariaDB monitor. Commands end with ; or \g.
Your MariaDB connection id is 40
Server version: 5.5.56-MariaDB MariaDB Server

Copyright (c) 2000, 2017, Oracle, MariaDB Corporation Ab and
others.

Type 'help;' or '\h' for help. Type '\c' to clear the current
input statement.

MariaDB [drupal]> show tables;
+-------------------+
| Tables_in_drupal |
+-------------------+
| users |
+-------------------+
1 row in set (0.00 sec)
```

5. Verify that our default data has been loaded into the table:

```
MariaDB [drupal]> select * from users;
+----+-------------+--------------------------+
| id | title | body |
+----+-------------+--------------------------+
| 1 | First Node | Contents of first Node |
| 2 | Second Node | Contents of second Node |
+----+-------------+--------------------------+
2 rows in set (0.00 sec)

MariaDB [drupal]> \q
Bye
```

How it works...

We will start with the definition of the new `drupal` database:

```
mysql::db { 'drupal':
  host     => 'localhost',
  user     => 'drupal',
  password => 'Cookbook',
  sql      => '/root/drupal.sql',
  require  => File['/root/drupal.sql']
}
```

We specify that we'll connect from `localhost` using the `drupal` user. We give the password for the user and specify a SQL file that will be applied to the database after the database has been created. We require that the SQL file exists before we create the user; that way, the CREATE TABLE in the SQL file can be executed:

```
$drupal = @(DRUPAL)
  CREATE TABLE users (
    id INT PRIMARY KEY AUTO_INCREMENT,
    title VARCHAR(255),
    body TEXT);
  INSERT INTO users (id, title, body) VALUES (1,'First Node','Contents of
first Node');
  INSERT INTO users (id, title, body) VALUES (2,'Second Node','Contents of
second Node');
  | DRUPAL
file { '/root/drupal.sql':
  ensure  => present,
  content => $drupal,
}
```

We then ensure that the user has the appropriate privileges with a `mysql_grant` resource:

```
mysql_grant { 'drupal@localhost/drupal.nodes':
  ensure     => 'present',
  options    => ['GRANT'],
  privileges => ['ALL'],
  table      => 'drupal.nodes',
  user       => 'drupal@localhost',
}
```

There's more...

Using the `puppetlabs-mysql` and `puppetlabs-apache` modules, we can create an entire functioning web server. The `puppetlabs-apache` module will install Apache, and we can include the PHP module as well. We can then use the `puppetlabs-mysql` module to install the MariaDB server, and then create the required Drupal databases and seed the database with the data.

Deploying a new Drupal installation would be as simple as including a class on a node. There are numerous examples on the web of this workflow. Systems such as Wordpress and Django can be installed from scratch in this way.

8
Servers and Cloud Infrastructure

In this chapter, we will cover the following recipes:

- Managing firewalls with iptables
- Building high-availability services using Keepalived
- Managing NFS servers and file shares
- Using HAProxy to load balance multiple web servers
- Managing Docker with Puppet

Introduction

As powerful as Puppet is managing the configuration of a single server, it's even more useful when coordinating many machines. In this chapter, we'll explore different ways to use Puppet to help you create high-availability clusters, share files across your network, set up automated firewalls, use load balancing to get more out of the machines you have, and create new virtual machines on the cloud and your desktop. We'll use exported resources to communicate between nodes.

Managing firewalls with iptables

In this chapter, we will begin to configure services that require communication between hosts over a network. Most Linux distributions will default to running a host-based firewall, iptables or firewalld. If you want your hosts to communicate with each other, you have two options: turn off iptables or configure iptables to allow the communication.

I prefer to leave iptables turned on and configure access. Keeping iptables is just another layer in your defence across the network. Host-based firewalls aren't a magic solution that will make your system secure, but they will block access to services you didn't intend to expose to the network.

Configuring iptables properly is a complicated task, which requires a deep understanding of networking. The example presented here is a simplification. If you are unfamiliar with iptables, I suggest you research them before continuing. More information can be found at `http://wiki.centos.org/HowTos/Network/IPTables` or `https://help. ubuntu.com/ community/IptablesHowTo`. For more information on firewalld, consult `http://www. firewalld.org/documentation/`. The current version of the `puppetlabs-firewall` module disables firewalld on Red Hat/Fedora systems.

Getting ready

In the following examples, we'll be using the Puppet Labs `firewall` module to configure iptables. Prepare by installing the module in your Git repository with `puppet module install`:

```
t@mylaptop ~ $ puppet module install -i ~/puppet/modules puppetlabs-
firewall
Notice: Preparing to install into /home/thomas/puppet/modules ...
Notice: Downloading from https://forgeapi.puppet.com ...
Notice: Installing -- do not interrupt ...
/home/thomas/puppet/modules
└─┬ puppetlabs-firewall (v1.12.0)
  └── puppetlabs-stdlib (v4.25.0)
```

How to do it...

To configure the `firewall` module, we need to create a set of rules, which will be applied before all other rules. As a simple example, we'll create the following rules:

- Allow all traffic on the loopback (`lo`) interface
- Allow all ICMP traffic
- Allow all traffic that is part of an established connection (ESTABLISHED, RELATED)
- Allow all TCP traffic to port 22 (`ssh`)

We will create a `myfw` (my firewall) class to configure the `firewall` module. We will then apply the `myfw` class to a node to have iptables configured on that node:

1. Create a class to contain these rules and call it `myfw::pre`:

```
class myfw::pre {
 Firewall {
 require => undef,
 }

 firewall { '0000 Allow all traffic on loopback':
 proto   => 'all',
 iniface => 'lo',
 action  => 'accept',
 }
 firewall { '0001 Allow all ICMP':
 proto  => 'icmp',
 action => 'accept',
 }
 firewall { '0002 Allow all established traffic':
 proto  => 'all',
 state  => ['RELATED', 'ESTABLISHED'],
 action => 'accept',
 }
 firewall { '0022 Allow all TCP on port 22 (ssh)':
 proto  => 'tcp',
 dport  => '22',
 action => 'accept',
 }
}
```

2. When traffic doesn't match any of the previous rules, we want a final rule that will drop the traffic. Create the `myfw::post` class to contain the default drop rule:

```
class myfw::post {
  firewall { '8999 Drop all other traffic':
    proto  => 'all',
    action => 'drop',
    before => undef,
  }
}
```

Previous versions of this book used `9999` for the rule number here. However, there a bug occurs when using that number (`https://tickets.puppetlabs.com/browse/MODULES-6340`). 8999 appears to be the highest number that can used at the moment.

3. Create a `myfw` class, which will include `myfw::pre` and `myfw::post` to configure the firewall:

```
class myfw {
  include firewall
  # our rulesets
  include myfw::post
  include myfw::pre

  # clear all the rules
  resources { "firewall":
  purge => true
  }

  # resource defaults
  Firewall {
  before  => Class['myfw::post'],
  require => Class['myfw::pre'],
  }
}
```

4. Attach the `myfw` class to a node definition; I'll do this to my cookbook node:

```
node cookbook {
   include myfw
}
```

5. Run Puppet on `cookbook` to see whether the firewall rules have been applied:

```
[root@cookbook ~]# puppet agent -t
...
Info: Caching catalog for cookbook.example.com
Info: Applying configuration version '1522695427'
Notice: /Stage[main]/Myfw::Post/Firewall[8999 Drop all other
traffic]/ensure: created
```

```
Notice:
/Stage[main]/Firewall::Linux::Redhat/File[/etc/sysconfig/iptabl
es]/seluser: seluser changed 'unconfined_u' to 'system_u'
Notice:
/Stage[main]/Firewall::Linux::Redhat/File[/etc/sysconfig/iptabl
es]/seltype: seltype changed 'etc_t' to 'system_conf_t'
Notice:
/Stage[main]/Firewall::Linux::Redhat/File[/etc/sysconfig/ip6tab
les]/seluser: seluser changed 'unconfined_u' to 'system_u'
Notice:
/Stage[main]/Firewall::Linux::Redhat/File[/etc/sysconfig/ip6tab
les]/seltype: seltype changed 'etc_t' to 'system_conf_t'
Notice: Applied catalog in 0.24 seconds
```

6. Verify the new rules with `iptables-save`

```
[root@cookbook ~]# iptables-save
# Generated by iptables-save v1.4.21 on Mon Apr 2 19:02:19 2018
*filter
:INPUT ACCEPT [0:0]
:FORWARD ACCEPT [0:0]
:OUTPUT ACCEPT [60:26281]
-A INPUT -i lo -m comment --comment "0000 Allow all traffic on
loopback" -j ACCEPT
-A INPUT -p icmp -m comment --comment "0001 Allow all ICMP" -j
ACCEPT
-A INPUT -m state --state RELATED,ESTABLISHED -m comment --
comment "0002 Allow all established traffic" -j ACCEPT
-A INPUT -p tcp -m multiport --dports 22 -m comment --comment
"0022 Allow all TCP on port 22 (ssh)" -j ACCEPT
-A INPUT -m comment --comment "8999 Drop all other traffic" -j
DROP
COMMIT
# Completed on Mon Apr 2 19:02:19 2018
# Generated by iptables-save v1.4.7 on Sun Nov 9 01:18:30 2014
```

How it works...

This is a great example of how to use metaparameters to achieve complex ordering with little effort. Our myfw module achieves the following configuration:

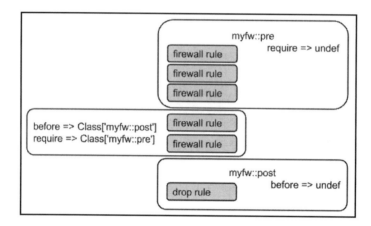

All the rules in the myfw::pre module are guaranteed to come *before* any other firewall rules we define. The rules in myfw::post are guaranteed to come *after* any other firewall rules. So, we have the rules in myfw::pre first, then any other rules, followed by the rules in myfw::post.

Our definition for the myfw class sets up this dependency with resource defaults:

```
# resource defaults
Firewall {
  before  => Class['myfw::post'],
  require => Class['myfw::pre'],
}
```

These defaults first tell Puppet that any firewall resource should be executed before anything in the myfw::post class. Then, they tell Puppet that any firewall resource should require that the resources in myfw::pre already have been executed.

When we defined the myfw::pre class, we removed the require statement in a random resource default. This ensures that the resources within the pre class don't require themselves before executing (Puppet will complain that we created a circular dependency otherwise):

```
Firewall {
  require => undef,
}
```

We use the same trick in our `myfw::post` definition. In this case, we only have a single rule in the `post` class, so we simply remove the `before` requirement:

```
firewall { '8999 Drop all other traffic':
  proto  => 'all',
  action => 'drop',
  before => undef,
}
```

Finally, we include a rule to purge all the existing iptables rules on the system. We do this to ensure that we have a consistent set of rules; only rules defined in Puppet will persist:

```
# clear all the rules
resources { "firewall":
  purge => true
}
```

`purge` is a metatype, it is mainly used to purge other resources. More information is available at `https://puppet.com/docs/puppet/5.3/type.html#resources`.

There's more...

As we suggested, we can now define firewall resources in our manifests and have them applied to the iptables configuration after the initialization rules (`myfw::pre`) but before the final drop (`myfw::post`). For example, to allow HTTP traffic on our cookbook machine, modify the node definition as follows:

```
include myfw
firewall {'0080 Allow HTTP':
  proto  => 'tcp',
  action => 'accept',
  dport  => 80,
}
```

Run Puppet on cookbook:

```
[root@cookbook ~]# puppet agent -t
...
Info: Caching catalog for cookbook.example.com
Info: Applying configuration version '1522697815'
Notice: /Stage[main]/Main/Node[cookbook]/Firewall[0080 Allow HTTP]/ensure:
created
Notice:
```

```
/Stage[main]/Firewall::Linux::Redhat/File[/etc/sysconfig/iptables]/seluser:
seluser changed 'unconfined_u' to 'system_u'
Notice:
/Stage[main]/Firewall::Linux::Redhat/File[/etc/sysconfig/iptables]/seltype:
seltype changed 'etc_t' to 'system_conf_t'
Notice: Applied catalog in 0.24 seconds
```

Verify that the new rule has been added after the last `myfw::pre` rule (`dports 22, ssh`):

```
[root@cookbook ~]# iptables-save
. . .
-A INPUT -p tcp -m multiport --dports 22 -m comment --comment "0022 Allow
all TCP on port 22 (ssh)" -j ACCEPT
-A INPUT -p tcp -m multiport --dports 80 -m comment --comment "0080 Allow
HTTP" -j ACCEPT
```

The Puppet Labs `firewall` module has a built-in notion to put all of our firewall resource titles that begin with a number in order. This is a requirement. The module attempts to order resources based on their title. You should keep this in mind when naming your firewall resources.

In a production environment, it is useful to have firewall rules adjusted automatically using exported resources. For example, if you had a service that would only allow client connections from registered clients, you could have clients create an exported firewall rule, as follows:

```
@@firewall {"0099 Allow ${facts['hostname']} to foo":
  proto  => 'tcp',
  action => 'accept',
  source => $facts['ipaddress'],
  tag    => 'foo',
}
```

On the server, you would then create a collector for the firewall resources:

```
Firewall <<| tag == 'foo' |>>
```

In the next section, we'll use our `firewall` module to ensure that two nodes can communicate as required.

Building high-availability services using Keepalived

High-availability services are those that can survive the failure of an individual machine or network connection. The primary technique for high availability is redundancy, otherwise known as **throwing hardware at the problem**. Although the eventual failure of an individual server is certain, the simultaneous failure of two servers is unlikely enough that this provides a good level of redundancy for most applications.

One of the simplest ways to build a redundant pair of servers is to have them share an IP address using Keepalived. Keepalived is a daemon that runs on both machines and exchanges regular messages between the two. One of those servers is the primary one and normally has the virtual IP address (VIP). If the secondary server fails to detect the primary server, it can take over the VIP, ensuring continuity of service. In real-world scenarios, you may want more machines involved in the VIP, but for this example, two machines works well enough.

In this recipe, we'll set up two machines in this configuration using Puppet, and I'll explain how to use it to provide a high-availability service.

 In previous releases of this book, we used heartbeat in place of Keepalived. More information on heartbeat is available at `http://www.linux-ha.org/wiki/Heartbeat`. Heartbeat has been replaced by pacemaker, so new installations should be using pacemaker. More information can be found at `http://clusterlabs.org/`.

Getting ready

You'll need two machines, of course, and an extra IP address to use as the VIP. You can usually request this from your ISP, if necessary. In this example, I'll be using machines named `cookbook` and `cookbook2`, with `cookbook` being the primary. We'll add the hosts to the Keepalived configuration.

How to do it...

Follow these steps to build the example:

1. Create the `modules/keepalived/manifests/init.pp` file with the following contents:

```
class keepalived (
  String $interface = 'eth1',
  String $real_name = 'cookbook.example.com',
  Array $real_servers = {},
  String $auth_pass = 'PacktPub',
  String $vip = '',
) {

  package {'ipvsadm':
    ensure => 'installed',
  }
  package {'keepalived':
    ensure => 'installed',
  }
  service {'keepalived':
    ensure  => 'running',
    enable  => true,
    require => Package['keepalived'],
  }

  if $facts['hostname'] == 'cookbook' {
    $state = 'MASTER'
    $virtual_router_id = 50
    $priority = 150
  } else {
    $state = 'BACKUP'
    $virtual_router_id = 50
    $priority = 149
  }
  file {'/etc/keepalived/keepalived.conf':
    content => epp('keepalived/keepalived.conf.epp'),
    mode    => '0644',
    notify  => Service['keepalived'],
  }
}
```

2. Create the `modules/templates/keepalived.conf.epp` template with the following contents:

```
global_defs {
}

vrrp_script check_true {
  script "/sbin/true"
  interval 2
  weight 2
}

vrrp_instance VIP_KEEPALIVED {
  state <%= $keepalived::state %>
  interface <%= $keepalived::interface %>
  virtual_router_id <%= $keepalived::virtual_router_id %>
  priority <%= $keepalived::priority %>
  advert_int 1
  authentication {
    auth_type PASS
    auth_pass <%= $keepalived::auth_pass %>
  }
  virtual_ipaddress {
    <%= $keepalived::vip %>
  }
  track_script {
    check_true
  }
  track_interface { <%= $keepalived::interface %> }
}
```

3. Modify your `site.pp` file as follows. We populate `real_servers` with the IP addresses of our cookbook servers and `vip` with our VIP:

```
node cookbook,cookbook2 {
  class { 'keepalived':
    real_servers => ['192.168.50.10','192.168.50.8'],
    vip          => '192.168.50.200',
  }
}
```

4. Run Puppet on each of the two servers:

```
[root@cookbook ~]# puppet agent -t
Info: Applying configuration version '1523034790'
Notice: /Stage[main]/Keepalived/Package[ipvsadm]/ensure:
created
Notice: /Stage[main]/Keepalived/Package[keepalived]/ensure:
created
Info: Computing checksum on file
/etc/keepalived/keepalived.conf
Info:
/Stage[main]/Keepalived/File[/etc/keepalived/keepalived.conf]:
Filebucketed /etc/keepalived/keepalived.conf t
o puppet with sum 968d3992f248f7c764c5d91c84db4f3f
Notice:
/Stage[main]/Keepalived/File[/etc/keepalived/keepalived.conf]/c
ontent: content changed '{md5}968d3992f248f7
c764c5d91c84db4f3f' to '{md5}a816083a30ed5a39d13841794673993a'
Info:
/Stage[main]/Keepalived/File[/etc/keepalived/keepalived.conf]:
Scheduling refresh of Service[keepalived]
Notice: /Stage[main]/Keepalived/Service[keepalived]/ensure:
ensure changed 'stopped' to 'running'
Info: /Stage[main]/Keepalived/Service[keepalived]: Unscheduling
refresh on Service[keepalived]
Notice: Applied catalog in 38.18 seconds

[root@cookbook2 ~]# puppet agent -t
...
Info:
/Stage[main]/Keepalived/File[/etc/keepalived/keepalived.conf]:
Scheduling refresh of Service[keepalived]
Notice: /Stage[main]/Keepalived/Service[keepalived]: Triggered
'refresh' from 1 event
Notice: Applied catalog in 9.48 seconds
```

The VIP should be on cookbook at this point; note that you will need to use the `ip` command as `ifconfig` will not show the address.

5. Verify that the VIP is running on one of the nodes:

```
[root@cookbook ~]# ip addr show dev eth1
3: eth1: <BROADCAST,MULTICAST,UP,LOWER_UP> mtu 1500 qdisc
pfifo_fast state UP qlen 1000
  link/ether 08:00:27:b0:8d:92 brd ff:ff:ff:ff:ff:ff
```

```
inet 192.168.50.10/24 brd 192.168.50.255 scope global eth1
valid_lft forever preferred_lft forever
inet 192.168.50.200/32 scope global eth1
valid_lft forever preferred_lft forever
inet6 fe80::a00:27ff:feb0:8d92/64 scope link
valid_lft forever preferred_lft forever
```

 You may need to disable SELinux to have the preceding code work. Alternatively, you can make a policy to allow Keepalived to create the VIP.

How it works...

We need to install Keepalived first of all, using the `keepalived` class:

```
package {'ipvsadm':
  ensure => 'installed',
}
package {'keepalived':
  ensure => 'installed',
}
service {'keepalived':
  ensure  => 'running',
  enable  => true,
  require => Package['keepalived'],
}
```

Next, we use the `keepalived.conf.epp` template to create a Keepalived configuration file:

```
global_defs {
}

vrrp_script check_true {
  script "/sbin/true"
  interval 2
  weight 2
}

vrrp_instance VIP_KEEPALIVED {
  state <%= $keepalived::state %>
  interface <%= $keepalived::interface %>
  virtual_router_id <%= $keepalived::virtual_router_id %>
  priority <%= $keepalived::priority %>
```

```
advert_int 1
authentication {
  auth_type PASS
  auth_pass <%= $keepalived::auth_pass %>
}
virtual_ipaddress {
  <%= $keepalived::vip %>
}
track_script {
  check_true
}
track_interface { <%= $keepalived::interface %> }
  }
}
```

As you can see, the class includes an `interface` parameter; by default, the VIP will be configured on `eth1`, but if you need to use a different interface, you can pass it in using this parameter.

Each pair of servers that we configure with a virtual IP will use the `keepalived` class with the same parameters. These will be used in the template to declare the IP address of each node.

In this simple example, we won't ever move the VIP from `cookbook` to `cookbook2`, unless the `cookbook` node goes offline. In a production setting, we would have the `check` in the following code verify that a service was running on our node:

```
vrrp_script check_true {
  script "/sbin/true"
  interval 2
  weight 2
}
```

Later, we'll expand on this example by adding HAProxy to our configuration, providing a high-availability service.

There's more...

With Keepalived set up as described in the example, the virtual IP address will be configured on `cookbook` by default. If something happens to interfere with this (for example, if you halt or reboot `cookbook`, stop the Keepalived service, or the machine loses network connectivity), `cookbook2` will immediately take over the virtual IP.

One common use for a Keepalived-managed virtual IP is to provide a highly-available website or service. To do this, you need to set the DNS name for the service (for example, cat-pictures.com) to point to the virtual IP. Requests for the service will be routed to whichever of the two servers currently has the virtual IP. If that server should go down, requests will go to the other, with no interruption in service visible to users.

Keepalived works great for the previous example but is not in widespread use in this form. The newer pacemaker project should be used for more complex setups. More information on heartbeat, pacemaker, Corosync, and other clustering packages can be found at `http://www.linux-ha.org/wiki/Main_Page`.

Managing cluster configurations is one area where exported resources are useful. Each node in a cluster will export information about itself, which will then be collected by the other members of the cluster. Using the `Puppet labs-concat` module, you can build up a configuration file from exported `concat` fragments from all of the nodes in the cluster.

Remember to look at the Puppet Forge before starting your own module. If nothing else, you'll get some ideas that you can use in your own module. Corosync can be managed with the `Puppet labs` module at `https://forge.puppetlabs.com/puppetlabs/corosync`.

Managing NFS servers and file shares

NFS (Network filesystem) is a protocol to mount a shared directory from a remote server. For example, a pool of web servers might all mount the same NFS share to serve static assets, such as images and style sheets. Although NFS is generally slower and less secure than local storage or a clustered filesystem, the ease with which it can be used makes it a common choice in data centers. We'll use our `myfw` module from before to ensure that the local firewall permits `nfs` communication. We'll also use the `puppetlabs-concat` module to edit the list of exported filesystems on our NFS server.

How to do it...

In this example, we'll configure an `nfs` server to share (export) a filesystem via NFS:

1. Create an `nfs` module with the following `nfs::exports` class, which defines a `concat` resource:

```
class nfs::exports {
  exec {'nfs::exportfs':
    command   => 'exportfs -a',
```

```
    refreshonly => true,
    path        => '/usr/bin:/bin:/sbin:/usr/sbin',
  }
  concat {'/etc/exports':
    notify => Exec['nfs::exportfs'],
  }
}
```

2. Create the `nfs::export` defined type. We'll use this definition for any NFS exports we create:

```
define nfs::export (
  String $where          = $title,
  String $who            = '*',
  String $options        = 'async,ro',
  String $mount_options  = 'defaults',
  String $tag            = 'nfs'
) {
  # make sure the directory exists
  # export the entry locally, then export a resource to be
picked up later.
  file {$where:
    ensure => 'directory',
    before => Concat['/etc/exports'],
  }
  include nfs::exports
  concat::fragment { "nfs::export::${where}":
    content => "${where} ${who}(${options})\n",
    target  => '/etc/exports'
    require => File[$where],
  }
  @@mount { "nfs::export::${where}::${::ipaddress_eth1}":
    ensure  => 'mounted',
    name    => $where,
    fstype  => 'nfs',
    options => $mount_options,
    device  => "${::ipaddress_eth1}:${where}",
    tag     => $tag,
  }
}
```

3. Create the `nfs::server` class, which will include the OS-specific configuration for the server:

```
class nfs::server {
  # ensure nfs server is running
  # firewall should allow nfs communication
```

```
      include nfs::exports
      case $::osfamily {
        'RedHat': { include nfs::server::redhat }
        'Debian': { include nfs::server::debian }
        default: { fail('nfs::server only works on redhat or
debian') }
      }
      include myfw
      firewall {'2049 NFS TCP communication':
        proto  => 'tcp',
        dport  => '2049',
        action => 'accept', }
      firewall {'2049 UDP NFS communication':
        proto  => 'udp',
        dport  => '2049',
        action => 'accept',
      }
      firewall {'0111 TCP PORTMAP':
        proto  => 'tcp',
        dport  => '111',
        action => 'accept',
      }
      firewall {'0111 UDP PORTMAP':
        proto  => 'udp',
        dport  => '111',
        action => 'accept',
      }
      firewall {'4000 TCP STAT':
        proto  => 'tcp',
        dport  => '4000-4010',
        action => 'accept',
      }
      firewall {'4000 UDP STAT':
        proto  => 'udp',
        dport  => '4000-4010',
        action => 'accept',
      }
    }
```

4. Create the `nfs::server::redhat` class:

```
    class nfs::server::redhat {
      package {'nfs-utils':
        ensure => 'installed',
      }
      service {'nfs':
        ensure => 'running',
        enable => true
```

```
   }
   file {'/etc/sysconfig/nfs':
     source => 'puppet:///modules/nfs/nfs',
     mode   => '0644',
     notify => Service['nfs'],
   }
 }
```

5. Create the `/etc/sysconfig/nfs` support file for Red Hat systems in the `files` directory of our `nfs` repository (`modules/nfs/files/nfs`):

```
STATD_PORT=4000
STATD_OUTGOING_PORT=4001
RQUOTAD_PORT=4002
LOCKD_TCPPORT=4003
LOCKD_UDPPORT=4003
MOUNTD_PORT=4004
```

6. Create the support class for Debian systems, `nfs::server::debian`:

```
# debian specific
class nfs::server::debian {
  # install the package
  package {'nfs':
    ensure => 'installed',
    name   => 'nfs-kernel-server',
  }
  # config
  file {'/etc/default/nfs-common':
    source => 'puppet:///modules/nfs/nfs-common',
    mode   => '0644',
    notify => Service['nfs-server']
  }
  # services
  service {'nfs-server':
    ensure => 'running',
    enable => true,
  }
  service {'nfs':
    ensure => 'running',
    name   => 'nfs-kernel-server',
    enable => true,
  }
}
```

7. Create the `nfs-common` configuration for Debian (which will be placed in `modules/nfs/files/nfs-common`):

```
STATDOPTS="--port 4000 --outgoing-port 4001"
```

8. Apply the `nfs::server` class to a node and then create an export on that node:

```
node debian {
  include nfs::server
  nfs::export {'/srv/home':
    tag => "srv_home"
  }
}
```

We provided the `nfs::server::redhat` class in case your NFS server machine is a Red Hat machine. In this example, we will use a Debian-based NFS server.

9. Create a collector for the exported resource created by the `nfs::server` class in the preceding code snippet:

```
node cookbook {
  Mount <<| tag == "srv_home" |>> {
    name => '/mnt',
  }
}
```

10. Run Puppet on the Debian node to create the exported resource:

```
root@debian:~# puppet agent -t
Info: Using configured environment 'production'
Info: Retrieving pluginfacts
Info: Retrieving plugin
Info: Loading facts
Info: Caching catalog for debian.example.com
Info: Applying configuration version '1524264325'
Notice: /Stage[main]/Nfs::Server::Debian/File[/etc/default/nfs-
common]/ensure: defined content as
'{md5}c4fc525f14d07f668ec4cbff0f7c2f39'
Info: /Stage[main]/Nfs::Server::Debian/File[/etc/default/nfs-
common]: Scheduling refresh of Service[nfs-server]
Notice: /Stage[main]/Nfs::Server::Debian/Service[nfs-
server]/ensure: ensure changed 'stopped' to 'running'
Info: /Stage[main]/Nfs::Server::Debian/Service[nfs-server]:
Unscheduling refresh on Service[nfs-server]
Notice: /Stage[main]/Nfs::Server::Debian/Service[nfs]/ensure:
```

```
ensure changed 'stopped' to 'running'
Info: /Stage[main]/Nfs::Server::Debian/Service[nfs]:
Unscheduling refresh on Service[nfs]
Notice: /Stage[main]/Myfw::Post/Firewall[8999 Drop all other
traffic]/ensure: created
Notice: /Stage[main]/Myfw::Pre/Firewall[0000 Allow all traffic
on loopback]/ensure: created
Notice: /Stage[main]/Myfw::Pre/Firewall[0001 Allow all
ICMP]/ensure: created
Notice: /Stage[main]/Myfw::Pre/Firewall[0002 Allow all
established traffic]/ensure: created
Notice: /Stage[main]/Myfw::Pre/Firewall[0022 Allow all TCP on
port 22 (ssh)]/ensure: created
Notice: /Stage[main]/Nfs::Server/Firewall[2049 NFS TCP
communication]/ensure: created
Notice: /Stage[main]/Nfs::Server/Firewall[2049 UDP NFS
communication]/ensure: created
Notice: /Stage[main]/Nfs::Server/Firewall[0111 TCP
PORTMAP]/ensure: created
Notice: /Stage[main]/Nfs::Server/Firewall[0111 UDP
PORTMAP]/ensure: created
Notice: /Stage[main]/Nfs::Server/Firewall[4000 TCP
STAT]/ensure: created
Notice: /Stage[main]/Nfs::Server/Firewall[4000 UDP
STAT]/ensure: created
Notice:
/Stage[main]/Main/Node[debian]/Nfs::Export[/srv/home]/File[/srv
/home]/ensure: created
Notice:
/Stage[main]/Nfs::Exports/Concat[/etc/exports]/File[/etc/export
s]/content:
--- /etc/exports 2018-04-20 22:42:10.032966834 +0000
+++ /tmp/puppet-file20180420-1236-si7nnd 2018-04-20
22:45:25.598700833 +0000
@@ -0,0 +1 @@
+/srv/home *(async,ro,no_subtree_check)

Info: Computing checksum on file /etc/exports
Info: FileBucket got a duplicate file
{md5}d41d8cd98f00b204e9800998ecf8427e
Info:
/Stage[main]/Nfs::Exports/Concat[/etc/exports]/File[/etc/export
s]: Filebucketed /etc/exports to puppet with sum
d41d8cd98f00b204e9800998ecf8427e
Notice:
/Stage[main]/Nfs::Exports/Concat[/etc/exports]/File[/etc/export
s]/content: content changed
'{md5}d41d8cd98f00b204e9800998ecf8427e' to
```

```
'{md5}e0ac48093bd5d197e308092e0d07de41'
Info: Concat[/etc/exports]: Scheduling refresh of
Exec[nfs::exportfs]
Notice: /Stage[main]/Nfs::Exports/Exec[nfs::exportfs]:
Triggered 'refresh' from 1 event
Notice: Applied catalog in 1.93 seconds
```

11. The export has been created, now we just have to run Puppet on cookbook (the client) to mount the filesystem:

```
[root@cookbook ~]# puppet agent -t
Info: Using configured environment 'production'
Info: Retrieving pluginfacts
Info: Retrieving plugin
Info: Loading facts
Info: Caching catalog for test.example.com
Info: Applying configuration version '1524264493'
Notice: tagged cookbook
Notice: /Stage[main]/Main/Node[cookbook]/Notify[tagged
cookbook]/message: defined 'message' as 'tagged cookbook'
Notice:
/Stage[main]/Main/Node[cookbook]/Mount[nfs::export::/srv/home::
192.168.50.20]/ensure: defined 'ensure' as 'mounted'
Info: Computing checksum on file /etc/fstab
Info:
/Stage[main]/Main/Node[cookbook]/Mount[nfs::export::/srv/home::
192.168.50.20]: Scheduling refresh of
Mount[nfs::export::/srv/home::192.168.50.20]
Info:
Mount[nfs::export::/srv/home::192.168.50.20](provider=parsed):
Remounting
Notice:
/Stage[main]/Main/Node[cookbook]/Mount[nfs::export::/srv/home::
192.168.50.20]: Triggered 'refresh' from 1 event
Info:
/Stage[main]/Main/Node[cookbook]/Mount[nfs::export::/srv/home::
192.168.50.20]: Scheduling refresh of
Mount[nfs::export::/srv/home::192.168.50.20]
Notice: Applied catalog in 0.08 seconds
```

12. Verify the mount with mount:

```
[root@cookbook ~]# mount -t nfs4
192.168.50.20:/srv/home on /mnt type nfs4
(rw,relatime,vers=4.0,rsize=65536,wsize=65536,namlen=255,hard,p
roto=tcp,port=0,timeo=600,retrans=2,sec=sys,clientaddr=192.168.
50.10,local_lock=none,addr=192.168.50.20)
```

How it works...

The `nfs::exports` class defines an `exec`, which runs `exportfs -a`, to export all filesystems defined in `/etc/exports`. Next, we define a `concat` resource to contain `concat::fragments`, which we will define next in our `nfs::export` class. `concat` resources specify the file that the fragments are to be placed into; `/etc/exports` in this case. Our `concat` resource has a `notify` for the previous `exec`. This has the effect that whenever `/etc/ exports` is updated, we run `exportfs -a` again to export the new entries:

```
class nfs::exports {
  exec {'nfs::exportfs':
    command    => 'exportfs -a',
    refreshonly => true,
    path       => '/usr/bin:/bin:/sbin:/usr/sbin',
  }
  concat {'/etc/exports':
    notify    => Exec['nfs::exportfs'],
  }
}
```

We then created an `nfs::export` defined type, which does all the work. The defined type adds an entry to `/etc/exports` via a `concat::fragment` resource:

```
# defined typ for nfs export
define nfs::export (
  String $where = $title,
  String $who = '*',
  String $options = 'async,ro,no_subtree_check',
  String $mount_options = 'defaults',
  String $tag = 'nfs'
) {
  # make sure the directory exists
  # export the entry locally, then export a resource to be picked up later.
  file {$where:
    ensure => 'directory',
    before => Concat['/etc/exports'],
  }
  include nfs::exports
  concat::fragment { "nfs::export::${where}":
    content => "${where} ${who}(${options})\n",
    target  => '/etc/exports',
    require => File[$where],
  }
  ...
}
```

In the definition, we use the `$where` attribute to define which filesystem we are exporting. We use `$who` to specify who can mount the filesystem. The `$options` attribute contains the exporting options, such as `rw` (read-write) and `ro` (read-only). Next, we have the options that will be placed in `/etc/fstab` on the client machine, the mount options, stored in `$mount_` options. The `nfs::exports` class is included here so that `concat::fragment` has a `concat` target defined.

Next, the exported `mount` resource is created; this is done on the server, so the `${::ipaddress_eth1}` variable holds the IP address of the server. We use this to define the device for the mount.

 We use `ipaddress_eth1` because I am using Vagrant, and each host has the same IP address for `eth0`. My `Vagrantfile` defines a private network, which is assigned to each host's `eth1` interface.

The device is the IP address of the server, a colon, and then the filesystem being exported. In this example, it is **192.168.50.20:/srv/home**:

```
@@mount { "nfs::export::${where}::${::ipaddress_eth1}":
    ensure    => 'mounted',
    name      => $where,
    fstype    => 'nfs',
    options   => $mount_options,
    device    => "${::ipaddress_eth1}:${where}",
    tag       => $tag,
}
```

We reuse our `myfw` module and include it in the `nfs::server` class. This class illustrates one of the things to consider when writing your modules: not all Linux distributions are created equal. Debian and Red Hat deal with NFS server configuration quite differently. The `nfs::server` module deals with this by including OS-specific subclasses:

```
# setup the server
class nfs::server {
  # ensure nfs server is running
  # firewall should allow nfs communication
  include nfs::exports
  case $::osfamily {
    'RedHat': { include nfs::server::redhat }
    'Debian': { include nfs::server::debian }
    default: { fail('nfs::server only works on redhat or debian') }
  }
```

The `nfs::server` module opens several firewall ports for NFS communication. NFS traffic is always carried over port 2049, but ancillary systems, such as locking, quota, and file status daemons, use ephemeral ports chosen by the portmapper, by default. The portmapper itself uses port 111. So our module needs to allow 2049, 111, and a few other ports. We attempt to configure the ancillary services to use ports 4000 through 4010:

```
include myfw
firewall { '2049 NFS TCP communication':
 proto => 'tcp',
 dport => '2049',
 action => 'accept',
}
firewall {'2049 UDP NFS communication':
 proto  => 'udp',
 dport  => '2049',
 action => 'accept',
}
firewall {'0111 TCP PORTMAP':
 proto  => 'tcp',
 dport  => '111',
 action => 'accept',
}
firewall {'0111 UDP PORTMAP':
 proto  => 'udp',
 dport  => '111',
 action => 'accept',
}
firewall {'4000 TCP STAT':
 proto  => 'tcp',
 dport  => '4000-4010',
 action => 'accept',
}
firewall {'4000 UDP STAT':
 proto  => 'udp',
 dport  => '4000-4010',
 action => 'accept',
}
```

In the `nfs::server::redhat` class, we modify `/etc/sysconfig/nfs` to use the ports specified. Also, we install the `nfs-utils` package and start the NFS service:

```
# redhat specific
class nfs::server::redhat {
  package {'nfs-utils':
    ensure => 'installed',
  }
  service {'nfs':
```

```
      ensure => 'running',
      enable => true
    }
    file {'/etc/sysconfig/nfs':
      source => 'puppet:///modules/nfs/nfs',
      mode    => '0644',
      notify => Service['nfs'],
    }
  }
```

We do the same for Debian-based systems in the `nfs::server::debian` class. The packages and services have different names, but overall the process is similar:

```
  # debian specific
  class nfs::server::debian {
    # install the package
    package {'nfs':
      ensure => 'installed',
      name => 'nfs-kernel-server',
    }
    # config
    file {'/etc/default/nfs-common':
      source => 'puppet:///modules/nfs/nfs-common',
      mode    => '0644',
      notify => Service['nfs-server']
    }
    # services
    service {'nfs-server':
      ensure => 'running',
      enable => true,
    }
    service {'nfs':
      ensure => 'running',
      name    => 'nfs-kernel-server',
      enable => true,
    }
  }
```

With everything in place, we include the server class to configure the NFS server and then define an export:

```
  node debian {
    include nfs::server
    nfs::export {'/srv/home':
      tag => 'srv_home'
    }
  }
```

What's important here is that we defined `tag`, which will be used in the exported resource we collect in the following code snippet:

```
Mount <<| tag == "srv_home" |>> {
  name => '/mnt',
}
```

We use the spaceship syntax (`<<|  |>>`) to collect all the exported mount resources that have the tag we defined earlier (`srv_home`). We then use a syntax called **override on collect** to modify the `name` attribute of the mount, which specifies where to mount the filesystem.

Using this design pattern with exported resources, we can change the server exporting the filesystem and have any nodes that mount the resource updated automatically. We can have many different nodes collecting the exported mount resource.

Using HAProxy to load balance multiple web servers

Load balancers are used to spread a load among a number of servers. Hardware load balancers are still somewhat expensive, whereas software balancers can achieve most of the benefits of a hardware solution.

HAProxy is the software load balancer of choice for most people: fast, powerful, and highly configurable.

My example Vagrantfile will be using Red Hat-based systems for this example, so we'll need to install the `selinux` module to configure SELinux:

```
t@mylaptop $ puppet module install puppet-selinux --modulepath
~/puppet/modules
Notice: Preparing to install into /home/thomas/puppet/modules ...
Notice: Downloading from https://forgeapi.puppet.com ...
Notice: Installing -- do not interrupt ...
/home/thomas/puppet/modules
└─┬ puppet-selinux (v1.5.2)
  └── puppetlabs-stdlib (v4.25.0)
```

How to do it...

In this recipe, I'll show you how to build an HAProxyserver to load balance web requests across web servers. We'll use exported resources to build the `haproxy` configuration file, just as we did for the NFS example:

1. Create the `modules/haproxy/manifests/master.pp` file with the following contents:

```
# the master member of the proxy group
class haproxy::master (
  String $app = 'myapp'
) {
  # The HAProxy master server
  # will collected haproxy::slave resources and add to it's
balancer
  package { 'haproxy': ensure => installed }
```

2. Set the SELinux Boolean for `haproxy_connect_any` to on. This will allow Haproxy to connect to services:

```
selinux::boolean{ 'haproxy_connect_any':
  ensure => 'on',
  before => Service['haproxy'],
}
```

3. Turn on the `haproxy` service:

```
service { 'haproxy':
  ensure  => running,
  enable  => true,
  require => Package['haproxy'],
}
```

4. Configure the `haproxy` service:

```
include haproxy::config
concat::fragment { 'haproxy.cfg header':
  target  => 'haproxy.cfg',
  source  => 'puppet:///modules/haproxy/haproxy.cfg',
  order   => '001',
  require => Package['haproxy'],
  notify  => Service['haproxy'],
}
# pull in the exported entries
```

```
Concat::Fragment <<| tag == $app |>> {
  target => 'haproxy.cfg',
  notify => Service['haproxy'],
}
```

5. Allow `haproxy` **through the host firewall (iptables):**

```
# firewall configuration
include myfw
firewall {'8080 haproxy statistics':
  proto  => 'tcp',
  dport  => 8080,
  action => 'accept'
}
firewall {'0080 http haproxy':
  proto  => 'tcp',
  dport  => 80,
  action => 'accept'
}
}
```

6. Create the `modules/haproxy/files/haproxy.cfg` file with the following contents:

```
global
        daemon
        user haproxy
        group haproxy
        pidfile /var/run/haproxy.pid

defaults
        log global
        stats enable
        mode http
        option httplog
        option dontlognull
        option dontlog-normal
        retries 3
        option redispatch
        timeout connect 4000
        timeout client 60000
        timeout server 30000

listen stats :8080
        mode http
        stats uri /
        stats auth haproxy:topsecret
```

```
listen myapp 0.0.0.0:80
        balance leastconn
```

7. Create the `slave` server configuration in the `haproxy::slave` class:

```
class haproxy::slave (
  String $app = 'myapp',
  Integer $localport = 8000
) {
  # haproxy slave, export haproxy.cfg fragment
  # configure simple webserver on different port
  @@concat::fragment { "haproxy.cfg ${::fqdn}":
    content => "\t\tserver ${::hostname}
${::ipaddress_eth1}:${localport} check maxconn 100\n",
    target  => 'haproxy.cfg',
    order   => '0010',
    tag     => $app,
  }
  include myfw
  firewall {"${localport} Allow HTTP to haproxy::slave":
    proto  => 'tcp',
    dport  => $localport,
    action => 'accept',
  }
}
```

8. Add an `selinux::port` resource to allow HAProxy to use port 8000:

```
selinux::port { 'allow-http-haproxy':
  ensure   => 'present',
  seltype  => 'http_port_t',
  protocol => 'tcp',
  port     => 8000,
  before   => Class['apache']
}
```

9. Include the `apache` class with the correct port and document root (`docroot`):

```
class {'apache': }
  apache::vhost { 'haproxy.example.com':
    port    => 8000,
    docroot => '/var/www/haproxy',
  }
  file {'/var/www/haproxy':
    ensure  => 'directory',
    mode    => '0755',
    require => Class['apache'],
  }
```

10. Create the `index` file, with the fully qualified domain name of the HAProxy slave server:

```
$index = @("INDEX")
  <html>
    <body>
      <h1>${::fqdn} haproxy::slave</h1>
    </body>
  </html>
  | INDEX
file {'/var/www/haproxy/index.html':
  mode    => '0644',
  content => $index,
  require => File['/var/www/haproxy'],
  }
}
```

11. Create the `concat` container resource in the `haproxy::config` class, as follows:

```
class haproxy::config {
  concat {'haproxy.cfg':
    path   => '/etc/haproxy/haproxy.cfg',
    order  => 'numeric',
    mode   => '0644',
    notify => Service['haproxy'],
  }
}
```

12. Modify `site.pp` to define the `master` and `slave` nodes:

```
node master {
  class {'haproxy::master':
    app => 'cookbook' }
}
node slave1,slave2 {
  class {'haproxy::slave':
    app => 'cookbook' }
}
```

13. Run Puppet on each of the slave servers:

```
[root@slave1 ~]# puppet agent -t
Info: Using configured environment 'production'
Info: Retrieving pluginfacts
Info: Retrieving plugin
Info: Loading facts
```

```
Info: Caching catalog for slave1.example.com
Info: Applying configuration version '1524599354'
Notice: /Stage[main]/Haproxy::Slave/Selinux::Port[allow-http-
haproxy]/Selinux_port[tcp_8000-8000]/seltype: seltype
changed 'soundd_port_t' to 'http_port_t'
...
Notice: /Stage[main]/Apache::Service/Service[httpd]/ensure:
ensure changed 'stopped' to 'running'
Info: /Stage[main]/Apache::Service/Service[httpd]: Unscheduling
refresh on Service[httpd]
Notice: Applied catalog in 2.16 seconds
```

14. Run Puppet on the `master` node to configure and run `haproxy`:

```
[root@master ~]# puppet agent -t
Info: Using configured environment 'production'
Info: Retrieving pluginfacts
Info: Retrieving plugin
Info: Loading facts
Info: Caching catalog for master.example.com
Info: Applying configuration version '1524601278'
Notice:
/Stage[main]/Haproxy::Master/Selinux::Boolean[haproxy_connect_a
ny]/Selboolean[haproxy_connect_any]/value: value changed 'off'
to 'on'
...
Info: Concat[haproxy.cfg]: Scheduling refresh of
Service[haproxy] Notice:
/Stage[main]/Haproxy::Master/Service[haproxy]: Triggered
'refresh' from 1 event
Notice: Applied catalog in 0.49 seconds
```

15. Check the HAProxy stats interface on master port 8080 in your web browser (`http://master.example.com:8080`) to make sure everything is okay (the username and password are in `haproxy.cfg`, `haproxy`, and `topsecret`). Try going to the proxied service as well. Notice that the page changes on each reload, as the service is redirected from `slave1` to `slave2` (`http://master.example.com`).

If you are using my example Vagrantfile, the *192.168.50.0/24* subnet is a private network. To connect to the network, use an `ssh socks` proxy: `t@mylaptop $ vagrant ssh puppet -- -D8000`. Then, configure your browser to connect to the `socks` proxy on *127.0.0.1:8000*.

How it works...

We built a complex configuration from various components of the previous sections. This type of deployment becomes easier the more you do it. At the top level, we configured the master to collect exported resources from slaves. The slaves exported their configuration information to allow HAProxy to use them in the load balancer. As slaves are added to the system, they can export their resources and be added to the balancer automatically.

Our nodes are running Centos 7, so we needed to add the `puppet-selinux` module to allow our configuration to work without disabling SELinux.

We used our `myfw` module to configure the firewall on the slaves and the master to allow communication.

We used the `Forge Apache` module to configure the listening web server on the slaves. We were able to generate a fully functioning website with 5 lines of code (10 more to place `index.html` on the website).

There are several things going on here. We have the firewall configuration and the Apache configuration, in addition to the HAProxy configuration. We'll focus on how the exported resources and the HAProxy configuration fit together.

In the `haproxy::config` class, we created the `concat` container for the HAProxy configuration:

```
class haproxy::config {
  concat {'haproxy.cfg':
    path   => '/etc/haproxy/haproxy.cfg',
    order  => 'numeric',
    mode   => '0644',
    notify => Service['haproxy']
  }
}
```

We reference this container in `haproxy::slave`:

```
# slave member of proxy
class haproxy::slave (
  String $app = 'myapp',
  Integer $localport = 8000
) {
  # haproxy slave, export haproxy.cfg fragment
  # configure simple webserver on different port
  @@concat::fragment { "haproxy.cfg ${::fqdn}":
```

```
    content => "\t\tserver ${::hostname} ${::ipaddress_eth1}:${localport}
check maxconn 100\n",
    target  => 'haproxy.cfg',
    order   => '0010',
    tag     => $app,
  }
```

We add a `notify` so that the HAProxy service is restarted when we add a new host to the configuration. Another important point here is that we set the order attribute of the slave configurations to *0010* when we define the header for the `haproxy.cfg` file; we use an order value of *0001* to ensure that the header is placed at the beginning of the file:

```
concat::fragment { 'haproxy.cfg header':
  target  => 'haproxy.cfg',
  source  => 'puppet:///modules/haproxy/haproxy.cfg',
  order   => '001',
  require => Package['haproxy'],
  notify  => Service['haproxy'],
}
```

We include an `selinux::port` definition to allow HAProxy to use port 8000 with SELinux enabled:

```
selinux::port { 'allow-http-haproxy':
  ensure   => 'present',
  seltype  => 'http_port_t',
  protocol => 'tcp',
  port     => 8000,
  before   => Class['apache']
}
```

The rest of the `haproxy::master` class is concerned with configuring the firewall, as we did in previous examples.

There's more...

HAProxy has a vast range of configuration parameters, which you can explore; see the HAProxy website at `http://haproxy.1wt.eu/#docs`.

Although it's most often used as a web server, HAProxy can proxy a lot more than just HTTP. It can handle any kind of TCP traffic, so you can use it to balance the load of MySQL servers, SMTP, video servers, or anything you like.

You can use the design we have shown here to attack many problems with the coordination of services between multiple servers. This type of interaction is very common; you can apply it to many configurations for load balancing or distributed systems. You can use the workflow described previously to have nodes export firewall resources (`@@firewall`) to permit their own access.

Managing EC2 instances

Using the Puppet `AWS` module, you can manage several aspects of your AWS deployments. In this section, we'll show how to build an EC2 instance automatically, including the required networks/interfaces and security groups.

Getting ready

You'll need to install the `aws-sdk` gem:

```
t@mylaptop ~/cookbook $ sudo /opt/puppetlabs/puppet/bin/gem install aws-sdk
Fetching: aws-sigv4-1.0.2.gem (100%)
...
Done installing documentation for aws-sigv4, aws-partitions, ..., aws-sdk-
workspaces, aws-sdk-xray, aws-sdk-resources, aws-sdk after 105 seconds
```

You'll need an AWS account; create one if you haven't already. The Free tier will work for the examples in this section. Log in to your AWS Console and create an API user. You will use the API user to create your AWS resources. Start by selecting **IAM** from the main console:

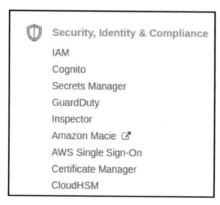

From IAM, select **Users**, then **Add user**. On the next screen, give your user a name and select **Programmatic access**, then click **Next**:

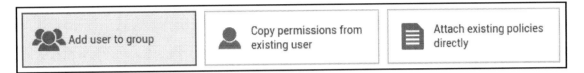

Select Attach existing policies directly and then select:

- `AmazonEC2FullAccess`
- `AmazonVPCFullAccess`

Click **Review**, and then click **Create user**.

After the user is created, go back to the **Users** tab and select the user:

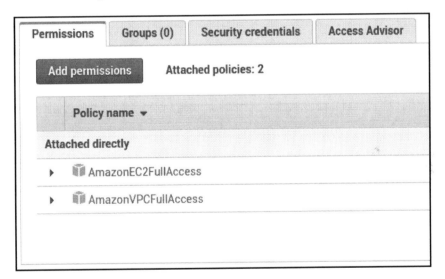

Click on **Security Credentials**, then click on **Create access key**. Download the csv file to ensure that you have a copy of the credentials:

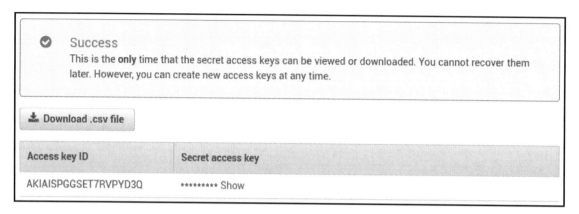

You will now need to use these AWS credentials. You can either add them to your shell configuration file (`.bashrc`) or add them on the command line:

```
export AWS_SECRET_ACCESS_KEY=EL2R+uL6/***********************pnbLwtu
export AWS_ACCESS_KEY_ID=AKI***************YYA
export AWS_REGION=us-west-2
```

Finally, go to the EC2 dashboard and select **Key Pairs** under **Network & Security**:

Click **Create Key Pair** and give the key pair a name (`cookbook` is a good one). After clicking **create**, the key will download automatically. Save this file—we'll need it when we `ssh` to our node later.

How to do it...

We'll create a simple instance in this example. To create an instance, we need a minimum environment. We need a VPC (a Virtual Private Cloud). Our VPC will need a network, a security group, and a default route:

1. Create a new module to hold the code. You can use PDK, puppet module generate, or just make the directories. I'm using the name cookbook_aws.

2. Create an init.pp file to contain the cookbook_aws class:

```
# AWS class
class cookbook_aws (
  String $availability_zone = 'us-west-2a',
  String $region = 'us-west-2',
  String $vpc = 'cookbook_aws',
) {
  include cookbook_aws::instance
  include cookbook_aws::network
  include cookbook_aws::securitygroup
  include cookbook_aws::vpc
  Class['cookbook_aws::vpc']
    -> Class['cookbook_aws::securitygroup']
    -> Class['cookbook_aws::network']
    -> Class['cookbook_aws::instance']
}
```

3. Our main class defines the order in which we want our subclasses to apply; create a vpc.pp manifest with the following contents:

```
# virtual private cloud
class cookbook_aws::vpc {
  ec2_vpc {'cookbook_aws':
    ensure     => present,
    region     => $cookbook_aws::region,
    cidr_block => '10.0.0.0/16',
  }
  ec2_vpc_internet_gateway {'cookbook_aws-gateway':
    ensure => present,
    region => $cookbook_aws::region,
    vpc    => $cookbook_aws::vpc,
  }
}
```

4. Define networks in `network.pp` as follows:

```
# network definitions
class cookbook_aws::network {
  # public network
  ec2_vpc_routetable { 'cookbook_aws-route-public':
    ensure => present,
    region => $cookbook_aws::region,
    vpc    => $cookbook_aws::vpc,
    routes => [
      {
        destination_cidr_block => '10.0.0.0/16',
        gateway                => 'local',
      },{
        destination_cidr_block => '0.0.0.0/0',
        gateway                => 'cookbook_aws-gateway',
      }
    ],
  }

  ec2_vpc_subnet {'cookbook_aws-public':
    ensure            => present,
    region            => $cookbook_aws::region,
    vpc               => $cookbook_aws::vpc,
    cidr_block        => '10.0.10.0/24',
    availability_zone => $cookbook_aws::availability_zone,
    route_table       => 'cookbook_aws-route-public',
  }
}
```

5. Define security groups for the network in `securitygroup.pp` as follows:

```
# security group
class cookbook_aws::securitygroup {
  ec2_securitygroup { 'cookbook-securitygroup':
    ensure      => present,
    region      => $cookbook_aws::region,
    vpc         => $cookbook_aws::vpc,
    description => 'Security group for cookbook',
    ingress     => [ {
      protocol => 'tcp',
      port     => 22,
      cidr     => '0.0.0.0/0',
    }]
  }
}
```

6. Define the test instance in `instance.pp`:

```
# an instance
class cookbook_aws::instance (
 String $image_id      = 'ami-07eb707f',
 String $instance_type = 't2.micro',
) {
 ec2_instance {'cookbook':
 ensure                        => running,
 region                        => $cookbook_aws::region,
 image_id                      => $image_id,
 instance_type                 => $instance_type,
 monitoring                    => false,
 key_name                      => 'cookbook',
 security_groups               => ['cookbook-securitygroup'],
 subnet                        => 'cookbook_aws-public',
 associate_public_ip_address => true,
 }
}
```

 AMI IDs change frequently. Log in to the console to retrieve the current ID and replace it in `$image_id`.

7. Run Puppet to create the VPC, security group, network, and routing:

```
t@mylaptop ~/cookbook $ puppet apply -e 'include cookbook_aws'
--modulepath ~/cookbook/modules
Notice: Compiled catalog for mylaptop.strangled.net in
environment production in 0.14 seconds
Notice:
/Stage[main]/Cookbook_aws::Vpc/Ec2_vpc[cookbook_aws]/ensure:
created
Notice:
/Stage[main]/Cookbook_aws::Vpc/Ec2_vpc_internet_gateway[cookboo
k_aws-gateway]/ensure: created
Notice:
/Stage[main]/Cookbook_aws::Network/Ec2_vpc_routetable[cookbook_
aws-route-public]/ensure: created
Notice:
/Stage[main]/Cookbook_aws::Network/Ec2_vpc_subnet[cookbook_aws-
public]/ensure: created
Notice:
/Stage[main]/Cookbook_aws::Network/Ec2_vpc_routetable[cookbook_
aws-route-private]/ensure: created
Notice:
```

```
/Stage[main]/Cookbook_aws::Network/Ec2_vpc_subnet[cookbook_aws-
private]/ensure: created
Notice:
/Stage[main]/Cookbook_aws::Instance/Ec2_instance[cookbook]/ensu
re: changed absent to running
Notice: Applied catalog in 2.06 seconds
```

8. Retrieve the IP address of your instance:

```
t@mylaptop ~/cookbook $ puppet resource ec2_instance
ec2_instance { 'cookbook':
  ensure            => 'running',
  availability_zone => 'us-west-2a',
  block_devices     => [
  {
    'device_name'           => '/dev/xvda',
    'delete_on_termination' => true
  }],
  ebs_optimized => false,
  hypervisor    => 'xen',
  image_id      => 'ami-07eb707f',
  instance_id   => 'i-0f86aeb8703e871eb',
  instance_type => 't2.micro',
  interfaces    => {
  'eni-06c0ff5fd98510ef6' => {
    'security_groups'     => [
      {
        'group_name'      => 'cookbook-securitygroup',
        'group_id'        => 'sg-07bb3eb50529ff3cd'
      }]
  }
},
  key_name            => 'cookbook',
  monitoring          => false,
  private_dns_name    => 'ip-10-0-10-31.us-
west-2.compute.internal',
  private_ip_address  => '10.0.10.31',
  public_dns_name     => 'ec2-54-244-26-203.us-
west-2.compute.amazonaws.com',
  public_ip_address   => '54.244.26.203',
  region              => 'us-west-2',
  security_groups     => ['cookbook-securitygroup'],
  subnet              => 'cookbook_aws-public',
  tenancy             => 'default',
  virtualization_type => 'hvm',
}
```

9. Add your previously defined `ssh` key to your running `ssh-agent`:

```
t@mylaptop ~/cookbook $ ssh-add ~/.ssh/cookbook
Identity added: /home/thomas/.ssh/cookbook
(/home/thomas/.ssh/cookbook)
```

10. `ssh` to your instance:

```
t@mylaptop ~/cookbook $ ssh ec2-user@54.244.26.203
X11 forwarding request failed on channel 0

       __|  __|_  )
       _|  ( / Amazon Linux 2 AMI
      ___|\___|___|

https://aws.amazon.com/amazon-linux-2/
No packages needed for security; 20 packages available
Run "sudo yum update" to apply all updates.
```

You can use Puppet to stop your instance when you are done, using `puppet resource`:

```
t@mylaptop ~/cookbook $ puppet resource ec2_instance cookbook
ensure=stopped region='us-west-2'
Notice: /Ec2_instance[cookbook]/ensure: changed running to
stopped
ec2_instance { 'cookbook':
  ensure        => 'stopped',
  ebs_optimized => false,
  monitoring    => false,
  region        => 'us-west-2',
  tenancy       => 'default',
}
t@mylaptop ~/cookbook $ puppet resource ec2_instance cookbook
ensure=absent region='us-west-2'
Notice: /Ec2_instance[cookbook]/ensure: changed stopping to
absent
ec2_instance { 'cookbook':
  ensure => 'absent',
}
```

How it works...

Puppet uses your AWS credentials to communicate with the AWS API and perform operations on your behalf. In our example, we created the minimum networking and security groups required to gain access to our node. Using the AWS module, you can quickly deliver infrastructure and nodes. If parts of the infrastructure already exist, Puppet will not recreate them. You can safely run the Puppet `apply` command several times without creating new instances, VPCs, or networks.

There's more...

You can define more networks and create a whole suite of machines within AWS. AWS now supports Puppet Enterprise as well, so you can have a Puppet Enterprise master configuration that lives within AWS. More information is available at `https://puppet.com/products/managed-technology/aws`.

Managing virtual machines with Vagrant

Vagrant is a tool for quickly deploying Virtual Machines locally. You can use Vagrant with VM platforms such as VirtualBox, KVM, AWS, and even VMware. Vagrant's images are called boxes. You may build your own boxes or download boxes from the public catalog of available boxes. Many of the popular Linux distributions are available. In this section, I'll show you how I built the machines used to test the code used in this book.

Getting ready

First, you'll need to install Vagrant. Vagrant is available for Windows, macOS, and Linux. You may download it from `https://www.vagrantup.com/downloads.html`. With Vagrant installed, select a working directory. In my examples, I've used the Puppet Git repository to hold my Vagrant configuration information. To ensure our Vagrant hosts can communicate properly with each other, we'll use the `vagrant-hosts` plugin. Install that as follows:

```
[thomas@mylaptop: ~] $ vagrant plugin install vagrant-hosts
Installing the 'vagrant-hosts' plugin. This can take a few minutes...
Fetching: vagrant-hosts-2.8.0.gem (100%)
Installed the plugin 'vagrant-hosts (2.8.0)'!
```

How to do it...

We'll create a Vagrantfile, which is how Vagrant defines virtual machines:

1. In the directory you wish to work with, initialize vagrant with `vagrant init`:

```
[thomas@mylaptop: ~] $ mkdir cookbook
[thomas@mylaptop: ~] $ cd cookbook
/home/thomas/cookbook
[thomas@mylaptop: cookbook] $ vagrant init
A `Vagrantfile` has been placed in this directory. You are now
ready to `vagrant up` your first virtual environment! Please
read
the comments in the Vagrantfile as well as documentation on
`vagrantup.com` for more information on using Vagrant.
```

2. The default `Vagrantfile` has a lot of comments; you can safely remove them to make it more readable:

```
[thomas@mylaptop: cookbook] $ sed -i -e '3,${/^\s*#/d}'
Vagrantfile
```

3. Edit the `Vagrantfile` to include a script to install Puppet. In our examples, we use Debian and RHEL, so we'll have two scripts. Add these lines before the `Vagrant.configure("2")` line:

```
$rhel = <<EOF
rpm -q puppet-agent
if [ $? -ne 0 ]; then
  yum install -y
http://yum.puppet.com/puppet5/puppet5-release-el-7.noarch.rpm
  yum install -y puppet-agent
fi
EOF
$debian = <<EOF
dpkg -s puppet-agent >/dev/null
if [ $? -ne 0 ]; then
  wget https://apt.puppet.com/puppet5-release-stretch.deb
  dpkg -i puppet5-release-stretch.deb
  apt-get update
  apt-get install -y puppet-agent
fi
EOF
```

4. Create a definition for our `cookbook` machine. This should be between the `Vagrant.configure("2")` line and the `end` line:

```
config.vm.define "cookbook" do |cookbook|
    cookbook.vm.box = "centos/7"
    cookbook.vm.provision "shell", inline: $rhel
    cookbook.vm.hostname = "cookbook.example.com"
    cookbook.vm.network "private_network", ip: "192.168.50.10",
        virtualbox__intnet: "puppet"
    cookbook.vm.provision :hosts
end
```

5. The `cookbook` machine will require a Puppet server. Define one now (put it directly after the `cookbook` line):

```
config.vm.define "puppet" do |puppet|
    puppet.vm.box = "centos/7"
    puppet.vm.provision "shell", inline: $rhel
    puppet.vm.hostname = "puppet.example.com"
    puppet.vm.network "private_network", ip: "192.168.50.100",
        virtualbox__intnet: "puppet"
    puppet.vm.provider "virtualbox" do |v|
      v.memory = 1500
    end
    puppet.vm.provision :hosts
end
```

6. Ensure that your Vagrantfile is correct with `vagrant status`:

```
[thomas@mylaptop: cookbook] $ vagrant status
Current machine states:

cookbook not created (virtualbox)
puppet not created (virtualbox)

This environment represents multiple VMs. The VMs are all
listed
above with their current state. For more information about a
specific
VM, run `vagrant status NAME`.
```

7. Create your puppet and cookbook nodes with vagrant up:

```
[thomas@mylaptop: cookbook] $ vagrant up puppet
Bringing machine 'puppet' up with 'virtualbox' provider...
==> puppet: Importing base box 'centos/7'...
==> puppet: Matching MAC address for NAT networking...
==> puppet: Checking if box 'centos/7' is up to date...
...
    puppet: Installed:
    puppet: puppet-agent.x86_64 0:5.5.1-1.el7
    puppet:
    puppet: Complete!
==> puppet: Running provisioner: hosts...
```

How it works...

Vagrant uses the Vagrantfiles to define virtual machines. You may include provisioning scripts in your Vagrantfiles to provision hosts. In this example, we simply installed puppet-agent and the associated yum/apt repositories:

```
$rhel = <<EOF
rpm -q puppet-agent
if [ $? -ne 0 ]; then
  yum install -y
http://yum.puppet.com/puppet5/puppet5-release-el-7.noarch.rpm
  yum install -y puppet-agent
fi
EOF
```

We use this definition in the call to vm.provision, as shown here:

```
cookbook.vm.provision "shell", inline: $rhel
```

We also make a call to the vagrant-hosts plugin to update the /etc/hosts file on our nodes:

```
cookbook.vm.provision :hosts
```

There's more...

Vagrant includes built-in support for Puppet. You can use Puppet in your provisioning steps. Both the `puppet agent` and `puppet apply` methods are supported. If you are starting from scratch, you'll use the `puppet apply` provisioner. First, create a `manifests` directory, and then a `default.pp` manifest within that directory:

```
$motd = @("MOTD")
 Welcome to ${facts['hostname']}
 This machine is managed by Puppet.
 | MOTD
file {'/etc/motd':
 content => $motd,
 mode    => '0644'
}
```

Your node will need to have the VirtualBox additions installed (or the equivalent for your VM system). With the preceding CentOS-based image, you'll need to install the `kernel-headers` and `kernel-devel rpm`, then update the `kernel rpm`, and reboot. This will make the `vboxsf` module available to mount the `/vagrant` filesystem. To achieve a consistent provision, install the `vagrant-reload` plugin and add the following to the provision script we defined earlier:

```
# setup vboxsf
modprobe vboxsf
if [ $? -ne 0 ]; then
yum install -y kernel-devel kernel-headers
yum update -y kernel
fi
```

Then, add `cookbook.vm.provision :reload` after the `$rhel` provision.

Add a call to Puppet to your `provision` section of the `cookbook` config, as follows:

```
cookbook.vm.provision "puppet"
```

Now, run `vagrant provision` to have `puppet apply` run against your manifest:

```
[thomas@mylaptop: cookbook] $ vagrant provision cookbook
==> cookbook: Running provisioner: shell...
    cookbook: Running: inline script
    cookbook: puppet-agent-5.5.1-1.el7.x86_64
==> cookbook: Running provisioner: puppet...
==> cookbook: Running Puppet with default.pp...
```

```
==> cookbook: Notice: Compiled catalog for cookbook.example.com in
environment production in 0.02 seconds
==> cookbook: Notice: /Stage[main]/Main/File[/etc/motd]/content: content
changed '{md5}d41d8cd98f00b204e9800998ecf8427e' to
'{md5}272b0de6c200008ed48e9c4dcafc852a'
==> cookbook: Notice: Applied catalog in 0.02 seconds
==> cookbook: Running provisioner: hosts...
```

Finally, use `vagrant ssh` to verify that the message of the day has been updated:

```
[thomas@mylaptop: cookbook] $ vagrant ssh cookbook
Last login: Fri Apr 27 20:03:56 2018 from 10.0.2.2
Welcome to cookbook
This machine is managed by Puppet.
```

Managing Docker with Puppet

Docker is a platform for the rapid deployment of containers. Containers are like lightweight virtual machines that might only run a single process. The containers in Docker are called docks and are configured with files called Dockerfiles. Puppet can be used to configure a node to not only run Docker but also configure and start several docks. You can then use Puppet to ensure that your docks are running and are consistently configured.

Getting ready

Download and install the Puppet Docker module from the Puppet Forge (https://forge.puppet.com/puppetlabs/docker):

```
t@mylaptop ~$ puppet module install puppetlabs-docker --modulepath
~/puppet/modules
Notice: Preparing to install into /home/thomas/puppet/modules ...
Notice: Downloading from https://forgeapi.puppet.com ...
Notice: Installing -- do not interrupt ...
/home/thomas/puppet/modules
└─┬ puppetlabs-docker (v1.0.4)
  ├── puppetlabs-apt (v4.5.1)
  ├── puppetlabs-stdlib (v4.25.0)
  └── stahnma-epel (v1.3.0)
```

Add all of these modules to your Puppet repository. The `stahnma-epel` module is required for Enterprise Linux-based distributions; it contains the extra packages for the Enterprise Linux YUM repository.

How to do it...

Perform the following steps to manage Docker with Puppet:

1. To install Docker on a node, we just need to include the `docker` class. We'll do more than install Docker; we'll also download an image and start an application on our `test` node. In this example, we'll create a new machine, called `shipyard`. Add the following node definition to `site.pp`:

```
node shipyard {
  class {'docker': }
  docker::image {'phusion/baseimage': }
  docker::run {'cookbook':
    image   => 'alpine',
    expose  => '8080',
    ports   => '8080',
    command => 'nc -k -l 8080',
  }
}
```

2. Run Puppet on your `shipyard` node to install Docker. This will also download the `alpine docker` image:

```
[root@shipyard ~]# puppet agent -t
Info: Using configured environment 'production'
Info: Retrieving pluginfacts
Info: Retrieving plugin
Info: Loading facts
Info: Caching catalog for shipyard.example.com
Info: Applying configuration version '1524672253'
...
Notice: /Stage[main]/Docker::Install/Package[docker]/ensure:
created
Notice: /Stage[main]/Docker::Service/Service[docker]/ensure:
ensure changed 'stopped' to 'running'
Info: /Stage[main]/Docker::Service/Service[docker]:
Unscheduling refresh on Service[docker]
...
Notice: /Stage[main]/Main/
# nc -v localhost 32768
# nc -v localhost 32768
Node[shipyard]/Docker::Run[cookbook]/Service[docker-
cookbook]/ensure: ensure changed 'stopped' to 'running'
Info: /Stage[main]/Main/Node[
# nc -v localhost 32768
shipyard]/Docker::Run[cookbook]/Service[docker-cookbook]:
```

```
Unscheduling refresh on Service[docker-cookbook]
Notice: Applied catalog in 13.08 seconds
# nc -v localhost 32768
# nc -v localhost 32768
```

3. Verify that your container is running on `shipyard` using `docker ps`:

```
[root@shipyard ~]# docker ps
CONTAINER ID IMAGE COMMAND CREATED STATUS PORTS NAMES
bd59783da467 alpine "nc -k -l 8080" 47 seconds ago Up 46
seconds 0.0.0.0:32768->8080/tcp cookbook
```

4. Verify that the `dock` is running `netcat` on port 8080 by connecting to the port listed previously (32768):

```
[root@shipyard ~]# nc -v localhost 32768
Ncat: Version 6.40 ( http://nmap.org/ncat )
Ncat: Connected to 127.0.0.1:32768.
Hello World!
Ncat: 13 bytes sent, 0 bytes received in 5.22 seconds.
```

How it works...

We began by installing the `docker` module from the Puppet Forge. This module installs the `docker` package on our node, along with any required dependencies.

We then defined a `docker::image` resource. This instructs Puppet to ensure that the named image is downloaded and available to Docker. On our first run, Puppet will make Docker download the image. We used `alpine` as our example because it is quite small, well-known, and includes the `netcat` daemon we used in the example. More information on alpine can be found at `http://phusion.github.io/baseimage-docker/`.

We then went on to define a `docker::run` resource. This example isn't terribly useful; it simply starts `netcat` in listen mode on port 8080. We need to expose that port to our machine, so we define the `expose` attribute of our `docker::run` resource. There are many other options available for the `docker::run` resource. Refer to the source code for more details.

We then used `docker ps` to list the running docks on our `shipyard` machine. We parsed the listening port on our local machine and verified that `netcat` was listening.

There's more...

Docker is a great tool for rapid deployment and development. You can spin as many docks as you need on even the most modest hardware. One great use for Docker is having docks act as test nodes for your modules. You can create a Docker image, which includes Puppet, and then have Puppet run within the dock. For more information on Docker, visit `http://www.docker.com/`.

External Tools and the Puppet Ecosystem

9

In this chapter, we will cover the following recipes:

- Creating custom facts
- Adding external facts
- Setting facts as environment variables
- Generating manifests with the `puppet resource` command
- Generating manifests with other tools
- Using PDK
- Using an external node classifier
- Creating your own resource types
- Creating your own providers
- Creating custom functions
- Testing your Puppet manifests with `rspec-puppet`

Introduction

Puppet is a useful tool by itself, but you can get much greater benefits by using Puppet in combination with other tools and frameworks. We'll look at some ways of getting data into Puppet, including the use of custom Facter facts, external facts, and tools to generate Puppet manifests automatically from the existing configuration.

You'll also learn how to extend Puppet by creating your own custom functions, resource types, and providers; how to use an external node classifier script to integrate Puppet with other parts of your infrastructure; and how to test your code with `rspec-puppet`.

Creating custom facts

While Facter's built-in facts are useful, it's actually quite easy to add your own facts. For example, if you have machines in different data centers or hosting providers, you could add a custom fact for this so that Puppet can determine whether any local settings need to be applied (for example, local DNS servers or network routes).

How to do it...

Here's an example of a simple custom fact:

1. Create the `modules/facts/lib/facter` directory and then create the `modules/facts/lib/facter/hello.rb` file with the following contents:

   ```
   Facter.add(:hello) do
       setcode do
       "Hello, world"
     end
   end
   ```

2. Use `puppet plugin` to download the new fact definition:

   ```
   [root@cookbook ~]# puppet plugin download
   Notice:
   /File[/opt/puppetlabs/puppet/cache/lib/facter/hello.rb]/ensure:
   defined content as '{md5}f66d5e290459388c5ffb3694dd22388b'
   Downloaded these plugins:
   /opt/puppetlabs/puppet/cache/lib/facter/hello.rb
   ```

3. Run `facter` to see your new fact value:

   ```
   [root@cookbook ~]# facter -p hello
   Hello, world
   ```

How it works...

Facter facts are defined in Ruby files that are distributed with Facter. Puppet can add additional facts to Facter by creating files within the `lib/facter` subdirectory of a module. These files are then transferred to client nodes, as we saw earlier with the `puppetlabs-stdlib` module. To have the command-line `facter` use these `puppet facts`, append the `-p` option to `facter`, as shown in the following command line:

```
[root@cookbook ~]# facter hello
[root@cookbook ~]# facter -p hello
Hello, world
```

Running `facter -p` is deprecated in Puppet 5; you may see issues when running `facter` separately from the command line. It is now preferred you use `puppet facts` when retrieving facts. The only caveat when running `puppet facts` is that you cannot search for a specific fact; you will receive all the facts from the system. The output returned will be in JSON format, suitable for manipulation by JSON tools, such as `jq`.

Facts can contain any Ruby code, and the last value evaluated inside the `setcode do ...` `end` block will be the value returned by the fact. For example, you could make a more useful fact that returns the number of users currently logged in to the system:

```
Facter.add(:users) do
  setcode do
    %x{/usr/bin/who |wc -l}.chomp
  end
end
```

To reference the fact in your manifests, just use its name like a built-in fact:

```
notify { "${::users} users logged in": }
```

This would return the following output:

```
Notice: 2 users logged in
```

You can add custom facts to any Puppet module. When creating facts that will be used by multiple modules, it may make sense to place them in a facts module. In most cases, the custom fact is related to a specific module and should be placed in that module.

There's more...

The name of the Ruby file that holds the fact definition is irrelevant. You can name this file whatever you wish; the name of the fact comes from the `Facter.add()` function call. You may also call this function several times within a single Ruby file to define multiple facts as necessary. For instance, you could grep the `/proc/meminfo` file and return several facts based on memory information, as shown in the `meminfo.rb` file in the following code snippet:

```
File.open('/proc/meminfo') do |f|
  f.each_line { |line|
    if (line[/^Active:/])
```

```
      Facter.add(:memory_active) do
        setcode do line.split(':')[1].to_i
        end
      end
    end
    if (line[/^Inactive:/])
      Facter.add(:memory_inactive) do
        setcode do line.split(':')[1].to_i
        end
      end
    end
  }
end
```

You can extend the use of facts to build a completely nodeless Puppet configuration; in other words, Puppet can decide what resources to apply to a machine, based solely on the results of facts. Jordan Sissel has written about this approach at `http://www.semicomplete. com/blog/geekery/puppet-nodeless-configuration/`.

You can find out more about custom facts, including how to make sure that OS-specific facts work only on the relevant systems, and how to weigh facts so that they're evaluated in a specific order at the puppetlabs website: `https://puppet.com/docs/facter/latest/ custom_facts.html`.

Adding external facts

The *Creating custom facts* recipe describes how to add extra facts written in Ruby. You can also create facts from simple files or from scripts with external facts instead. External facts may be written in YAML, JSON, or txt format.

External facts live in the `/etc/facter/facts.d` directory and have a simple `key=value` format:

```
message="Hello, world"
```

Getting ready

Here's what you need to do to prepare your system to add external facts.

You'll need to create the external `facts` directory, using the following command:

```
[root@cookbook ~]# mkdir -p /etc/facter/facts.d
```

How to do it...

In this example, we'll create a simple external fact that returns a message, as shown in the *Creating custom facts* recipe:

1. Create the `/etc/facter/facts.d/local.txt` file with the following contents:

   ```
   model=ED-209
   ```

2. Run the following command:

   ```
   [root@cookbook ~]# facter model
   ED-209
   ```

3. Well, that was easy! You can add more facts to the same file, or other files, of course, as follows:

   ```
   model=ED-209
   builder=OCP
   directives=4
   ```

However, what if you need to compute a fact in some way, for example, the number of logged-in users? You can create executable facts to do this:

1. Create the `/etc/facter/facts.d/users.sh` file with the following contents:

   ```
   #!/bin/sh
   echo users=`who |wc -l`
   ```

2. Make this file executable with the following command:

   ```
   [root@cookbook ~]# chmod a+x /etc/facter/facts.d/users.sh
   ```

3. Check the users value with the following command:

   ```
   [root@cookbook ~]# facter users
   2
   ```

How it works...

In this example, we'll create an external fact by creating files on the node. We'll also show you how to override a previously defined fact:

1. Current versions of Facter will look into `/etc/facter/facts.d` for files with `.txt`, `.json`, or `.yaml` extensions. If `facter` finds a text file, it will parse the file for `key=value` pairs and add the key as a new fact:

   ```
   [root@cookbook ~]# facter model
   ED-209
   ```

2. If the file is a YAML or JSON file, then `facter` will parse the file for `key=value` pairs in the respective format. For YAML, for instance, it will do the following:

   ```
   ---
   registry: NCC-68814
   class: Andromeda
   shipname: USS Prokofiev
   ```

3. The resulting output will be as follows:

   ```
   [root@cookbook ~]# facter registry class shipname
      class    => Andromeda
      registry => NCC-68814
      shipname => USS Prokofiev
   ```

4. In the case of executable files, Facter will assume that their output is a list of `key=value` pairs. It will execute all the files in the `facts.d` directory and add their output to the internal fact hash. In Windows, batch files or PowerShell scripts may be used in the same way that executable scripts are used in Linux.

5. In the users example, Facter will execute the `users.sh` script, which results in the following output:

   ```
   users=2
   ```

6. It will then search this output for users and return the matching value:

   ```
   [root@cookbook ~]# facter users
   2
   ```

7. If there are multiple matches for the key you specified, Facter determines which fact to return based on a weight property. In my version of Facter, the weight of external facts is 10,000 (https://github.com/puppetlabs/facter/blob/3.11.x/ lib/inc/facter/facts/collection.hpp#L88). This high value is to ensure that the facts you define can override the supplied facts, for example:

```
[root@cookbook ~]# facter architecture
x86_64
[root@cookbook ~]# echo
"architecture=ppc64">>/etc/facter/facts.d/ myfacts.txt
[root@cookbook ~]# facter architecture
ppc64
```

There's more...

Since all external facts have a weight of 10,000, the order in which they are parsed within the /etc/facter/facts.d directory sets their precedence (with the last one encountered having the highest precedence). To create a fact that will be favored over another, you will have to carefully craft the name of the file to ensure it is read last by facter:

```
[root@cookbook ~]# facter architecture
ppc64
[root@cookbook ~]# echo "architecture=r10000"
>>/etc/facter/facts.d/architecture.txt
[root@cookbook ~]# facter architecture
r10000
```

Debugging external facts

If you're having trouble getting Facter to recognize your external facts, run facter in debug mode to see what's happening:

```
ubuntu@cookbook:~/puppet$ facter -d robin
Fact file /etc/facter/facts.d/myfacts.json was parsed but returned an empty
data set
```

The Fact file X was parsed but returned an empty dataset error, which means Facter didn't find any key=value pairs in the file or, in the case of an executable fact, in its output.

Note that if you have external facts present, Facter parses or runs all the facts in the `/etc/facter/facts.d` directory every time you query Facter. If some of these scripts take a long time to run, that can significantly slow down anything that uses Facter. Unless a particular fact needs to be recomputed every time it's queried, consider replacing it with a cron job that computes it every so often and writes the result to a text file in the `Facter` directory.

Using external facts in Puppet

Any external facts you create will be available to both Facter and Puppet. To reference external facts in your Puppet manifests, just use the fact name in the same way you would for a built-in or custom fact:

```
notify { "There are ${facts['users']} people logged in right now.": }
```

Unless you are specifically attempting to override a defined fact, you should avoid using the name of a predefined fact. Running `facter -p` is now deprecated; you should be using the newer syntax, `puppet facts`. Running `puppet facts` has the disadvantage that all facts are returned; there is no way to query for specific facts. However, using `puppet facts` ensures that a full Puppet runtime environment is created when evaluating facts. You may get unexpected results when running `facter -p`.

Setting facts as environment variables

Another handy way to get information into Puppet and Facter is to pass it using environment variables. Any environment variable whose name starts with `FACTER_` will be interpreted as a fact. For example, ask `facter` the value of `hello` using the following command:

```
[root@cookbook ~]# facter -p hello
Hello, world
```

Now, override the value with an environment variable and ask again:

```
[root@cookbook ~]# FACTER_hello='Howdy!' facter -p hello
Howdy!
```

It works just as well with Puppet, so let's run through an example.

How to do it...

In this example, we'll set a fact using an environment variable:

1. Keep the node definition for cookbook the same as our last example:

```
node cookbook {
  notify {"$::hello": }
}
```

2. Run the following command:

```
[root@cookbook ~]# FACTER_hello="Hallo Welt" puppet agent -t
Info: Caching catalog for cookbook.example.com
Info: Applying configuration version '1416212026'
Notice: Hallo Welt
Notice: /Stage[main]/Main/Node[cookbook]/Notify[Hallo Welt]/
message: defined 'message' as 'Hallo Welt'
Notice: Finished catalog run in 0.03 seconds
```

Generating manifests with the Puppet resource command

If you have a server that is already configured as it needs to be, or nearly so, you can capture that configuration as a Puppet manifest. The puppet resource command generates Puppet manifests from the existing configuration of a system. For example, you can have puppet resource generate a manifest that creates all the users found on the system. This is very useful to take a snapshot of a working system and get its configuration quickly into Puppet.

How to do it...

Here are some examples of using puppet resource to get data from a running system:

1. To generate the manifest for a particular user, run the following command:

```
t@mylaptop $ puppet resource user thomas
user { 'thomas':
  ensure  => 'present',
  comment => 'Thomas Uphill',
  gid     => 1000,
```

```
            groups  => ['wheel', 'audio', 'pulse-rt',    'jackuser',
         'vboxusers', 'docker'],
            home    => '/home/thomas',
            shell   => '/bin/bash',
            uid     => 1000,
         }
```

2. For a particular service, run the following command:

```
t@mylaptop $ puppet resource service sshd
service { 'sshd':
  ensure => 'running',
  enable => 'true',
}
```

3. For a package, run the following command:

```
t@mylaptop $ puppet resource package kernel
package { 'kernel':
  ensure => '4.16.6-302.fc28',
}
```

There's more...

You can use puppet resource to examine each of the resource types available in Puppet. In the preceding examples, we generated a manifest for a specific instance of the resource type, but you can also use puppet resource to dump all instances of the resource:

```
t@mylaptop $ puppet resource service |head -40
service { 'ModemManager.service':
  ensure => 'running',
  enable => 'true',
}
service { 'NetworkManager-dispatcher.service':
  ensure => 'stopped',
  enable => 'true',
}
service { 'NetworkManager-wait-online.service':
  ensure => 'running',
  enable => 'true',
}
service { 'NetworkManager.service':
  ensure => 'running',
  enable => 'true',
```

```
}
service { 'abrt-ccpp.service':
  ensure => 'stopped',
  enable => 'false',
}
...
```

This will output the state of each `service` on the system; this is because each `service` is an enumerable resource. When you try the same command with a resource that is not enumerable, you get an error message:

```
t@mylaptop $ puppet resource file
Error: Could not run: Listing all file instances is not supported. Please
specify a file or directory, e.g. puppet resource file /etc
```

Asking Puppet to describe each file on the system will not work; that's something best left to an audit tool such as Tripwire (a system designed to look for changes on every file on the system: http://www.tripwire.com).

Generating manifests with other tools

If you want to quickly capture the complete configuration of a running system as a Puppet manifest, there are a couple of tools available to help. In this example, we'll look at Blueprint, which is designed to examine a machine and dump its state as the Puppet code.

Getting ready

Here's what you need to do to prepare your system to use Blueprint. On RHEL systems, the `python-pip` package is included in the EPEL repository. Use Puppet to install `pip`:

```
[root@cookbook ~]# puppet resource package epel-release ensure=installed
Notice: /Package[epel-release]/ensure: created
package { 'epel-release':
  ensure => '7-9',
}
[root@cookbook ~]# puppet resource package python-pip ensure=installed
Notice: /Package[python-pip]/ensure: created
package { 'python-pip':
  ensure => '8.1.2-6.el7',
}
```

Now use the `pip` package provider to install `blueprint`:

```
[root@cookbook ~]# puppet resource package blueprint ensure=installed
provider=pip
Notice: /Package[blueprint]/ensure: created
package { 'blueprint':
  ensure => '3.4.2',
}
```

You may need to install Git on your `cookbook` node if it is not already installed.

How to do it...

These steps will show you how to run Blueprint:

1. Run the following commands:

```
[root@cookbook ~]# mkdir blueprint && cd blueprint
[root@cookbook blueprint]# blueprint create -P blueprint_test
# [blueprint] please give Git your name and email address so
commits have an author
# [blueprint]
# [blueprint] git config --global user.email "you@example.com"
# [blueprint] git config --global user.name "Your Name"
# [blueprint]
```

2. Configure Git with a username and email, as shown in the output:

```
[root@cookbook blueprint]# git config --global user.email
"thomas@narrabilis.com"
[root@cookbook blueprint]# git config --global user.name
"Thomas Uphill"
```

3. Re-run the `blueprint` command:

```
[root@cookbook blueprint]# blueprint create -P blueprint_test
# [blueprint] searching for APT packages to exclude
# [blueprint] searching for Yum packages to exclude
...
# [blueprint] searching for PEAR/PECL packages
# [blueprint] searching for service dependencies
blueprint_test/manifests/init.pp
```

4. Read the `blueprint_test/manifests/init.pp` file to see the generated code:

```
#
# Automatically generated by blueprint(7). Edit at your own
risk.
#
class blueprint_test {
 Exec {
    path =>
'/usr/local/sbin:/sbin:/bin:/usr/sbin:/usr/bin:/opt/puppetlabs/
bin:/root/bin',
 }
 Class['files'] -> Class['packages']
 class files {
 file {
 . . .
```

The `blueprint_test` module created should be seen as a starting point only, it will need some modification on your end to work as expected.

There's more...

Blueprint just takes a snapshot of the system as it stands; it makes no intelligent decisions, and Blueprint captures all the files on the system and all the packages. It will generate a configuration much larger than you may actually require. For instance, when configuring a server, you may specify that you want the Apache package installed. The dependencies for the Apache package will be installed automatically and you need to specify them. When generating the configuration with a tool such as Blueprint, you will capture all those dependencies and lock the versions that are installed on your system currently. Looking at our generated Blueprint code, we can see that this is the case:

```
class yum {
  package {
        'NetworkManager': ensure       => '1:1.0.6-30.el7_2.x86_64';
        'NetworkManager-libnm': ensure => '1:1.0.6-30.el7_2.x86_64';
        'NetworkManager-team': ensure  => '1:1.0.6-30.el7_2.x86_64';
        'NetworkManager-tui': ensure   => '1:1.0.6-30.el7_2.x86_64';
        'acl': ensure                  => '2.2.51-12.el7.x86_64';
  . . .
```

If you were creating this manifest yourself, you would likely specify `ensure =>` `installed` instead of a specific version.

Packages install default versions of files. Blueprint has no notion of this and will add all the files to the manifest, even those that have not changed. By default, Blueprint will indiscriminately capture all the files in /etc as file resources.

Blueprint and similar tools have a very small use case generally, but may help you to get familiar with the Puppet syntax and give you some ideas on how to specify your own manifests. I would not recommend blindly using this tool to create a system, however.

There's no shortcut to good configuration management; those who hope to save time and effort by cutting and pasting someone else's code as a whole (as with public modules) are likely to find that it saves neither.

Using PDK

The **PDK (Puppet Development Kit)** is a set of tools for developing and testing modules. Puppet released the PDK to make developing modules easier and, more importantly, consistent.

Getting ready

To use the PDK, install the PDK following the directions at https://puppet.com/docs/pdk/latest/pdk_install.html.

For RHEL installations, pdk can be installed with the puppet5 YUM repo using the following:

```
[root@cookbook ~]# yum install pdk
Loaded plugins: fastestmirror
...
Running transaction
  Installing : pdk-1.5.0.0-1.el7.x86_64 1/1
  Verifying  : pdk-1.5.0.0-1.el7.x86_64 1/1

Installed:
  pdk.x86_64 0:1.5.0.0-1.el7

Complete!
```

Debian/Ubuntu LTS releases, such as Trusty and Xenial, have the PDK available in the apt repository: http://apt.puppet.com/dists/xenial/puppet5/binary-amd64/

macOS and Windows have their own packages, available at `https://puppet.com/download-puppet-development-kit`.

The PDK will be installed into `/opt/puppetlabs/pdk`; add `/opt/puppetlabs/pdk/bin` to your `PATH` variable.

How to do it...

To use the PDK to create a new module, use the `new module` command:

1. Run the new command; use your `forge` username if you have one:

   ```
   [t@mylaptop ~]$ pdk new module thing1 [12/1820]
   pdk (INFO): Creating new module: thing1
   We need to create the metadata.json file for this module, so
   we're going to ask you 4
   questions.
   If the question is not applicable to this module, accept the
   default option shown afte
   r each question. You can modify any answers at any time by
   manually updating the metadata.json file.

   [Q 1/4] If you have a Puppet Forge username, add it here.
   We can use this to upload your module to the Forge when it's
   complete.
   --> uphillian
   ```

2. You may use your own name for the module author name; or any pseudo-name you prefer:

   ```
   [Q 2/4] Who wrote this module?
   This is used to credit the module's author.
   --> Thomas Uphill
   ```

3. Select a license from the list at `https://spdx.org/licenses/`, and enter the key exactly as shown, or use one of the following options:

   ```
   [Q 3/4] What license does this module code fall under?
   This should be an identifier from https://spdx.org/licenses/.
   Common values are "Apache-2.0", "MIT", or "proprietary".
   --> GPL-3.0
   ```

4. Select Linux, Debian-based Linux, and Windows as the types of OS you support:

```
[Q 4/4] What operating systems does this module support?
Use the up and down keys to move between the choices, space to
select and enter to continue.
--> RedHat based Linux, Debian based Linux, Windows (Use arrow
or number (1-7) keys, p
--> RedHat based Linux, Debian based Linux, Windows
```

5. Choose yes to have your module created:

```
Metadata will be generated based on this information, continue?
Yes
pdk (INFO): Module 'thing1' generated at path
'/home/thomas/puppet/modules/thing1', from template
'file:///opt/puppetlabs/pdk/share/cache/pdk-templates.git'.
pdk (INFO): In your module directory, add classes with the 'pdk
new class' command.
```

6. Create the default manifest with the new class command (this will only work within the thing1 directory):

```
[t@mylaptop ~]$ cd thing1
/home/thomas/puppet/modules/thing1
[t@mylaptop thing1]$ pdk new class thing1
pdk (INFO): Creating
'/home/thomas/puppet/modules/thing1/manifests/init.pp' from
template.
pdk (INFO): Creating
'/home/thomas/puppet/modules/thing1/spec/classes/thing1_spec.rb
'
from template.
```

7. Edit the manifests/init.pp file and add the following:

```
file {'/tmp/foo':
  content => 'foo'
}
```

8. Test your module using pdk:

```
[t@mylaptop thing1] $ pdk test unit
pdk (INFO): Using Ruby 2.4.4
pdk (INFO): Using Puppet 5.5.1
```

```
[√] Preparing to run the unit tests.
[×] Running unit tests.
  Evaluated 9 tests in 1.829098921 seconds: 3 failures, 0
pending.
[√] Cleaning up after running unit tests.
failed: rspec: ./spec/classes/thing1_spec.rb:8: error during
compilation: Parameter path failed on File[/tmp/foo]: File
paths must be fully qualified, not '/tmp/foo' (file:
/home/thomas/puppet/modules/thing1/spec/fixtures/modules/thing1
/manifests/init.pp, line: 8)
...
```

The test failed because we created a file with a Unix-style path, but our module is marked as supporting Windows. The PDK did the work of writing our test cases.

How it works...

The PDK uses templates to create directories that contain the files needed for testing our module. The PDK also uses the responses to our questions to create a `metadata.json` file. This file describes our module and any dependencies it may require.

We created the `init` class for our module using `new class thing1`; this creates the `manifests/init.pp` file to contain our default class. PDK does not create a default manifest because some modules have no manifests; they may include fact definitions in `lib/facter` or functions in `lib/puppet/functions`, or even types and providers.

The PDK will use our responses to create `rspec` tests and the supporting files for the tests. Using `pdk test unit`, we are able to run `rspec` against our manifests.

Using the PDK, we can automate some of the testing we have to do on our modules. In the preceding example, we found that our definition of the `/tmp/foo` file caused compilation problems on Windows. We can fix that by modifying the code to read as follows:

```
$foo = $facts['osfamily'] ? {
  'windows' => 'C:/temp/foo',
    default  => '/tmp/foo'
}
file {$foo:
  content  => 'bar'
}
```

Now, when we run `pdk test unit`, we see the expected results:

```
[t@mylaptop thing1]$ pdk test unit
pdk (INFO): Using Ruby 2.4.4
pdk (INFO): Using Puppet 5.5.1
[√] Preparing to run the unit tests.
[√] Running unit tests.
  Evaluated 7 tests in 0.776962162 seconds: 0 failures, 0 pending.
[√] Cleaning up after running unit tests.
```

There's more...

The PDK also supports creating defined types. Explore the options and experiment. For instance, try creating a `foo` defined type:

```
[t@mylaptop thing1]$ pdk new defined_type foo
pdk (INFO): Creating '/home/vagrant/thing1/manifests/foo.pp' from template.
pdk (INFO): Creating '/home/vagrant/thing1/spec/defines/foo_spec.rb' from template.
```

The PDK is actively developed and new features are always being added. I find the templates are useful as a starting point for my `rspec` tests.

Using an external node classifier

When Puppet runs on a node, it needs to know which classes should be applied to that node. For example, if it is a web server node, it might need to include an Apache class. The normal way to map nodes to classes is in the Puppet manifest itself, for example, in your `site.pp` file:

```
node 'web1' {
  include apache
}
```

Alternatively, you can use an **External Node Classifier** (**ENC**) to do this job. An ENC is any executable program that can accept the **fully-qualified domain name** (**FQDN**) as the first command-line argument ($1). The script is expected to return a list of classes, and parameters, and an optional environment to apply to the node. The output is expected to be in the standard YAML format. When using an ENC, you should keep in mind that the classes applied through the standard `site.pp` are merged with those provided by the ENC.

Parameters returned by the ENC are available as top-scope variables to the node.

An ENC could be a simple shell script, for example, or a wrapper around a more complicated program or API that can decide how to map nodes to classes. The Foreman project uses an ENC to decide which classes are applied to nodes. More information on The Foreman can be found at `https://theforeman.org/manuals/1.17/index.html#3.5.5FactsandtheENC`. The Puppet Enterprise classifier is an alternative to an ENC, more information on the classifier can be found at `https://puppet.com/docs/pe/latest/managing_nodes/grouping_and_classifying_nodes.html`.

In this example, we'll build the simplest of ENCs, a shell script that simply prints a list of classes to include. We'll start by including an `enc` class that defines `notify` which, in turn, will print a top-scope `$enc` variable.

Getting ready

We'll start by creating our enc class to include with the enc script:

1. Run the following command:

   ```
   t@mylaptop ~/puppet $ mkdir -p modules/enc/manifests
   ```

2. Create the `modules/enc/manifests/init.pp` file with the following contents:

   ```
   class enc {
     notify {"We defined this from $enc": }
   }
   ```

How to do it...

Here's how to build a simple external node classifier. We'll perform all these steps on our Puppet master server. If you are running masterless, then do these steps on a node:

1. Create the /etc/puppetlabs/cookbook.sh file with the following contents:

```
#!/bin/bash
cat <<EOF
---
classes:
    enc:
parameters:
    enc: $0
EOF
```

2. Run the following command:

   root@puppet:/etc/puppetlabs # chmod a+x cookbook.sh

3. Modify your /etc/puppetlabs/puppet/puppet.conf file as follows:

```
node_terminus  = exec
external_nodes = /etc/puppetlabs/cookbook.sh
```

4. Restart the puppetserver services to make the change effective:

   [root@puppet ~]# systemctl restart puppetserver

5. Ensure your site.pp file has the following empty definition for the default node:

```
node default {}
```

6. Run Puppet:

   ```
   [root@enctest ~]# puppet agent -t
   . . .
   Notice: We defined this from /etc/puppetlabs/cookbook.sh
   Notice: /Stage[main]/Enc/Notify[We defined this from
   /etc/puppetlabs/cookbook.sh]/message: defined 'message' as 'We
   defined this from /etc/puppetlabs/cookbook.sh'
   Notice: Applied catalog in 0.03 seconds
   ```

How it works...

When an ENC is set in `puppet.conf`, Puppet will call the specified program with the node's FQDN as the first command-line argument. In our example script, this argument is ignored, and it just outputs a fixed list of classes (actually, just one class).

Obviously, this script is not terribly useful; a more sophisticated script might check a database to find the class list, or look up the node in a hash, an external text file, or a database (often an organization's configuration management database–CMDB). Hopefully, this example is enough to get you started with writing your own external node classifier. Remember that you can write your script in any language you prefer.

There's more...

An ENC can supply a whole list of classes to be included in the node, in the following (YAML) format:

```
---
classes:
  CLASS1:
  CLASS2:
  CLASS3:
```

For classes that take parameters, you can use this format:

```
---
classes:
  mysql:
    package: percona-server-server-5.5
    socket: /var/run/mysqld/mysqld.sock
    port: 3306
```

You can also produce top-scope variables using an ENC with this format:

```
---
parameters:
  message: 'Anyone home MyFly?'
```

Variables that you set in this way will be available in your manifest using the normal syntax for a top-scope variable, for example `$::message`.

When you are done testing your ENC, be sure to remove the configuration from `puppet.conf`, as the ENC will interfere with the recipes in the following sections.

See also

- See the puppetlabs ENC page for more information on writing and using ENCs: `https://puppet.com/docs/puppet/latest/nodes_external.html`

Creating your own resource types

As you know, Puppet has a bunch of useful built-in resource types: packages, files, users, and so on. Usually, you can do everything you need to do by using either combinations of these built-in resources, or `define`, which you can use more or less in the same way as a resource (see `Chapter 3`, *Writing Better Manifests*, for information on definitions).

In the early days of Puppet, creating your own resource type was more common as the list of core resources was shorter than it is today. Before you consider creating your own resource type, I suggest searching the Forge for alternative solutions. Even if you can find a project that only partially solves your problem, you will be better served by extending and helping out that project, rather than trying to create your own. However, if you need to create your own resource type, Puppet makes it quite easy. The native types are written in Ruby, and you will need a basic familiarity with Ruby in order to create your own.

Let's refresh our memory on the distinction between types and providers. A type describes a resource and the parameters it can have (for example, the `package` type). A provider tells Puppet how to implement a resource type for a particular platform or situation (for example, the apt/dpkg providers implement the package type for Debian-like systems).

A single type (package) can have many providers (APT, YUM, Fink, and so on). If you don't specify a provider when declaring a resource, Puppet will choose the most appropriate one for the platform in question.

We'll use Ruby in this section; if you are not familiar with Ruby, check out `http://www.ruby-doc.org/docs/Tutorial/` or `http://www.codecademy.com/tracks/ruby/`.

How to do it...

In this section, we'll see how to create a custom type that we can use to manage Git repositories, and in the next section, we'll write a provider to implement this type.

Create the `modules/cookbook/lib/puppet/type/gitrepo.rb` file with the following contents:

```
Puppet::Type.newtype(:gitrepo) do
  ensurable

  newparam(:source) do
  isnamevar
  end

  newparam(:path)
end
```

This will define our type; a type without a provider cannot be used though. In the next section, we'll create a provider for this type.

How it works...

Custom types can live in any module, in a `lib/puppet/type` subdirectory, and in a file named for the type (in our example, that's `modules/cookbook/lib/puppet/type/gitrepo.rb`). The first line of `gitrepo.rb` tells Puppet to register a new type, named `gitrepo`:

```
Puppet::Type.newtype(:gitrepo) do
```

The `ensurable` line automatically gives the type an `ensure` property, such as Puppet's built- in resources:

```
ensurable
```

We'll now give the type some parameters. For the moment, all we need is a `source` parameter for the Git source URL, and a `path` parameter to tell Puppet where the repo should be created in the filesystem:

```
newparam(:source) do
  isnamevar
end
```

The `isnamevar` declaration tells Puppet that the source parameter is the type's `namevar`. So when you declare an instance of this resource, whatever name you give, it will be the value of source, for example:

```
gitrepo { 'git://github.com/puppetlabs/puppet.git':
  path => '/home/ubuntu/dev/puppet',
}
```

Finally, we tell Puppet that the type accepts the `path` parameter:

```
newparam(:path)
```

There's more...

When deciding whether or not you should create a custom type, you should ask a few questions about the resource you are trying to describe:

- Is the resource enumerable? Can you easily obtain a list of all the instances of the resource on the system?
- Is the resource atomic? Can you ensure that only one copy of the resource exists on the system (This is particularly important when you want to use `ensure=>absent` on the resource.)
- Is there any other resource that describes this resource? In such a case, a defined type based on the existing resource would, in most cases, be a simpler solution.

Documentation

Our example is deliberately simple, but when you move on to developing real custom types for your production environment, you should add documentation strings to describe what the type and its parameters do, for example:

```
Puppet::Type.newtype(:gitrepo) do
  @doc = "Manages Git repos"
  ensurable
  newparam(:source) do
    desc "Git source URL for the repo"
    isnamevar
  end
  newparam(:path) do
    desc "Path where the repo should be created"
  end
end
```

Validation

You can use parameter validation to generate useful error messages when someone tries to pass bad values to the resource. For example, you could validate that the directory where the repo is to be created actually exists:

```
newparam(:path) do
  desc "Path where the repo should be created"
  validate do |value|
    basepath = File.dirname(value)
    unless File.directory?(basepath)
      raise ArgumentError, "The path %s doesn't exist" % basepath
    end
  end
end
```

You can also specify the list of allowed values that the parameter can take:

```
newparam(:breakfast) do
  newvalues(:bacon, :eggs, :sausages)
end
```

Creating your own providers

In the previous section, we created a new custom type named `gitrepo` and told Puppet that it takes two parameters, `source` and `path`. However, so far, we haven't told Puppet how to actually check out the repo, in other words, how to create a specific instance of this type. That's where the provider comes in.

We saw that a type will often have several possible providers. In our example, there is only one sensible way to instantiate a Git repo, so we'll only supply one provider: git. If you were to generalize this type to just repo, say it's not hard to imagine creating several different providers depending on the type of repo, for example, `git`, `svn`, `cvs`, and so on.

How to do it...

We'll add the `git` provider, and create an instance of a `gitrepo` resource to check that it all works. You'll need Git installed for this to work, but if you're using the Git-based manifest management setup described in Chapter 2, *Puppet Infrastructure*, we can safely assume that Git is available:

1. Create the `modules/cookbook/lib/puppet/provider/gitrepo/git.rb` file with the following contents:

```
require 'fileutils'

Puppet::Type.type(:gitrepo).provide(:git) do
  commands :git => "git"

  def create
    git "clone", resource[:source], resource[:path]
  end

  def exists?
    File.directory? resource[:path]
  end
end
```

2. Modify your `site.pp` file as follows:

```
node 'cookbook' {
  gitrepo { 'https://github.com/puppetlabs/puppetlabs-git':
    ensure => present,
    path   => '/tmp/puppet',
  }
}
```

3. Run Puppet:

```
[root@cookbook ~]# puppet agent -t
Info: Using configured environment 'production'
Info: Retrieving pluginfacts
Info: Retrieving plugin
Info: Loading facts
Info: Caching catalog for cookbook.example.com
Info: Applying configuration version '1525968630'
Notice:
/Stage[main]/Main/Node[cookbook]/Gitrepo[https://github.com/puppetl
abs/puppetlabs-git]/ensure: created
Notice: Applied catalog in 0.43 seconds
```

How it works...

Custom providers can live in any module, in a `lib/puppet/provider/TYPE_NAME` subdirectory in a file named after the provider. (The provider is the actual program that is run on the system; in our example, the program is Git and the provider is in `modules/cookbook/lib/puppet/provider/gitrepo/git.rb`. Note that the name of the module is irrelevant.)

After an initial require line in `git.rb`, we tell Puppet to register a new provider for the `gitrepo` type with the following line:

```
Puppet::Type.type(:gitrepo).provide(:git) do
```

When you declare an instance of the `gitrepo` type in your manifest, Puppet will first of all check whether the instance already exists, by calling the `exists?` method on the provider. So we need to supply this method, complete with code to check whether an instance of the `gitrepo` type already exists:

```
def exists?
  File.directory? resource[:path]
end
```

This is not the most sophisticated implementation; it simply returns `true` if a directory exists matching the path parameter of the instance. A better implementation of `exists?` might check, for example, whether there is a `.git` subdirectory and that it contains valid Git metadata. But this will do for now.

If `exists?` returns true, Puppet will take no further action because the specified resource exists (as far as Puppet knows). If it returns `false`, Puppet assumes the resource doesn't yet exist, and will try to create it by calling the provider's `create` method.

Accordingly, we supply some code for the create method that calls the `Git clone` command to create the repo:

```
def create
  git "clone", resource[:source], resource[:path]
end
```

The method has access to the instance's parameters, which we need in order to know where to check out the repo from and which directory to create it in. We get this by looking at `resource[:source]` and `resource[:path]`.

There's more...

You can see that custom types and providers in Puppet are very powerful. In fact, they can do anything–at least, anything that Ruby can do. If you are managing some parts of your infrastructure with complicated `define` statements and `exec` resources, you may want to consider replacing these with a custom type. However, as stated previously, it's worth looking around to see whether someone else has already done this before implementing your own.

Our example was very simple, and there is much more to learn about writing your own types. If you're going to distribute your code for others to use, or even if you aren't, it's a good idea to include tests with it. Puppetlabs has a useful page on the interface between custom types and providers:

```
https://puppet.com/docs/puppet/latest/custom_types.html
```

There is another one on implementing providers:

```
https://puppet.com/docs/puppet/latest/provider_development.html
```

They also offer a complete worked example of developing a custom type and provider, which is a little more advanced than that presented in this book:

```
https://puppet.com/docs/puppet/latest/complete_resource_example.html
```

Creating custom functions

If you've read the *Using GnuPG to encrypt secrets* recipe in Chapter 4, *Working with Files and Packages*, then you've already seen an example of a custom function (in that example, we created a secret function that shelled out to GnuPG). Let's look at custom functions in a little more detail now and build an example. There are two Ruby APIs available when writing custom functions, the legacy and the modern API. Legacy functions are instantiated with `Puppet::Parser::Functions`, modern functions are instantiated with `Puppet::Functions.create_function`. In our example, we will use the modern API.

How to do it...

If you've read the *Efficiently distributing cron jobs* recipe in Chapter 5, *Users and Virtual Resources*, you might remember that we used the inline_epp function to set a random time for cron jobs to run, based on the hostname of the node. In this example, we'll take that idea and turn it into a custom function called random_minute:

1. Create the modules/cookbook/lib/puppet/parser/functions/random_minute.rb file with the following contents:

```
Puppet::Functions.create_function(:random_minute) do
  dispatch :randMin do end

  def randMin()
    scope = closure_scope
    hostname = scope['facts']['hostname']
    hostname.sum % 60
  end
end
```

2. Modify your site.pp file as follows:

```
node 'cookbook' {
  cron { 'randomised_cron_job':
    command => '/bin/echo "Hello, world">>/tmp/hello.txt',
    hour    => '*',
    minute  => random_minute(),
  }
}
```

3. Run Puppet:

```
[root@cookbook ~]# puppet agent -t
Info: Using configured environment 'production'
Info: Retrieving pluginfacts
Info: Retrieving plugin
Info: Loading facts
Info: Caching catalog for cookbook.example.com
Info: Applying configuration version '1526013433'
Notice:
/Stage[main]/Main/Node[cookbook]/Cron[randomised_cron_job]/ensu
re: created
Notice: Applied catalog in 0.15 seconds
```

4. Check `crontab` with the following command:

```
[root@cookbook ~]# crontab -l
# HEADER: This file was autogenerated at 2018-05-11 04:37:13
+0000 by puppet.
# HEADER: While it can still be managed manually, it is
definitely not recommended.
# HEADER: Note particularly that the comments starting with
'Puppet Name' should
# HEADER: not be deleted, as doing so could cause duplicate
cron jobs.
# Puppet Name: randomised_cron_job
15 * * * * /bin/echo "Hello, world">>/tmp/hello.txt
```

How it works...

Custom functions can live in any module, in the `lib/puppet/functions` subdirectory in a file named after the function (in our example, `random_minute.rb`). Functions can be namespaced as well. For example we could have a `cookbook::random_minute` function, this would be in `lib/puppet/functions/cookbook/random_minute.rb`. You can now have all your functions prefaced with your company or project, to avoid namespace collisions.

Functions are created with a `create_function` call. The arguments to the function are handled via a dispatch method. You define multiple dispatch methods to account for variations in input parameters for your function. In this way, your function can deal with different input forms. When a set of input matches the dispatch call, the referenced function is called. In the preceding example, we do not have any arguments, so the `randMin` function is called with no input parameters.

Our `randMin` function needs to know the value of the hostname `fact`, to do this, we assign the current scope to a `scope` variable. We then look in the `facts` array within the `scope` variable to retrieve the value for hostname. Then we simply call the built-in `Ruby hash` function and we simply call the built-in `Ruby hash` function to return an integer. We then modulus (%) that integer with 60 to return a number between 0 and 60.

There's more...

You can, of course, do a lot more with custom functions. In fact, anything you can do in Ruby, you can do in a custom function. You also have access to all the facts and variables that are in scope at the point in the Puppet manifest where the function is called, by calling scope, as shown in the example. You can also work on arguments, for example, a general-purpose hashing function that takes two arguments: the size of the hash table and optionally the thing to hash. Create `modules/cookbook/lib/puppet/functions/hashtable.rb` with the following contents:

```
Puppet::Functions.create_function(:hashtable) do
  dispatch :hashtable do
    param 'String', :input
  end
  dispatch :hashhost do end
  def hashtable(input)
    input.sum
  end
  def hashhost()
    scope = closure_scope
    hostname = scope['facts']['hostname']
    hostname.sum
  end
end
```

Now, we'll create a test for our hashtable function and alter `site.pp` as follows:

```
node cookbook {
  $hours = hashtable(24)
  $minutes = hashtable()
  $days = hashtable(30)
  $days_fqdn = hashtable(30,'fqdn')
  $days_ipaddress = hashtable(30,'ipaddress')
  notify {"\n hours=${hours}\n minutes=${minutes}\n days=${days}\n
days_fqdn=${days_fqdn}\n days_ipaddress=${days_ipaddress}\n":}
}
```

Now, run Puppet and observe the values that are returned:

```
[root@cookbook ~]# puppet agent -t
Info: Using configured environment 'production'
Info: Retrieving pluginfacts
Info: Retrieving plugin
Info: Loading facts
Info: Caching catalog for cookbook.example.com
Info: Applying configuration version '1526272299'
Notice:
 hours=15
 minutes=15
 days=15
 days_fqdn=4
 days_ipaddress=15
Notice: Applied catalog in 0.05 seconds
```

Our simple definition quickly grew when we added the ability to add arguments. As with all programming, care should be taken when working with arguments to ensure that you do not have any error conditions. With the dispatch framework, we were able to write several different versions of the function based on the input supplied.

To find out more about what you can do with custom functions, see the puppetlabs website:
`https://puppet.com/docs/puppet/latest/functions_basics.html`

Testing your puppet manifests with rspec-puppet

It would be great if we could verify that our Puppet manifests satisfy certain expectations without even having to run Puppet. The `rspec-puppet` tool is a nifty tool for this. Based on RSpec, a testing framework for Ruby programs, `rspec-puppet` lets you write test cases for your Puppet manifests that are especially useful for catching regressions (bugs introduced when fixing another bug) and refactoring problems (bugs introduced when reorganizing your code).

Getting ready

Here's what you'll need to do to install `rspec-puppet`.

Run the following commands:

```
t@mylaptop $ sudo /opt/puppetlabs/puppet/bin/gem install rspec-puppet
Fetching: rspec-support-3.7.1.gem (100%)
Successfully installed rspec-support-3.7.1
...
Installing ri documentation for rspec-puppet-2.6.11
Done installing documentation for rspec-support, rspec-core, diff-lcs,
rspec-expectati
ons, rspec-mocks, rspec, rspec-puppet after 4 seconds
7 gems installed
```

This uses the Gem included with `puppet agent`. You may also install using the system gem but be aware that different versions of Ruby have different gem behaviour. You may also try using the gem provider and `puppet resource` like this:

```
puppet resource package rspec-puppet ensure=installed provider=gem
```

This, too would use the system gem.

How to do it...

Let's create an example class, `thing`, and write some tests for it.

1. Define the `thing` class:

```
class thing {
  service {'thing':
    ensure  => 'running',
    enable  => true,
    require => Package['thing'],
  }
  package {'thing':
    ensure => 'installed'
  }
  file {'/etc/thing.conf':
    content => 'fubar\n',
    mode    => '0644',
    require => Package['thing'],
    notify  => Service['thing'],
  }
}
```

2. Create a `metadata.json` file in the root directory of your module:

```
{
  "name": "thomas-thing",
  "version": "0.0.1",
  "author": "Thomas Uphill",
  "summary": "Does a thing",
  "license": "Apache-2.0",
  "source": "https://github.com/uphillian/thomas-thing",
  "project_page": "https://github.com/uphillian/thomas-thing",
  "dependencies": [
    { "name":"puppetlabs/stdlib","version_requirement":">=
4.13.1 < 5.0.0" }
  ],
  "data_provider": "hiera",
  "description": "Useless module that should do a thing, it
doesn't though."
}
```

3. Run the following commands:

```
t@mylaptop ~/puppet]$cd modules/thing
t@mylaptop ~/puppet/modules/thing $ rspec-puppet-init
t@mylaptop $ rspec-puppet-init
 + spec/
 + spec/classes/
 + spec/defines/
 + spec/functions/
 + spec/hosts/
 + spec/fixtures/
 + spec/fixtures/manifests/
 + spec/fixtures/modules/
 + spec/fixtures/modules/thing
 + spec/fixtures/manifests/site.pp
 + spec/spec_helper.rb
 + Rakefile
```

4. Create the `spec/classes/thing_spec.rb` file with the following contents:

```
require 'spec_helper'
describe 'thing' do
 it { should create_class('thing') }
 it { should contain_package('thing') }
 it { should contain_service('thing').with('ensure' =>
'running' ) }
 it { should contain_file('/etc/things.conf') }
end
```

5. Run the following commands:

```
t@mylaptop $ rake
/opt/puppetlabs/puppet/bin/ruby -
I/opt/puppetlabs/puppet/lib/ruby/gems/2.4.0/gems/rspec-
support-3.7.1/lib:/opt/puppetlabs/puppet/lib/ruby/gems/2.4.0/ge
ms/rspec-core-3.7.1/lib
/opt/puppetlabs/puppet/lib/ruby/gems/2.4.0/gems/rspec-
core-3.7.1/exe/rspec --pattern
spec/\*\*\{,/\*/\*\*\}/\*_spec.rb
...F...F

Failures:

  1) thing should contain File[/etc/things.conf]
     Failure/Error: it { should
contain_file('/etc/things.conf') }
       expected that the catalogue would contain
File[/etc/things.conf]
     # ./spec/classes/thing_spec.rb:6:in `block (2 levels) in
<top (required)>'

  2) thing should contain File[/etc/things.conf]
     Failure/Error: it { should
contain_file('/etc/things.conf') }
       expected that the catalogue would contain
File[/etc/things.conf]
     #
./spec/fixtures/modules/thing/spec/classes/thing_spec.rb:6:in
`block (2 levels) in <top (required)>'

Finished in 1.04 seconds (files took 1.03 seconds to load)
8 examples, 2 failures

Failed examples:

rspec ./spec/classes/thing_spec.rb:6 # thing should contain
File[/etc/things.conf]
rspec
./spec/fixtures/modules/thing/spec/classes/thing_spec.rb:6 #
thing should contain File[/etc/things.conf]

/opt/puppetlabs/puppet/bin/ruby -
I/opt/puppetlabs/puppet/lib/ruby/gems/2.4.0/gems/rspec-
support-3.7.1/lib:/opt/puppetlabs/puppet/lib/ruby/gems/2.4.0/ge
ms/rspec-core-3.7.1/lib
/opt/puppetlabs/puppet/lib/ruby/gems/2.4.0/gems/rspec-
```

```
core-3.7.1/exe/rspec --pattern
spec/\*\*\{,/\*/\*\*\}/\*_spec.rb failed
```

How it works...

The `rspec-puppet-init` command creates a framework of directories for you to put your specs (test programs) in. At the moment, we're just interested in the `spec/classes` directory. This is where you'll put your class specs, one per class, named after the class it tests, for example, `thing_spec.rb`:

1. The spec code itself begins with the following statement, which sets up the RSpec environment to run the specs:

   ```
   require 'spec_helper'
   ```

2. A `describe` block follows:

   ```
   describe 'thing' do
   .. end
   ```

3. `describe` identifies the class we're going to test (thing) and wraps the list of assertions about the class inside a `do .. end` block.

4. Assertions are our stated expectations of the thing class. For example, the first assertion is the following:

   ```
   it { should create_class('thing') }
   ```

5. The `create_class` assertion is used to ensure that the named class is actually created. Here is the next line:

   ```
   it { should contain_package('thing') }
   ```

6. The `contain_package` assertion means what it says: the class should contain a package resource named thing.

7. Test for the existence of the thing service:

   ```
   it { should contain_service('thing').with('ensure' => 'running'
   ) }
   ```

8. The preceding code actually contains two assertions. First, that the class contains a `thing` service:

```
contain_service('thing')
```

9. The second assertion is that the service has an `ensure` attribute with the `running` value:

```
with('ensure' => 'running' )
```

10. You can specify any attributes and values you want using the `with` method, as a comma-separated list. For example, the following code asserts several attributes of a file resource:

```
it { should contain_file('/tmp/hello.txt').with(
  'content' => "Hello, world\n",
  'owner'   => 'ubuntu',
  'group'   => 'ubuntu',
  'mode'    => '0644' )
}
```

11. In our thing example, we need to only test that the `thing.conf` file is present, using the following code:

```
it { should contain_file('/etc/thing.conf') }
```

12. When you run the `rake spec` command, `rspec-puppet` will compile the relevant Puppet classes, run all the specs it finds, and display the results:

```
...F Failures:
1) thing should contain File[/etc/things.conf]
Failure/Error: it { should contain_file('/etc/things.conf') }
expected that the catalogue would contain
File[/etc/things.conf] # ./spec/classes/thing_spec.rb:9:in
`block (2 levels) in <top (required)>' Finished in 1.66 seconds
4 examples, 1 failure
```

13. As you can see, we defined the file in our test as `/etc/things.conf` but the file in the manifests is `/etc/thing.conf`, so the test fails. Edit `thing_spec.rb` and change `/etc/things.conf` to `/etc/thing.conf`:

```
it { should contain_file('/etc/thing.conf') }
```

14. Run `rake` again:

```
t@mylaptop $ rake
/opt/puppetlabs/puppet/bin/ruby -
I/opt/puppetlabs/puppet/lib/ruby/gems/2.4.0/gems/rspec-
support-3.7.1/lib:/opt/puppetlabs/puppet/lib/ruby/gems/2.4.0/ge
ms/rspec-core-3.7.1/lib
/opt/puppetlabs/puppet/lib/ruby/gems/2.4.0/gems/rspec-
core-3.7.1/exe/rspec --pattern
spec/\*\*\{,/\*/\*\*\}/\*_spec.rb
........

Finished in 0.85703 seconds (files took 0.8356 seconds to load)
8 examples, 0 failures

manifests/init.pp - WARNING: class not documented on line 1
```

There's more...

There are many conditions you can verify with `rspec`. Any resource type can be verified with `contain_<resource type>(title)`. In addition to verifying that your classes will apply correctly, you can also test functions and definitions by using the appropriate sub-directories within the `spec` directory (classes, defines, or functions).

You can find more information about `rspec-puppet`, including complete documentation for the assertions available and a tutorial, at `http://rspec-puppet.com/`.

When you want to start testing how your code applies to nodes, there are a few options. Beaker can be used for this or Serverspec, as well. More information on Beaker is available at `https://github.com/puppetlabs/beaker`. Serverspec information can be found at `https://serverspec.org/`.

10
Monitoring, Reporting, and Troubleshooting

In this chapter, we will cover the following recipes:

- Noop—the don't-change-anything option
- Logging the command output
- Logging debug messages
- Generating reports
- Producing automatic HTML documentation
- Drawing dependency graphs
- Understanding Puppet errors
- Inspecting configuration settings

Introduction

Most of us had the experience of sitting in an exciting presentation about some new technology and then rushing home to play with it. Of course, once you start experimenting with it, you immediately run into problems. What's going wrong? Why doesn't it work? How can I see what's happening under the hood? This chapter will help you answer some of these questions, and give you the tools to solve common Puppet problems.

We'll also see how to generate useful reports on your Puppet infrastructure and how Puppet can help you monitor and troubleshoot your network as a whole.

Noop—the don't-change-anything option

Sometimes, your Puppet manifest doesn't do exactly what you expected, or perhaps someone else has checked in changes you didn't know about. Either way, it's good to know exactly what Puppet is going to do before it does it.

When you are retrofitting Puppet into an existing infrastructure, you might not know whether Puppet is going to update a config file or restart a production service. Any such change could result in unplanned downtime. Also, sometimes, manual configuration changes are made on a server that Puppet would overwrite.

To avoid these problems, you can use Puppet's `noop` mode, which means *no operation* or do nothing. When run with the noop option, Puppet only reports what it would do, but doesn't actually do anything. One caveat here is that even during a `noop` run, `pluginsync` still runs and any `lib` directories in modules will be synced to nodes. This will update external fact definitions and possibly Puppet's types and providers. If you are using PuppetDB for reporting, the fact values for a node are also updated on a `noop` run.

How to do it...

You may run the `noop` mode when running `puppet agent` or `puppet apply` by appending the `--noop` switch to the command. You may also create a `noop=true` line in your `puppet.conf` file within the `[agent]` or `[main]` sections:

1. Create a `noop.pp` manifest that creates a file, as follows:

   ```
   file {'/tmp/noop':
     content => 'nothing',
     mode    => '0644',
   }
   ```

2. Run puppet agent with the `noop` switch:

   ```
   t@mylaptop.example.com $ puppet apply noop.pp --noop
   Notice: Compiled catalog for mylaptop.example.com.strangled.net
   in environment production in 0.02 seconds
   Notice: /Stage[main]/Main/File[/tmp/noop]/ensure: current_value
   'absent', should be 'file' (noop)
   Notice: Class[Main]: Would have triggered 'refresh' from 1
   event
   Notice: Stage[main]: Would have triggered 'refresh' from 1
   event
   Notice: Applied catalog in 0.02 seconds
   ```

3. Run it without the `noop` option to see that the file is created:

```
t@mylaptop.example.com $ puppet apply noop.pp
Notice: Compiled catalog for mylaptop.example.com.strangled.net
in environment production in 0.01 seconds
Notice: /Stage[main]/Main/File[/tmp/noop]/ensure: defined
content as '{md5}3e47b75000b0924b6c9ba5759a7cf15d'
Notice: Applied catalog in 0.02 seconds
```

How it works...

In the `noop` mode, Puppet does everything it would normally, with the exception of actually making any changes to the machine (the exec resources, for example, won't run). It tells you what it would have done, and you can compare this with what you expected to happen. If there are any differences, double-check the manifest or the current state of the machine.

Note that when we ran with `--noop`, Puppet warned us that it would have created the `/tmp/noop` file. This may or may not be what we want, but it's useful to know in advance. If you are making changes to the code applied to your production servers, it's useful to run puppet agent with the `--noop` option to ensure that your changes will not affect the production services.

There's more...

You can also use noop mode as a simple auditing tool. It will tell you whether any changes have been made to the machine since Puppet last applied its manifest. Some organizations require all config changes to be made with Puppet, which is one way of implementing a change-control process. Unauthorized changes to the resources managed by Puppet can be detected using Puppet in noop mode and you can then decide whether to merge the changes back into the Puppet manifest or undo them.

You can also use the `--debug` switch in Puppet to see the details of every resource Puppet considers in the manifest. This can be helpful when trying to figure out whether Puppet is loading a particular class, or to see in which order things are happening.

If you are running a master, you can compile the catalog for a node on the master with the `--trace` option in addition to `--debug`. If the catalog is failing to compile, this method will also fail to compile the catalog (if you have an old definition for the cookbook node that is failing, try commenting it out before running this test). This produces a lot of debugging output. For example, to compile the catalog for our cookbook, host on our master and place the results in `/tmp/cookbook.log`:

```
[root@puppet ~]# puppet master --compile cookbook.example.com --debug --
trace --logdest /tmp/cookbook.log
{
 "tags": [
 "settings",
 "cookbook",
 "node"
 ],
 "name": "cookbook.example.com",
 "version": 1526923109,
 "code_id": null,
 "catalog_uuid": "f0efb635-8711-4c28-b5d6-245e813f1425",
 ...
```

After compiling the catalog, Puppet will print out the catalog to the command line. The log file (`/tmp/cookbook.log`) will have a lot of information on how the catalog was compiled.

See also

- The *Auditing resources* recipe in Chapter 5, *Users and Virtual Resources*
- The *Automatic syntax-checking with Git hooks* recipe in Chapter 2, *Puppet Infrastructure*
- The *Generating reports* recipe in this chapter
- The *Testing your Puppet manifests with rspec-puppet* recipe in Chapter 9, *External Tools and the Puppet Ecosystem*

Logging the command output

When you use the exec resources to run commands on the node, Puppet will give you an error message such as the following if a command returns a non-zero exit status:

```
Notice: /Stage[main]/Main/Exec[/bin/cat /tmp/missing]/returns: /bin/cat:
/tmp/missing: No such file or directory
Error: /bin/cat /tmp/missing returned 1 instead of one of [0]
Error: /Stage[main]/Main/Exec[/bin/cat /tmp/missing]/returns: change from
notrun to 0 failed: /bin/cat /tmp/missing returned 1 instead of one of [0]
```

As you can see, Puppet not only reports that the command failed, but shows its output:

```
/bin/cat: /tmp/missing: No such file or directory
```

This is useful for figuring out why the command didn't work, but sometimes the command actually succeeds (in that it returns a zero exit status) but still doesn't do what we wanted. In that case, how can you see the command output? You can use the `logoutput` attribute.

How to do it...

Follow these steps in order to log the command output:

1. Define an exec resource with the `logoutput` parameter, as shown in the following code snippet:

```
exec { 'exec with output':
  command  => '/bin/cat /etc/hostname',
  logoutput => true,
}
```

2. Run Puppet:

```
t@mylaptop $ puppet apply exec.pp
Notice: Compiled catalog for mylaptop.example.com in
environment production in 0.05 seconds
Notice: /Stage[main]/Main/Exec[exec with output]/returns:
mylaptop.example.com
Notice: /Stage[main]/Main/Exec[exec with output]/returns:
executed successfully
Notice: Applied catalog in 0.02 seconds
```

3. As you can see, even though the command succeeds, Puppet prints the output:

   mylaptop.example.com

How it works...

The `logoutput` attribute has three possible settings:

- `false`: This never prints the command output
- `on_failure`: This only prints the output if the command fails (the default setting)
- `true`: This always prints the output, whether the command succeeds or fails

There's more...

You can set the default value of `logoutput` to always display the command output for all exec resources by defining the following in your `site.pp` file:

```
Exec { logoutput => true, }
```

What's this Exec syntax? It looks like an exec resource, but it's not. When you use `Exec` with a capital E, you're setting the resource default for exec. You may set the resource default for any resource by capitalizing the first letter of the resource type. Anywhere that Puppet sees that resource within the current scope or a nested subscope, it will apply the defaults you define.

If you never want to see the command output, whether it succeeds or fails, use:

```
logoutput => false,
```

More information is available at `https://docs.puppetlabs.com/references/latest/type.html#exec`.

Logging debug messages

It can be very helpful when debugging problems if you can print out information at a certain point in the manifest. This is a good way to tell, for example, whether a variable isn't defined or has an unexpected value. Sometimes, it's useful just to know that a particular piece of code has been run. Puppet's notify resource lets you print out such messages.

How to do it...

Define a `notify` resource in your manifest at the point you want to investigate:

```
notify { 'Got this far!': }
```

How it works...

When this resource is applied, Puppet will print out the message:

```
notice: Got this far!
```

There's more...

In addition to simple messages, we can output variables within our notify statements. Additionally, we can treat the notify calls the same as other resources, having them require or be required by other resources.

By printing out variable values, you can refer to variables in the message:

```
notify {"operating system is ${facts['os']['name']}": }
```

Puppet will interpolate the values in the printout:

```
Notice: operating system is Fedora
```

Resource ordering

Puppet compiles your manifests into a catalog. The order in which resources are executed on the client (node) may not be the same as the order of the resources within your source files. When you are using a notify resource for debugging, you should use resource chaining to ensure that the notify resource is executed before or after your failing resource.

For example, if the `exec failing exec` is failing, you can chain a notify resource to run directly before the failed exec resource, as shown here:

```
notify{"failed exec on ${hostname}": }
  -> exec {'failing exec':
      command   => "/bin/grep ${hostname} /etc/hosts",
      logoutput => true,
    }
```

If you don't chain the resource or use a metaparameter, such as `before` or `require`, there is no guarantee that your `notify` statement will be executed near the other resources you are interested in debugging. More information on resource ordering can be found at `https://docs.puppetlabs.com/puppet/latest/reference/lang_relationships.html`.

For example, to have your notify resource run after `failing exec` in the preceding code snippet, use:

```
notify { 'Resource X has been applied':
  require => Exec['failing exec'],
}
```

Note, however, that in this case the notify resource will fail to execute, since the exec failed. When a resource fails, all the resources that depended on that resource are skipped:

```
notify {'failed exec failed': require => Exec['failing exec'] }
```

When we run Puppet, we see that the notify resource is skipped:

```
t@mylaptop ~/puppet/manifests $ puppet apply fail.pp
...
Error: /bin/grepmylaptop /etc/hosts returned 1 instead of one of [0]
Error: /Stage[main]/Main/Exec[failing exec]/returns: change from notrun to
0 failed: /bin/grepmylaptop /etc/hosts returned 1 instead of one of [0]
Notice: /Stage[main]/Main/Notify[failed exec failed]: Dependency
Exec[failing exec] has failures: true
Warning: /Stage[main]/Main/Notify[failed exec failed]: Skipping because of
failed dependencies
Notice: Finished catalog run in 0.06 seconds
```

Generating reports

If you're managing a lot of machines, Puppet's reporting facility can give you some valuable information on what's actually happening out there.

How to do it...

To enable reports, just add this to a client's `puppet.conf`, within the `[main]` or `[agent]` sections:

```
report = true
```

 In recent versions of Puppet, `report = true` is the default setting.

How it works...

With reporting enabled, Puppet will generate a report file, containing data such as:

- Date and time of the run
- Total time for the run
- Log messages output during the run
- List of all the resources in the client's manifest
- Whether Puppet changed any resources, and how many
- Whether the run succeeded or failed

By default, these reports are stored on the node at `/opt/puppetlabs/puppet/cache/reports/` in a directory named after the certname of the node (the FQDN), but you can specify a different destination using the `reportdir` option in `puppet.conf`. You can create your own scripts to process these reports (which are in YAML format). When we run puppet agent on `cookbook.example.com`, the following file is created on the master:

```
/opt/puppetlabs/server/data/puppetserver/reports/201805140434.yaml
```

There's more...

If you have more than one master server, you can have all your reports sent to the same server by specifying `report_server` in the `[agent]` section of `puppet.conf`.

If you just want one report, or you don't want to enable reporting all the time, you can disable reporting by specifying `report = false` in `puppet.conf` and then add the `--report` switch to the command line when you run Puppet manually:

```
[root@cookbook ~]# puppet agent -t --report
Notice: Finished catalog run in 0.34 seconds
```

You won't see any output, but a report file will be generated in the report directory.

You can also see some overall statistics about a Puppet run by supplying the `--summarize` switch:

```
[root@cookbook ~]# puppet agent -t --report --summarize
Info: Using configured environment 'production'
Info: Retrieving pluginfacts
Info: Retrieving plugin
Info: Loading facts
Info: Caching catalog for cookbook.example.com
Info: Applying configuration version '1526924636'
Notice: Applied catalog in 0.05 seconds
Changes:
Events:
Resources:
            Total: 7
Time:
         Schedule: 0.00
   Transaction evaluation: 0.02
   Convert catalog: 0.04
   Catalog application: 0.05
   Node retrieval: 0.16
   Config retrieval: 0.31
      Plugin sync: 0.65
   Fact generation: 1.23
         Last run: 1526924636
       Filebucket: 0.00
            Total: 2.47
Version:
           Config: 1526924636
           Puppet: 5.5.0
```

Other report types

Puppet can generate different types of reports with the reports option in the `[main]` section of `puppet.conf` on your Puppet master servers. There are several built-in report types, listed at `https://docs.puppetlabs.com/references/latest/report.html`. In addition to the built-in report types, there are some community-developed reports that are quite useful. The Foreman (`http://theforeman.org`), for example, provides a Foreman report type that you can enable to forward your node reports to the Foreman.

See also

- The *Auditing resources* recipe in `Chapter 5`, *Users and Virtual Resources*

Producing automatic HTML documentation

As your manifests get bigger and more complex, it can be helpful to create HTML documentation for your nodes and classes using an automatic documentation tool, puppet strings. Previous versions of Puppet included the `doc` option, which was used to produce documentation. However, it was deprecated in favor of puppet strings, a ruby gem.

Getting ready...

Install the puppet strings ruby gem. First install the YARD gem, then puppet-strings:

```
t@mylaptop ~ $ sudo /opt/puppetlabs/puppet/bin/gem install yard
[sudo] password for thomas:
Fetching: yard-0.9.12.gem (100%)
-------------------------------------------------------------------------
-----
As of YARD v0.9.2:

RubyGems "--document=yri,yard" hooks are now supported. You can auto-
configure
YARD to automatically build the yri index for installed gems by typing:

$ yard config --gem-install-yri

See `yard config --help` for more information on RubyGems install hooks.

You can also add the following to your .gemspec to have YARD document your
```

```
gem
on install:

    spec.metadata["yard.run"] = "yri" # use "yard" to build full HTML docs.


--------------------------------------------------------------------------
-----
Successfully installed yard-0.9.12
Parsing documentation for yard-0.9.12
Installing ri documentation for yard-0.9.12
Done installing documentation for yard after 2 seconds
1 gem installed

t@mylaptop ~ $ sudo /opt/puppetlabs/puppet/bin/gem install puppet-strings
Fetching: rgen-0.8.2.gem (100%)
Successfully installed rgen-0.8.2
Fetching: puppet-strings-2.0.0.gem (100%)
Successfully installed puppet-strings-2.0.0
Parsing documentation for rgen-0.8.2
Installing ri documentation for rgen-0.8.2
Parsing documentation for puppet-strings-2.0.0
Installing ri documentation for puppet-strings-2.0.0
Done installing documentation for rgen, puppet-strings after 2 seconds
2 gems installed
```

How to do it...

We'll use the `thing1` module we created with PDK. PDK does a great job of filling out all the default comments that are used by puppet strings:

1. Use `puppet` strings to generate the HTML documentation as follows:

```
t@mylaptop $ cd
modules/thing1/home/thomas/puppet/modules/thing1
t@mylaptop $ puppet strings
Files: 1
Modules: 0 ( 0 undocumented)
Classes: 0 ( 0 undocumented)
Constants: 0 ( 0 ocumented)
Attributes: 0 ( 0 undocumented)
Methods: 0 ( 0 undocumented)
Puppet Classes: 1 ( 0 undocumented)
Puppet Defined Types: 0 ( 0 undocumented)
Puppet Types: 0 ( 0 undocumented)
Puppet Providers: 0 ( 0 undocumented)
Puppet Functions: 0 ( 0 undocumented)
```

```
Puppet Tasks: 0 ( 0 undocumented)
Puppet Plans: 0 ( 0 undocumented)
 100.00% documented
```

2. This will generate a set of HTML files in a directory named doc in the current directory. Open the top-level index file at `modules/thing1/doc/index.html`:

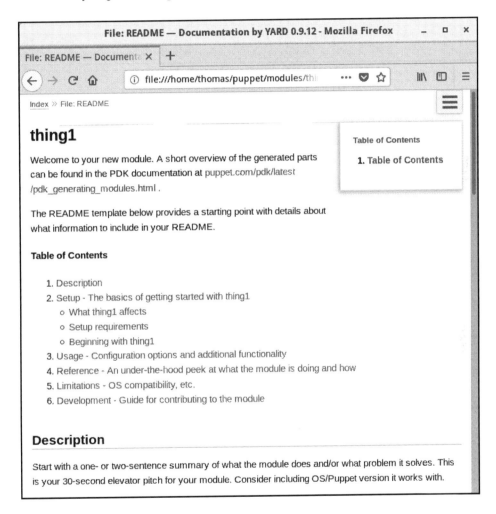

3. Click the **hamburger** menu on the right and select the `thing1` class:

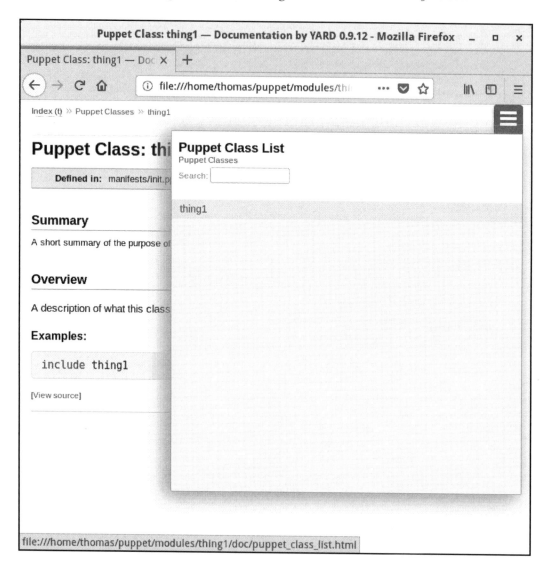

How it works...

The puppet strings command creates a structured HTML documentation tree similar to using YARD (YARD is similar to RDoc, which was used previously). Puppet-strings will use the comments in your code to generate the documentation. Properly formatting your comments will make it easier to produce quality documentation for your modules.

There's more...

Using the puppet strings server command, you can generate documentation for all the modules known in the current environment. Puppet strings will then start a web server and serve up your documentation. For example, we can run the server command on our Puppet server, as follows:

```
[root@puppet ~]# puppet strings server
Generating documentation for Puppet module 'concat'.
[warn]: Missing a description for Puppet resource property 'ensure' at
/etc/puppetlabs/code/environments/production/public/concat/lib/puppet/type/
concat_file.rb:24.
...
Starting YARD documentation server.
[2018-05-21 20:19:19] INFO WEBrick 1.3.1
[2018-05-21 20:19:19] INFO ruby 2.4.2 (2017-09-14) [x86_64-linux]
[2018-05-21 20:19:19] INFO WEBrick::HTTPServer#start: pid=25400 port=8808
::1 - - [21/May/2018:20:23:24 UTC] "GET / HTTP/1.1" 200 2838
- -> /
```

Now, when we point our web browser to port `8808` on our puppet server, we see documentation for all the modules in our environment:

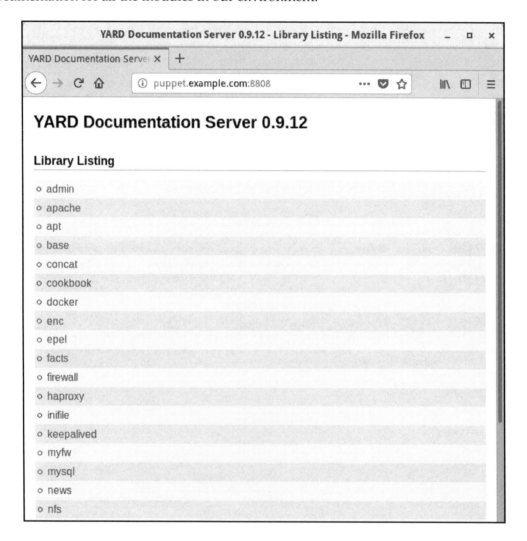

Drawing dependency graphs

Dependencies can get complicated quickly, and it's easy to end up with a circular dependency (where A depends on B, which depends on A) that will cause Puppet to complain and stop working. Fortunately, Puppet's `--graph` option makes it easy to generate a diagram of your resources and the dependencies between them, which can be a big help in fixing such problems.

Getting ready

Install the `graphviz` package to view the diagram files:

```
t@mylaptop ~ $ sudo puppet resource package graphviz ensure=installed
Notice: /Package[graphviz]/ensure: created
package { 'graphviz':
  ensure => '2.40.1-20.fc28',
}
```

How to do it...

Follow these steps to generate a dependency graph for your manifest:

1. Create a new `trifecta` module:

```
t@burnaby $ pdk new module trifecta
pdk (INFO): Creating new module: trifecta

We need to create the metadata.json file for this module, so
we're going to ask you 4 questions.
If the question is not applicable to this module, accept the
default option shown after each question. You can modify any
answers at any time by manually updating the metadata.json
file.

[Q 1/4] If you have a Puppet Forge username, add it here.\
We can use this to upload your module to the Forge when it's
complete.
--> uphillian

[Q 2/4] Who wrote this module?
This is used to credit the module's author.
--> Thomas Uphill
```

```
[Q 3/4] What license does this module code fall under?
This should be an identifier from https://spdx.org/licenses/.
Common values are "Apache-2.0", "MIT", or "proprietary".
--> GPL-3.0

[Q 4/4] What operating systems does this module support?
Use the up and down keys to move between the choices, space to
select and enter to continue.
--> RedHat based Linux, Debian based Linux, Windows (Use arrow
or number (1-7) keys, press Space to select and Ente--> RedHat
based Linux, Debian based Linux
Metadata will be generated based on this information, continue?
Yes
pdk (INFO): Module 'trifecta' generated at path
'/home/thomas/puppet/modules/trifecta', from template
'file:///opt/puppetlabs/pdk/share/cache/pdk-templates.git'.
pdk (INFO): In your module directory, add classes with the 'pdk
new class' command.
```

2. Create the `init` class:

```
t@burnaby $ cd
trifecta/home/thomas/puppet/modules/trifectat@burnaby
$ pdk new class trifecta
pdk (INFO): Creating
'/home/thomas/puppet/modules/trifecta/manifests/init.pp' from
template.
pdk (INFO): Creating
'/home/thomas/puppet/modules/trifecta/spec/classes/trifecta_spe
c.rb' from template.
```

3. Place the following code, containing a deliberate circular dependency, in the `init` class (can you spot the problem?):

```
# A description of what this class does
#
# @summary A short summary of the purpose of this class
#
# @example
# include trifecta
class trifecta {
  package { 'ntp':
    ensure  => installed,
    require => File['/etc/ntp.conf'],
  }

  service { 'ntp':
```

```
      ensure  => running,
      require => Package['ntp'],
    }

    file { '/etc/ntp.conf':
      source  => 'puppet:///modules/trifecta/ntp.conf',
      notify  => Service['ntp'],
      require => Package['ntp'],
    }
  }
```

4. Create a simple `ntp.conf` file in `modules/trifecta/files/ntp.conf` with the following content:

   server 127.0.0.1

5. Run `Puppet apply` to generate the graph:

   ```
   t@mylaptop $ puppet apply --modulepath ~thomas/puppet/modules -
   e 'include trifecta' --graph
   Notice: Compiled catalog for burnaby.strangled.net in
   environment production in 0.01 seconds
   Error: Found 1 dependency cycle:
   (File[/etc/ntp.conf] => Package[ntp] =>
   File[/etc/ntp.conf])\nCycle graph written to
   /home/thomas/.puppetlabs/opt/puppet/cache/state/graphs/cycles.d
   ot.
   Error: Failed to apply catalog: One or more resource dependency
   cycles detected in graph
   ```

6. Convert the `cycles.dot` file to a PNG using the dot command, as follows:

   ```
   t@mylaptop $ dot -Tpng
   /home/thomas/.puppetlabs/opt/puppet/cache/state/graphs/cycles.d
   ot -o cycles.png
   ```

7. View the PNG:

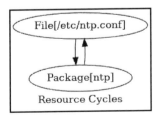

Resource Cycles

How it works...

When you run `puppet apply --graph` (or set `graph=true` in `puppet.conf`), Puppet will generate three graphs in the DOT format (a graphics language):

- `resources.dot`: This shows the hierarchical structure of your classes and resources, but without dependencies
- `relationships.dot`: This shows the dependencies between resources as arrows, as shown in the preceding image
- `expanded_relationships.dot`: This is a more detailed version of the relationships graph

If there is a dependency cycle in your code, then Puppet will also generate a `cycles.dot` file. For our preceding code, the `relationships.dot` file produces the following PNG:

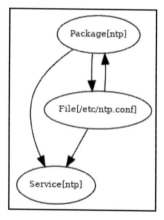

The dot tool (part of the graphviz package) will convert these to an image format, such as PNG, for viewing.

In the relationships graph, each resource in your manifest is shown as a balloon (known as a vertex), with arrowed lines connecting them to indicate the dependencies. You can see that, in our example, the dependencies between `File['/etc/ntp.conf']` and `Package['ntp']` are bidirectional. When Puppet tries to decide where to begin applying these resources, it can start at `File['/etc/ntp.conf']`, look for what depends on `File['/etc/ntp. conf']`, and end up at `Package['ntp']`.

When Puppet looks for the dependencies

This type of problem is known as a circular dependency problem; Puppet can't decide where to start because the two resources depend on each other.

To fix the circular dependency problem, all you need to do is remove one of the dependency lines and break the circle. The following code fixes the problem:

```
class trifecta {
  package { 'ntp':
    ensure => installed,
  }

  service { 'ntp':
    ensure  => running,
    require => Package['ntp'],
  }

  file { '/etc/ntp.conf':
    source  => 'puppet:///modules/trifecta/ntp.conf',
    notify  => Service['ntp'],
    require => Package['ntp'],
  }
}
```

Now, when we run puppet apply or agent with the `--graph` option, the resulting graph does not have any circular paths (cycles).

In this graph, it is easy to see that `Package[ntp]` is the first resource to be applied, then `File[/etc/ntp.conf]`, and finally `Service[ntp]`.

A graph such as that shown previously is known as a **Directed Acyclic Graph (DAG)**. Reducing the resources to a DAG ensures that Puppet can calculate the shortest path of all the vertices (resources) in linear time. For more information on DAGs, check out `http://en.wikipedia.org/wiki/Directed_acyclic_graph`.

There's more...

Resource and relationship graphs can be useful even when you don't have a bug to find. If you have a very complex network of classes and resources, for example, studying the resources graph can help you see where to simplify things. Similarly, when dependencies become too complicated to understand by reading the manifest, the graphs can be a useful form of documentation. For instance, a graph will make it readily apparent which resources have the most dependencies and which resources are required by the most other resources. Resources that are required by a large number of other resources will have numerous arrows pointing at them.

See also

- The *Using run stages* recipe in `Chapter 3`, *Writing Better Manifests*

Understanding Puppet errors

Puppet's error messages can sometimes be a little confusing. Updated and increasingly helpful error messages are one reason to upgrade your Puppet installation if you are running any version prior to Version 3.

Here are some of the most common errors you might encounter, and what to do about them.

How to do it...

Often, the first step is simply to search the web for the error message text and see what explanations you can find for the error, along with any helpful advice about fixing it. Here are some of the most common puzzling errors, with possible explanations.

Could not retrieve file metadata for XXX: getaddrinfo: Name or service not known

Where XXX is a file resource, you may have accidentally typed `puppet://modules...` in a file source instead of `puppet:///modules...` (note the triple slash).

Could not evaluate: Could not retrieve information from environment production source(s) XXX

The source file may not be present or may not be in the right location in the Puppet repo.

Error: Could not set 'file' on ensure: No such file or directory XXX

The file path may specify a parent directory (or directories) that doesn't exist. You can use separate file resources in Puppet to create these. You will see this error if, for example, you specified the /etc/myProduct/config.ini file and the /etc/myProduct directory did not exist.

Change from absent to file failed: Could not set 'file on ensure: No such file or directory

This is often caused by Puppet trying to write a file to a directory that doesn't exist. Check that the directory either exists already or is defined in Puppet, and that the file resource requires the directory (so that the directory is always created first).

 Another thing to consider is that SELinux rules may prevent the file from being created. Check the audit log for entries from Puppet attempting to create the file.
You may also encounter this with remote file systems (NFS, Samba), where the local root user does not have permission to create the file in question.

Undefined method 'closed?' for nil:NilClass

This unhelpful error message is roughly translated as *something went wrong*. It tends to be a catch-all error caused by many different problems, but you may be able to determine what is wrong from the name of the resource, the class, or the module. One trick is to add the --debug switch, to get more useful information:

```
[root@cookbook ~]# puppet agent -t --debug
```

If you check your Git history to see what was touched in the most recent change, this may be another way to identify what's upsetting Puppet:

Duplicate definition: X is already defined in [file] at line Y; cannot redefine at [file] line Y

This one has caused me a bit of puzzlement in the past. Puppet's complaining about a duplicate definition, and normally ,if you have two resources with the same name, Puppet will helpfully tell you where they are both defined. But in this case, it's indicating the same file and line number for both. How can one resource be a duplicate of itself?

The answer is, if it's a defined type (a resource created with the define keyword). If you create two instances of a defined type, you'll also have two instances of all the resources contained within the definition, and they need to have distinct names. For example:

```
define check_process() {
  exec { 'is-process-running?':
  command => "/bin/ps ax |/bin/grep ${name} >/tmp/pslist.${name}.txt",
  }
}
check_process { 'exim': }
check_process { 'nagios': }
```

When we run Puppet, the same error is printed twice:

```
t@mylaptop $ puppet apply duplicate.pp
Error: Evaluation Error: Error while evaluating a Resource Statement,
Evaluation Error: Error while evaluating a Resource Statement, Duplicate
declaration: Exec[is-process-running?] is already declared at (file:
/home/thomas/puppet/duplicate.pp, line: 2); cannot redeclare (file:
/home/thomas/puppet/duplicate.pp, line: 2) (file:
/home/thomas/puppet/duplicate.pp, line: 2, column: 5) (file:
/home/thomas/puppet/duplicate.pp, line: 7) on node burnaby.strangled.net
```

Because the exec resource is named is-process-running?, if you try to create more than one instance of the definition, Puppet will refuse because the result would be two exec resources with the same name. The solution is to include the name of the instance (or some other unique value) in the title of each resource:

```
exec { "is-process-${name}-running?":
```

The double quotes are required when you want Puppet to interpolate the value of a variable into a string.

See also

- The *Generating reports* recipe in this chapter
- The *Noop – the don't-change-anything option (doing a dry run)* recipe in this chapter
- The *Logging debug messages* recipe in this chapter

Inspecting configuration settings

You probably know that Puppet's configuration settings are stored in puppet.conf, but there are lots of parameters, and those that aren't listed in puppet.conf will take a default value. How can you see the value of any configuration parameter, regardless of whether or not it's explicitly set in puppet.conf? The answer is to use the puppet config print command.

How to do it...

Run the following command. This will produce a lot of output (it may be helpful to pipe it through less if you'd like to browse the available configuration settings):

```
[root@cookbook ~]# puppet config print --section agent |head -10
Resolving settings from section 'agent' in environment 'production'
agent_catalog_run_lockfile =
/opt/puppetlabs/puppet/cache/state/agent_catalog_run.lock
agent_disabled_lockfile =
/opt/puppetlabs/puppet/cache/state/agent_disabled.lock
allow_duplicate_certs = false
always_retry_plugins = true
app_management = false
autoflush = true
autosign = /etc/puppetlabs/puppet/autosign.conf
basemodulepath =
/etc/puppetlabs/code/modules:/opt/puppetlabs/puppet/modules
bindaddress = *
binder_config =
```

How it works...

Running `puppet config print` will output every configuration parameter and its current value (and there are lots of them).

To see the value for a specific parameter, add it as an argument to the puppet config print command:

```
[root@cookbook ~]# puppet config print modulepath --section agent
Resolving settings from section 'agent' in environment 'production'
/etc/puppetlabs/code/environments/production/modules:/etc/puppetlabs/code/m
odules:/opt/puppetlabs/puppet/modules
```

See also

- The *Generating reports* recipe in this chapter

Other Books You May Enjoy

If you enjoyed this book, you may be interested in these other books by Packt:

Puppet 5 Beginner's Guide - Third Edition
John Arundel

ISBN: 978-1-78847-290-6

- Understand the latest Puppet 5 features
- Install and set up Puppet and discover the latest and most advanced features
- Configure, build, and run containers in production using Puppet's industry-leading Docker support
- Deploy configuration files and templates at super-fast speeds and manage user accounts and access control
- Automate your IT infrastructure
- Use the latest features in Puppet 5 onward and its official modules
- Manage clouds, containers, and orchestration
- Get to know the best practices to make Puppet more reliable and increase its performance

Puppet 5 Essentials - Third Edition
Martin Alfke, Felix Frank

ISBN: 9-781-78728-471-5

- Understand declarative configuration management
- Make use of GIT-based deployment workflows
- Extend Factor with secure elements
- Create modular and reusable Puppet code
- Extend your code base with publicly available Puppet modules
- Separate logic from data by using Hiera
- Understand and develop Puppet Roles and Profiles

Leave a review - let other readers know what you think

Please share your thoughts on this book with others by leaving a review on the site that you bought it from. If you purchased the book from Amazon, please leave us an honest review on this book's Amazon page. This is vital so that other potential readers can see and use your unbiased opinion to make purchasing decisions, we can understand what our customers think about our products, and our authors can see your feedback on the title that they have worked with Packt to create. It will only take a few minutes of your time, but is valuable to other potential customers, our authors, and Packt. Thank you!

Index

Made in the USA
Middletown, DE
16 February 2020